ANSWERING THE CALL

ANSWERING THE CALL

The extraordinary life of
Sir Wesley Hall

Paul Akeroyd

Foreword by David Lloyd

J.W. McKENZIE

J.W. McKenzie Ltd
12 Stoneleigh Park Road,
Ewell, Epsom, Surrey KT19 0QT
Tel 0208 393 7700

Photographs appear by kind permission as follows:

Randy Brooks of Brooks LaTouche Photography, St Michael, Barbados:
for the portrait of Wes Hall on the front of the jacket

PA Images: (i) Wes Hall and Roy Gilchrist docking at Southampton, (ii) The
players leaving the field at Lord's in 1963 and (iii) Tom Graveney caught in 1966

Getty Images: (i) The Three Ws, (ii) Norman O'Neill on his backside
and (iii) Wes Hall, Jeffrey Stollmeyer and Garry Sobers

First published 2022

ISBN of standard edition: 978 0 94782144 9

ISBN of limited edition: 978 0 94782145 6

Printed and bound in Great Britain by
CPI Antony Rowe, Bumpers Way, Chippenham SN14 6LH

Contents

Foreword by David Lloyd   7

Introduction   8

PART ONE: From Unlikely Beginnings to Test Cricketer

1   Home Life and St Giles' School   11

2   Brotherly Love and Combermere   20

3   A Reluctant Fast Bowler   35

4   England 1957: A Difficult Tour   48

5   Back to Basics   56

6   Taking Test Cricket by Storm   64

7   Life in the Leagues   80

8   Australia 1960/61: The Series that Saved Cricket   86

9   The Tied Test   93

10   The Influence of Worrell: Planning a Career Path   100

11   England 1963: Hall and Griffith Unleashed   116

12   Behind the Celebrations   126

13   World Champions and the Tragedy of Worrell   138

14   A Team in Decline and Struggles with Injury   149

15   Cricketing Memories and Reflections   160

16   A Tribute to the Three Ws   171

PART TWO: Life After Cricket

17   A Career Crossroads   179

18   Businessman, Politician, Cricket Administrator   187

19   Member of Parliament and Government Minister   198

20   The Greatest Call to Serve   209

21   Meeting Nelson Mandela and Farewell to Politics   217

22   Managing West Indies in Turbulent Times   225

23   WICB Presidency   237

24   A Final Tally   246

25   Lessons Learned from Cricket   257

26   Cricket, Citizenship and Independence   269

27   A Crowning Moment   274

28   The Last Word   278

Statistics of Cricket Career   280

Acknowledgements and Bibliography   282

Index   284

Contents

Foreword by David Lloyd
Introduction

PART ONE

Foreword

David Lloyd

One of the most asked questions is: 'How did you get into cricket?'

For me, I was a youngster at Accrington Cricket Club and would spend all my spare time there with my friends. Making up games, practising in the nets and watching the team play at weekends.

The Lancashire League was famous for attracting the best players in the world. We signed Wesley Hall, a colossus among fast bowlers. I would practise with the Seconds. Wes took an interest in my left-arm wrist spin, and from time to time he would take me into the First XI nets. I made my League debut against Rishton in the same team as the great man!

The team would meet on Broadway in Accrington and travel to away games in a charabanc. Wes always turned up in his mackintosh ... hail, rain, or shine! What a character! The lads in the team – Lindon Dewhurst, the Rushtons, Jim Eland, Jack Collier, Jackie Hope, Derek Mark, Russ Cuddihy, Eddie Robinson – all held him in great affection, and I can honestly say there was never a dull moment with Wes around. He is one of the best pros that has graced the Lancashire League.

He visited the club a few years ago and, although not as sprightly as he used to be, insisted on going to the end of his run.

So, how did I get into cricket? Very simple ... 'Wesley Winfield Hall'. One of the very best 'Men of Cricket'.

Introduction

Wesley Winfield 'Wes' Hall, one of the most fearsome and popular fast bowlers of all time, was born in a working-class suburb of Bridgetown, Barbados in 1937. In the foreword to Hall's autobiography, *Pace Like Fire,* published 28 years later when his career was at its peak, his mentor and Test captain Sir Frank Worrell acknowledged the personal qualities that made both the cricket field and the dressing room more decent places when Wes was around. A respect for opponents, an absence of egotism and a penchant for fun – always close to the surface but which knew its place when more serious cricketing matters demanded – set him apart from other fast bowlers. Worrell went on to remark that Wes 'discusses cricket in any other terms except in the first person singular'.

In a cricketing context, of greater significance than bowling figures and batting averages, is the place occupied by Sir Wes (he was knighted in 2012) in the history of the game and particularly that of West Indian cricket. From the time West Indies joined the ranks of Test-playing nations in 1928, they had enjoyed limited success, propelled to the occasional eye-catching series victory by the brilliance of players such as Learie Constantine, Manny Martindale, George Headley, the Three Ws (Frank Worrell, Everton Weekes, and Clyde Walcott), Sonny Ramadhin, and Alf Valentine. Consistency had eluded them, but that was to change dramatically in the 1960s. From 1962 to 1967, West Indies won consecutive Test series against India and England (twice each), and Australia, to lay claim for the first time to the title of cricket's world champions. Led by the serene Worrell, West Indies' first permanent black captain, and inspired by the great Garfield Sobers, not only were they the best team in the world, West Indies also became synonymous with a brand of positive, exciting cricket. At a time when cricket's reputation had been tarnished by slow play and negative tactics, their vibrant approach gave the game a much-needed fillip. Flamboyant batting and explosive pace bowling came together irresistibly to lay down a blueprint for success which would be replicated so spectacularly by the all-conquering teams led by Clive Lloyd and Vivian Richards. Sobers, Rohan Kanhai, Conrad Hunte and Seymour

Nurse featured prominently in a powerful batting line-up; Lance Gibbs was a world-class off-spinner; and the team's cutting edge was provided by Wes Hall and Charlie Griffith. The blistering Hall-Griffith axis was the fastest bowling attack in the world in the 1960s, ensuring that their team was to be taken seriously and would not be bullied. As such, Sir Wes and Sir Charles represent a pivotal link in the West Indian fast-bowling tradition established in the 1930s by Constantine and Martindale, and which later formed the basis of West Indies' domination of world cricket for the best part of a generation. Fittingly, at a time when Caribbean colonies were moving towards independence, a team of West Indian cricketers could claim to be the greatest in the world.

In 1965, Sir Frank said of *Pace Like Fire*: 'This is Wes's first book, and I feel certain it won't be his last.' As on most occasions, Worrell's judgement was sound, although the 57-year hiatus between then and this biography is probably greater than even he envisaged. *Answering the Call* explores the man behind and beyond Wes Hall the cricketer, drawing from conversations with Sir Wes, who in his eighties remains lucid and insightful. It reveals a remarkable individual whose talents, ambition and devotion to duty have combined to produce a life of accomplishment in many fields and service to the game of cricket, to those in need, to his country, and to God.

Sir Wes identifies pivotal themes that have defined his life's path. The first was a burning ambition which revealed itself when he was just eight and was roundly dismissed as a childhood flight of fancy by those less convinced of his destiny. Later he benefitted from five pieces of advice imparted by his beloved mother when her wisdom was most needed. Finally, he describes a series of lifetime reference points in the form of occasions when he was asked to serve and to which he responded by answering the call.

Part One

From Unlikely Beginnings
to Test Cricketer

1

Home Life and St Giles' School

Wes Hall was born in Glebe Land – since re-named Goddings Road – in the Station Hill district in the parish of St Michael[1] on 12 September 1937, a year which had begun with widespread social unrest in Barbados. The country was sharply divided along lines of race, with a small white ruling class wielding economic and political power. The majority black population – largely employed in the agricultural sector – suffered from poverty, lack of opportunity and dismal labour conditions. On 26 July 1937, frustration at the injustices of the system erupted into the riots that became known as the Labour Rebellion. This 'People's Uprising' heralded a stage in the process of democratic reform which had begun with the fight against slavery and continued through the Second World War in opposition to colonialism. It eventually culminated in Barbados gaining independence from Britain in 1966 under the leadership of Errol Walton Barrow[2].

Wes's white paternal great-grandfather, Merlyn Ingram, arrived from Scotland on a whaler in 1850. He settled on the island and married a black woman, Hessie King. Their offspring – James, Lewis, and Brigham – all passed as white and as such enjoyed considerable social advantage in colonial Barbados, where they lived in the parish of Christ Church on the south coast. James was the father of Fred King-Ingram.

The ancestry on Wes's maternal side is pure African: his great, great-grandfather was a slave named James McClean, who worked on the 181-acre Hannay's plantation in the northern parish of St Lucy. On a visit to the plantation, Wes was fortunate to meet 83-year-old Grantley Cadogan who proved to be a valuable source of information. The slave huts have

[1] St Michael, which includes the capital of Barbados, Bridgetown, is one of the eleven parishes into which the island is divided.

[2] E.W. Barrow (1920-1987) became the first prime minister of Barbados when the island achieved independence in 1966. In 1998 he was named as one of the ten Barbadian National Heroes and is referred to as The Right Excellent Errol Walton Barrow.

been either torn down or developed into modern homes, but behind the houses sugar cane still grows in the fields where James McClean toiled his entire life. James' son Samuel McClean married Frances Elcock, the daughter of a slave, and they had seven children, one of whom, Louise McClean, married James Hall. Their four daughters included Ione Hall.

From their respective beginnings on the southern shores of the island and at its northern tip, Fred King-Ingram and Ione Hall met and became the parents of Llewellyn and, thirteen months later, Wesley.

Home for Llewellyn and Wes in Station Hill was a simple chattel house[3] which they shared with their mother, grandmother and Aunt Daphne. They had no electricity or running water, and the boys were required to fill the large water barrel with buckets of water from the nearby public pipe. Flanked by Glendairy Prison[4] on one side and District A Police Station a similar distance across the road, there were regular security patrols, and the neighbourhood was one of the safest on the island.

As was common throughout Barbados at that time, theirs was a religious household. Wes's mother was a Methodist, and his grandmother Louise was a member of Holligan Road Pentecostal church close to the famous Empire Cricket Club in nearby Bank Hall. To her displeasure, when Llewellyn was born in 1936, Louise was banished to the rear pews of her church on the basis that her daughter was an unmarried mother, and she was again 'put in the back seat' a few months later when Ione was pregnant with Wes. Nevertheless, their grandmother took both boys to that church as infants. Thereafter, they went with her to Mayers Road Pentecostal Church in a district known as The Ivy, just 400 yards from their home. As Wes became older and learned how his grandmother had been treated by her church, he began to feel resentful. He reasoned that if the church did not want his mother to have children out of wedlock, then effectively it was rejecting him. Later he came to understand the difference between rejection and temporary disqualification, although the unfairness of punishing his grandmother for her daughter's 'sins' still troubled him.

---

[3] Chattel houses are small, portable wooden dwellings, which were originally the homes of plantation workers who would literally move their house when they were required to relocate.

[4] The Glendairy jailhouse building is still there but, following riots and a fire, it has stood empty since the prison was relocated in 2005 to Her Majesty's Prison, Dodds, in the parish of St Philip.

Wes and his contemporaries attended church on Sunday morning, Sunday School at 3pm, and then Evensong later in the day. The boys' involvement in the church was immersive, and they gained a fundamental understanding of the Christian ethos. Duty and loyalty were central pillars of their lives, instilled in them from an early age in church, at school and by their family – especially their mother. Guided by her devout Christian beliefs, Ione was a constant source of support and wisdom, and the high standards that she demanded of her sons were matched by the love she gave in return. She compensated for her lack of secondary school education by reading avidly to become a font of self-acquired knowledge. She was a lady of few words, each one weighed carefully to achieve maximum effect: 'A quiet admonishment from her was as effective as six lashes.'

The boys' grandmother was an industrious businesswoman. She made a living selling cow heel and tripe for the Williams family. Beatrice Williams, the owner of the business, bought the heels and tripe wholesale in bulk from Goddard's icehouse on Broad Street in Bridgetown. She would then boil the cured meat and divide it out among the salespeople she employed at various locations across the town. Wes's grandmother sold her produce on the steps of Sam Adderley's general store and grocery in Eagle Hall. Ione was a sales assistant at the store and had been instrumental in gaining permission for her mother to occupy that prime position. Louise continued working there until she was eighty years old. In addition to her job as a saleswoman, she also worked a small plot of land, growing root crops which she would either sell or give to friends and neighbours.

Ione displayed such business acumen that in 1945 the large Barbados wholesale merchant Ince and Company offered her the opportunity to manage her own shop in St Lawrence in Christ Church. Goods and provisions were delivered to her by horse-drawn cart, and she ran the business. The shop also served as a bar selling liquor to local fishermen, and Ione typically worked more than twelve hours a day. Although the work was hard, it led to a significant improvement in the family's circumstances: at the back of the shop there was ample living accommodation, with the unaccustomed luxury of running water and an indoor lavatory. Ione's sister Daphne, a seamstress, made the move with her and helped in the shop while continuing her dressmaking work.

That same year, the family moved their chattel house from Station Hill to a plot in the Back Ivy neighbourhood close to the boys' primary school,

St Giles' Boys'. Louise continued to live there, and initially, Llewellyn and Wes split their time between St Lawrence and The Back Ivy, spending weekends with their mother and weekdays with their grandmother.

The boys had a strict upbringing. They were expected to display respect and humility, and their grandmother in particular was a disciplinarian. Any hopes they might have harboured of a more relaxed regime when staying with an indulgent grandparent were doomed from the outset. This did not deter Wes from trying to outflank her, with unintended consequences on one occasion. At St Giles', the boys and their friends liked to play cricket before classes began. Louise, on the other hand, was firmly of the view that getting to school early and returning late wasted time that should be spent at home resting or working. In a moment of genius, Wes – always the more daring of the two – came up with the idea of moving the time on the clock in the house forward by an hour. This would give him and his brother an hour's cricket before school. The ruse worked perfectly in the morning, but unfortunately Wes had overlooked one crucial detail: unless the clock was turned back, it would remain an hour fast. Sure enough, when it showed five o'clock and the boys were still not home, their agitated grandmother marched into the school to fetch them. In addition to his embarrassment, Wes also found himself in trouble when he got home!

Llewellyn and Wes became increasingly dissatisfied with Louise's regime, and their mother agreed that they could live permanently with her in St Lawrence provided they continued their education at St Giles'. They accepted her terms, despite the arduous daily commute: in the morning, they walked to the bus stop at Worthing View, where they would catch the bus to Culloden Road near the Garrison Savannah racecourse just outside Bridgetown. From there, the boys walked the final mile and a half up the hill to school. With the return journey every evening, they covered five miles a day walking to and from school, no doubt a foundation for the stamina Wes would display in his cricket career! A measure of the family's love for St Giles' was the fact that St Lawrence Primary School, itself highly regarded, was just 50 yards from their mother's house. In addition, the boys' religious devotion survived the change of location. Every Sunday they walked the short distance from their mother's shop to attend St Lawrence Anglican Church, where Wes was captivated by the lyrical beauty of the sung psalms and the Eucharist in preparation for the Holy Communion.

During his time in St Lawrence, Wes became very close to Ione's relatives and to his father's extended family, especially his grandfather James Ingram: 'I remember sitting on the knee of my flaxen-haired, blue-eyed grandfather. He was a wonderful old man. He never left the house without wearing a jacket – except, of course, when he was fishing!' The Ingram family of fishermen and sailors lived around the neighbouring villages of St Lawrence, Oistins and Maxwell Hill on the south coast of the island. They became renowned for their love of music, with a tradition of guitar-playing and singing passed down the generations.

Wes's father Fred – James' son – was an interesting, charismatic character. He worked as a successful salesman for the Barbadian distribution company, Frank B. Armstrong, and was a skilful tiller operator on sailing boats. He was also a noted banjo player but was better known as a middleweight and occasional cruiserweight boxer who rejoiced under the flamboyant ring name 'Dynamite Blues'. The father/son relationship between Fred and Wes was an unconventional one to say the least. Fred met and married another woman shortly before Wes was born; they had a daughter – Wes's sister Margaret – and Fred played very little part in the boys' upbringing. Wes bears no resentment towards him, preferring instead to focus on his father's engaging personality and ability in the ring:

> He was a skilful boxer and a good mover. When my son Sean was born, my father used to visit him with gifts. He was a proud grandfather. We never shook hands, shared a hug or even a meal, and the only time we spent under the same roof was the day he was buried. He was 54 and I loved him.

Wes has been known as 'Blues' by his school friends for over 70 years and is happy to share his father's nickname.

Wes's immediate family was completed by his father's other son. Llewellyn and Wes were members of the Police Boys Club in the mid-1950s, and they became very good friends with Merlyn Watts, a young private at Worthing Police Station, known to one and all as 'Lion Man'. A jovial, larger-than-life character and an excellent singer, Merlyn was a fast bowler for Sheffield in the Barbados Cricket League (BCL), and he went on to become a senior superintendent in the Royal Barbados Police Force: 'He would always say to me "I was first", though I never understood what he meant.' Years later, when Wes was in Trinidad, Margaret called to tell him that Lion Man was dead. She also cast light on the meaning of the words, 'I was first': Merlyn Watts was their older brother, the first of Fred's children, born in 1935 and named after their Scottish great-grandfather.

In 1942, five-year-old Llewellyn Hall started at St Giles', and a year later Wesley followed him through the school gates. It was a high-performing primary school whose many outstanding teachers placed great emphasis on such virtues as diligence, good manners and humility. Several teachers went on to become headmasters at other schools and, due to its outstanding reputation, St Giles' was extremely popular, with approximately 1,000 pupils in the 1940s. As a result, lessons took place wherever space could be found, often outside in the shade of a tree.

In those days, most teachers were male, but Wes had the good fortune to be taught by two exceptional female teachers, Miss Inniss – who had become one of the very few female teachers when she was just 18 years old – and later Miss Mullins. The former made a particular impression on Wes. She encouraged her pupils to read extensively and, from their first meeting when Wes was seven years old, Miss Inniss ignited in him a love of language and poetry:

> There was such a tapestry of love and goodness about her; she was loved by all the boys. Only three of us admitted that we loved her, but they all did – and maybe some of the masters too! And not just for her stunning visage, for she was a wonderful, caring teacher.

Given her exceptional teaching talent, it came as no surprise to Wes when – as Mrs Avis Carrington – she opened her own independent school, Merrivale Preparatory School, in St Michael, in 1959. This revolutionary move established her as a true pioneer amongst Barbadian women. Another groundbreaker, The Honourable Mia Amor Mottley, who in 2018 became the first female prime minister of Barbados, was one of the many outstanding pupils who attended Merrivale. Also in 2018, Avis – subsequently Dame Avis – celebrated her 100th birthday.

The year spent in Miss Inniss' class had a profound, settling effect on Wes and the other boys, all of whom had experienced the turmoil of local social unrest and the omnipresent backdrop of the Second World War. He looked up to her, and she was responsible for giving him the confidence that fuelled his dreams: 'By the time I left her class at the age of eight, my spinnaker was full of air, and I was ready to take on those brilliant teachers that I would meet in the next nine years!'

Around that time, Wes first gave voice to a dream that would shape his life. Motivated by a desire to improve his circumstances, he realised that a good education was essential, and he decided therefore that he must go to high school. Fine school as St Giles' was, primary education ended at the age of 14, and the only ways to extend one's schooling were either by paying or winning a scholarship to attend one of the secondary schools. The former route was not an option for the Halls, but the latter afforded outstanding pupils access to the fee-paying schools. Wes therefore boldly declared that he would be gaining a scholarship to the renowned Combermere School.

He had a particularly supportive ally in Mr J.O. Morris, a teacher at St Giles' who did everything in his power to ensure the continuation of his school's proud record of producing scholars. For a year, Wes regularly visited Mr Morris' house in Pinfold Street in Bridgetown for free private lessons in preparation for the Combermere scholarship exam. Mr Morris did the same for all of those boys who he felt had the potential to pass if they received extra tuition, but who could not afford to pay for it. These included Sir Louis Tull, an eminent lawyer and government minister, and Dr Martin Haynes, a distinguished surgeon, contemporaries of Wes at St Giles', who both won prestigious Barbados Scholarships to Harrison College in their final year.

Wes speaks in glowing terms of his primary school, which he credits with playing a pivotal role in his and Llewellyn's development. He is eternally grateful for the start it gave him. In addition to his outstanding education, it also instilled in him the work ethic and discipline so highly valued by the exclusive schools. He was bright, diligent and a keen reader but, without proper nurturing by an inspirational group of teachers, his potential may have remained unfulfilled.

Perhaps just as significantly, the small field to the side of the school is where Wes learned to play cricket. It was there that he first encountered the Sobers brothers – Garry and Gerald – when St Giles' played against their arch-rivals, Bay Street Boys' School. Garry was a year older than Wes and, even at the age of twelve, Sobers' extraordinary talent was obvious. He was mainly a spinner in those days, and Gerald was a star batsman. Wes and Garry faced each other just once in school matches before Wes left St Giles' at the end of 1949.

St Giles' School has honoured Wes by erecting a bust of him in the entrance hall, a reminder to the pupils who have followed him of what can be achieved through hard work and dedication. Much has changed over the intervening 70 years. Buildings have been added, and today there are only around 450 boys and girls on the roll. Happily, St Giles' high standards have been maintained, and the school is still thriving.

On a recent visit, Sir Wes was invited to give an impromptu address to a class of seven-year-olds. The children listened intently as he reiterated the values that the school taught him: 'Work hard, study for your exams and aim high – and as St Gilesians you can do it!'

Along with Harrison College and The Lodge, Combermere School was one of the island's three elite high schools, with Harrison considered the most illustrious. Despite St Giles' success in sending pupils on scholarships to Harrison College, Wes was fixated on Combermere for two sound reasons: gaining entry to Harrison College was so tough that it was considered viable only for the *crème de la crème*; and more importantly for a cricket-mad youngster, Combermere offered an excellent cricket programme. Every Saturday he would walk the short distance to watch the school's matches, and what he saw made a deep impression on him, especially the excellent Combermere First XI of 1946. That team included Wes's schoolboy hero Neville Grant, O.H. Wilkinson, Rudolph 'Huffie' Knight and Vernon Babb, all of whom would vie for selection for the Barbados team.

His dream of attending Combermere may have seemed extravagant, but it paled alongside his belief that he would also one day play cricket for West Indies. A familiar sight wandering around the streets near his home with a ball and a home-made bat in hand, he would proudly announce to all and sundry what the future held for him. The responses were hardly encouraging, yet Wes remained undeterred by the doubting voices, and the visions of his destiny continued to drive him on.

18

In 1949, the time came for him to deliver what he had been promising for the previous three years. As he walked to Combermere on the morning of the scholarship exam, he was passed by the boys who could afford to travel by bus and those being taken in their fathers' cars. All were heading for the grand, intimidating school hall, praying that their preferred questions came up. The heart-stopping moment when the invigilator solemnly utters the words: 'You may now turn over your papers', gave way to elation when Wes read the first question: 'List the coordinating conjunctions and construct sentences using them.' To a voracious reader, lover of language, and someone who knew those conjunctions off by heart, the examiner had, in Wes words, 'bowled me a lollipop, and I hit it out the ground!' The rest of the paper was similarly kind to Wes. He finished the exam in rapid time and handed his paper to the invigilator.

Passing the Combermere scholarship exam was the first significant achievement of Wes's life. It showed him the importance of vision: 'You need to dream big and set yourself targets. If you don't know where you're going, you won't know when you get there.'

The first part of Wes's audacious two-fold prediction had come true but, before the second could be realised, he had a great deal of learning to do, on and off the cricket field. Over the next eight years, on three occasions his mother's guidance would prove to be hugely influential in helping him come to terms with who he was, and three calls to serve would map out the most unlikely route to cricketing distinction.

2

Brotherly Love and Combermere

Llewellyn was very intelligent; according to Wes, he was 'much brighter than I was, and the teachers liked him.' However, Llewellyn and his mother were unaware of the scholarship opportunities until Wes learned of the scheme, unfortunately too late for Llewellyn. He had been under the impression that the only way to enter a high school was to pay the fees, which at the time were eight British West Indies dollars (BWI)[1] a term to attend Combermere. Even though this was inexpensive compared to the BWI 24 charged by Harrison College, it was still more than his mother could afford. Llewellyn stayed on at St Giles' to the age of 14 when he was awarded a bursary to enter the printing trade on a six-year apprenticeship with a Barbadian newspaper, *The Advocate*. The relationship between Llewellyn and Wes has always been a strong and loving one, greatly valued by both. Wes loved and looked up to his brother:

> He is the nicest person I have ever met. I didn't understand him when we were youngsters, but I now understood how James, the brother of Christ, would have felt in the presence of a brother who did nothing wrong! I could not believe it, everybody loved him. I would kick things, even a can in the street, and wreck my sneakers, but his lasted all year! He was even a better cricketer than me, and he became a good fast bowler for Springfield in the BCL.

The last term at St Giles' School was a metaphorical victory lap for Wes. Having won a scholarship, he had begun excitedly reading textbooks in preparation for the next year's studies, and he was intent on leaving the school 'with a bang' prior to starting at Combermere. He decided that the best way to achieve this would be to play Mr Marlow in the school production of Oliver Goldsmith's *She Stoops to Conquer*. There was a snag though: his brother was given the role. Wes acknowledged that Llewellyn

---

[1] The British West Indies dollar was the unit of currency used in the eastern Caribbean and British Guiana from 1949 until 1965, when it was replaced by the Eastern Caribbean dollar. In 1973, Barbados introduced the Barbados dollar.

was good but felt that he could bring more expression and passion to the part. By his own admission, he was a 'loquacious' boy, and this invited unfavourable comparisons with his brother; his pleas for the part – or any other part for that matter – were met with crushing rejection: 'You're an accident waiting to happen, Wes, we can't give you a part!' Reluctantly, he resigned himself to watching from the sidelines.

In the week leading up to the show, all tickets had been sold and there was much excitement as the big day approached. There was to be a full rehearsal on the Tuesday evening, but disaster struck for Llewellyn. He developed a sore throat and was unable to speak, leaving the rehearsal bereft of its leading man. Wes sensed his opportunity. He made sure that he caught the attention of the teacher in charge, Mr Oscar Robinson[2]. When asked where Llewellyn was, Wes replied that his brother was suffering from 'an inflammatory condition of the larynx, Sir.' Speaking in the style of Marlow was bound to impress the teacher and, furthermore, he reckoned that the ailment he had described sounded far more serious than a mere sore throat! When Mr Robinson said that he would have to call off the performance, Wes triumphantly informed him that such action was unnecessary as he knew the entire play word-for-word and could stand in for his brother. To prove his point, he recited extracts on demand and, upon hearing the lines perfectly delivered, Mr Robinson decided that Wes would replace Llewellyn. The new Mr Marlow ran home to tell his mother the good news. Initially overjoyed, her mood turned sombre when Wes explained the circumstances. She told Wes that such behaviour was not acceptable in her house. He needed to think about the person he was and who he really wanted to be, rather than how the world saw him. In the meantime, she would work on Llewellyn's sore throat to make sure he would be alright by Friday!

Through his disappointment, Wes could see that his mother was right; to seek popularity at others' expense was shallow and hubristic, and that lesson in humility had a profound impact on him. It taught him the need to strive to be honourable in his personal dealings and to be honest with himself: 'Since that day I have always felt that I would rather be hated for who I am than loved for something that I'm not. She was telling me to be true to myself.'

---

[2] O.M. (Oscar) Robinson (b. 1916) played cricket for Barbados and had scored a century against British Guiana in 1946.

Wes started at Combermere School in January 1950, and the second piece of maternal guidance came in the form of her words of solace after an extraordinary first day at his new school. Sitting in alphabetical order in their form room, the new boys were instructed to stand up one-by-one and announce their name and previous school. When his turn came, Wes rose and got as far as 'Wesley Hall, St ...' before the form master – Mr Eustace Taitt, also on his first day at his new school and eager to impose himself – interrupted him: 'Hold on, do you understand what I told you?'

'Yes, Sir. You asked me to say my name and then my school, Sir.'

'Very well, go ahead.'

'Wesley H...'

'You go to see the headmaster.'

Confused, Wes did as he was ordered, and when he explained to the headmaster's secretary, Miss Hunte, that he had been sent by 'the teacher', her response left him in no doubt that he was now in a very different world: 'Wesley, there are no teachers here. They are masters.' Seconds later the headmaster walked in. Major Cecil Noott was an imposing figure, a six-foot-six Welshman with a bearing befitting his army background. He addressed Wes as if he was barking orders at his company: 'What are you doing here?'

This time Wes was very careful to use the correct language: 'The master sent me, Sir.'

The headmaster strode over to the wall, took down a cane, instructed Wes to bend forward and delivered six lashes across his back. At this moment, the form master rushed into the room. The question was repeated: 'What are you doing here?'

Even in his dejected state, and smarting with pain, Wes was able to derive some satisfaction as Major Noott adopted the same tone to address the master! Mr Taitt explained the misunderstanding: Wesley Hall was – and still is – the name of a primary school in Barbados, and he thought Wes was being cheeky.

The intervention came too late for Wes. Upset and filled with a sense of injustice, he returned to his form room, his back burning and eyes brimming with tears. His new classmates warned him that they were not allowed to stay in the room during lunch, so he left and headed towards the canteen, not knowing that walking along the corridors was also forbidden. A voice called out to him: 'Hey you, get off the corridor!' The older boy came towards him and continued to shout at him: 'Hey, new boy, get off the corridor!'

The next thing Wes knew, he had been struck a fierce blow to the head. He stumbled forward, and in that instant he decided that enough was enough. He raised himself to his full height and punched his assailant, a fifth-form prefect, so hard that he knocked out a tooth. When Wes's classmates heard that the boy who had been beaten by the headmaster that morning had hit a prefect at lunch time, they gathered around him. Rawle Brancker – who would go on to play first-class cricket for Barbados and represent the West Indians on the 1966 tour of England – was full of admiration: 'Boy, I will walk with you for the balance of our time at this school! Nobody's ever going to mess around with you!' Unfortunately for Wes, reticence to tangle with him did not extend to the headmaster. The first lesson after lunch was French; Major Noott taught French. He strode into the classroom, grabbed Wes by the collar and marched him to his study. After reaching for the cane once more, Major Noott expressed some sympathy for Wes and even said he believed he would never have to beat Wes again; however, hitting a prefect was not acceptable ...

The headmaster's empathy failed to ease the pain of the additional six lashes, and Wes arrived home bloodied and distressed after his turbulent first day at Combermere. He felt angry that someone who did not know him should choose to beat him so unjustly. When he told his mother that he was never going back, her reply was unemotional. She repressed her instinct to rail against a system that had wronged her son so badly and instead offered words that she felt would help him: 'Wesley, be better, not bitter. Bitterness is a wasted emotion. You can be better than they are. Go back to school. I will take you there tomorrow.'

Tomorrow came. Wes did indeed return to Combermere, and thereafter he spent many happy days there, mercifully none as eventful as his first!

The call from Ronnie Hughes to keep wicket
Cricket was taken very seriously at Combermere School. Mr Ronnie Hughes was the master in charge of the teams, and he was assisted by another excellent teacher, Mr Harry Sealy. As an ardent cricket fan, the headmaster Major Noott was very proud of the school First XI's status in the island's leading men's competition, the first division of the Barbados

Cricket Association (BCA). He was a firm believer that the game instilled worthy qualities in the boys, and he made every effort to encourage them.

Wes was 14 years old when he first represented the Second XI in the BCA's lower – intermediate – division in 1952. Playing as an opening batsman, he scored heavily in his first season, including innings of 96 against Wanderers and 92 against Leeward Cricket Club. At the end of the season, Mr Hughes explained to Wes that, despite his success, the competition for places was so intense that he had little chance of progressing to the first team the following year unless he expanded his skills. Mr Hughes demanded that all his First XI players were versatile cricketers in that the batsmen should also be useful bowlers and *vice-versa*; therefore, Wes would need another string to his bow if he was to retain his place in the team when runs were scarce. Ronnie Hughes' innovative thinking was ahead of his time, for in the 1950s cricketers were usually either batsmen or bowlers and rarely did both. He accepted that his policy may lead to an occasional good player being missed, but he prophesied that in the future, cricket would require all players to be multi-dimensional.

Mr Hughes' insistence on a team of all-rounders led to Wes receiving his first call to serve, although the coach's vision of how Wes would develop his skill set to fit into the team could not have been more unexpected: 'You don't look like you can bowl; you're not a great fielder. I think I can let you keep wicket.' This was hardly the most resounding vote of confidence, but Wes was encouraged by the interest that Ronnie was taking in him and his cricket development. Mr Hughes gave him a copy of Godfrey Evans' autobiography, *Behind the Stumps*, and Wes's task was to study the book during the next nine months in order to learn the art of wicketkeeping. He would then be wicketkeeper and open the batting for the school in the BCA first division the following season. Unlike the other boys in the team, Wes had never played in that division. Moreover, Mr Hughes had not even seen him keep wicket, yet he was prepared to guarantee Wes a place in the team that would play in Barbados' elite division against the island's best cricketers, including many Test players!

Not surprisingly, Wes was astonished. Ronnie Hughes explained his belief that a good character and high standards of conduct were integral to cricketing success. He had seen those qualities in Wes, who had uncomplainingly attended every practice session and continued to score runs for the Second XI as he waited fruitlessly for a chance to play in the first team.

Mr Hughes' willingness to challenge convention had shown itself prior to the 1952 season. So strong was his faith in the crop of boys in Wes's year, he had taken the unprecedented – and audacious – step of dropping the senior players *en masse* from the first team and replacing them with the richly talented 14-year-olds. The team representing Combermere in the first division therefore comprised boys in short trousers (the schoolboys did not wear cricket flannels until they were in the fifth form) playing against Test cricketers. This incongruous spectacle became commonplace as the youngsters flourished and vindicated Ronnie's judgement, although as Wes wryly recalls: 'The men showed you no mercy just because you were in short pants. Instead, they viewed a match against boys as an opportunity for easy runs and cheap wickets!'

That Combermere First XI was exceptional, reckoned by many knowledgeable observers to be one of the finest teams in the history of Barbadian school cricket. Wes acknowledges that he wasn't a good enough batsman to force his way into a batting order that included Mr Hughes, a very capable batsman; the future West Indies Test batsman Peter Lashley; Rawle Brancker and Lionel Williams, both of whom became first-class cricketers; all-rounder Victor Callender; opening batsman Errie Inniss; and Francis Scott, regarded by Wes as the most gifted 14-year-old batsman he ever saw, including Sobers. Sadly, Scott never even played for Barbados. His progress was hampered by his belief that there is no such thing as a good ball; he considered that every delivery was there for a batsman to hit, and therefore it is batsmen who make balls appear 'good' by playing bad shots. Wes learned from the obvious flaws in Scott's approach and has since witnessed many young players (mainly batsmen!) succumb to a similar belief in their invincibility. The example of Scott alerted Wes to the danger of overstepping the line between confidence and bravado.

> He would get a pretty 30 or 40 and get out. That may be ok when you're twelve years old but, when you get to 16 or 17, anytime you go into a match thinking that a man can't bowl you a good ball, you're in trouble! He should try facing Shackleton in England – a bowler like that would bowl 95 out of 100 balls in the right area. You take chances with him and you're out.

The bowling in that school side was spearheaded by the West Indies pace bowler Frank King, at the time the fastest bowler in the Caribbean, and

Lionel Williams, who later represented Barbados. In a shrewd move, Major Noott had appointed King to the post of the school's head groundsman, taking advantage of the fact that as a member of staff he was eligible to play for the school team!

On the first day of practice for the 1953 season, Mr Hughes instructed Wes to fetch the gloves and stand behind the stumps to King. The first ball was fired down the leg side; Wes leapt to his left and took the ball cleanly. The other boys watched in disbelief. Wes had never been the nimblest of fielders, and they had no reason to suspect that he would be a good wicketkeeper. He continued to impress, however, and was duly given the job of keeping wicket and opening the batting – as Ronnie Hughes had planned – for the opening match of the season.

Wes's debut for the Combermere First XI marked the third occasion when his mother's influence had a profound effect on him. On the morning of the match, he was counting down the minutes before heading off to catch the bus to the ground. Not only would he be making his debut in Combermere's elite team, he would also be keeping wicket in a match for the first time in his life. The opening bowler would be the extremely quick Frank King; Lionel Williams, himself 'no slouch', would be bowling from the other end, followed by left-arm seamers Victor Callendar and Clyde Sealey. With a variety of spinners among the bowlers, Wes could be forgiven for feeling apprehensive that morning.

His mother sensed his anxiety, and her voice was gentle and calming: 'I have something for you Wesley.' (She was a Wesleyan, hence his name.) She handed him a small package and, upon opening it, Wes set eyes for the first time on the cross and chain that would mean so much to him. She had given the few pieces of jewellery she owned to her cousin, Clesbert McClean, a jeweller, and asked him to melt them down and make the crucifix. She removed it from its wrapping and placed it around her son's neck. Wes was so overcome with emotion that he was unable even to thank her. Sensing his discomfort, she held him in her arms and assured him that, despite his nerves, all he could do was to give of his best. The chain and the crucifix would remind him to allow God to be at the centre of everything he did in his life.

Determined not to let his mother see him cry, Wes got up, picked up his kit and ran down the road to the bus stop with tears streaming down his cheeks. At that moment he recognised the special qualities in his mother and vowed always to listen to her wisdom.

Apart from when having it cleaned, Wes has always had the same chain around his neck from that day when he was 15 years old, although he recalls having a scare in Adelaide when it came unhooked. Fearing it was lost, he was in a state of complete panic and remains eternally grateful to the journalist Crawford White from the *Daily Express* in London who stayed to search with him and eventually found it by the Adelaide Oval gates. Many words have been written about the chain and crucifix, none more compelling than Wes's expression of what it means to him:

> You see fellas nowadays with six chains around their neck: they have entered the oasis of prosperity, that's why they've got six chains. I have this to remind me, not of where I have come from, but where I am going. And to remind me, as my mother told me, to make sure that God is always at the centre of my endeavours.

During Wes's first season in the first team, his performances improved steadily. The following season, in addition to holding his own at the top of the batting order, he continued to make progress as a wicketkeeper and was considered by many observers to be the best schoolboy wicketkeeper in Barbados.

Combermere at that time provided unrivalled opportunities for a youngster obsessed with cricket. The headmaster had always been supportive of the cricketers; Mr Hughes offered his total commitment to them and expected nothing less in return. Despite Combermere's status as a great hockey school, he refused to allow members of the cricket team to play hockey, football or any other sport. Cricket was his sporting passion, and it was the boys' good fortune that he went to extreme lengths to help the team. He would regularly take twelve of them in a van from the school to his house in Pine Gardens, an affluent white suburb, having instructed the head groundsman Frank King to send a couple of men ahead to cut and roll a wicket in his front garden. Ronnie would then conduct practice sessions there, with the strict instruction that nobody was to risk upsetting the neighbours by hitting a house, although the spectacle of a dozen schoolboys playing cricket on his front lawn created quite a stir among the watching residents! He even arranged for his wife to cook for the boys, and the corned beef and rice made a welcome change from the biscuits and cheese that was the customary offering at cricket grounds.

Mr Hughes also ensured that money from the school games fund was allocated to provide every member of the First XI with a new bat and 'a flashy pair of boots', on the understanding that 'you couldn't get free shoes and come dirty'. For most of the boys, owning new equipment was a novel experience, and they took great pride in their appearance. Failure to do so was guaranteed to antagonise Mr Hughes, who was quick to enforce discipline when the boys failed to meet his high expectations, as Lionel Williams once discovered to his cost.

In the side principally as a fast bowler, Williams was also an accomplished batsman, the only 14-year-old Wes ever saw fearlessly hitting Frank King's bowling. Wes firmly believed that Williams was good enough to become a top batsman, but Ronnie was convinced that he had the potential to be a world-class fast bowler, so he shared the new ball with King and batted low down the order. In the match in question, Wes opened the batting as usual, and he and the other batsmen played solidly before Williams went in towards the end of the innings and struck a rapid 70. Afterwards, he voiced his frustration at the earlier batsmen, who he felt had shown too much respect to the bowlers instead of punishing what he obviously considered to be moderate bowling. When word reached Ronnie, he confronted Williams, who complained that he should be batting at number 3 in the order, not down at number 8. In the second innings, Williams was granted his wish and scored 94. Ronnie met him at the pavilion, congratulated him on a fine innings and, in the same sentence, reminded him that there was no place for *prima donnas* in the side, so he was dropped for the next match. Williams was upset, not so much a victim of his own misdemeanour as Ronnie Hughes' lofty principles.

Ronnie felt it was his job to teach the boys proper standards of behaviour and values and regularly arranged for guest speakers to come and talk to them. Everton Weekes was at the height of his career when he visited the school. He began by telling them to take pride in their appearance, always behave properly and to trust in their common sense. These were goals which they all could achieve, irrespective of their talent. Weekes went on to emphasise the need to set high standards and always perform to the best of one's ability. This resonated strongly with Wes, as it echoed his mother's words. All the boys listened intently, and much as they had enormous affection and respect for Mr Hughes he himself knew that they were more likely to heed lessons from people they hero-worshipped: stars such as Everton Weekes.

In addition to providing guidance for the boys on the cricket field, Mr Hughes was also an inspirational history teacher. The public examinations required the boys to study the textbook, *The New Groundwork of British History* by George Townsend Warner. It was a hefty and very expensive tome, and Ronnie was aware that a number of the boys could not afford to buy the book, so he condensed it into notes, and gave each of them a copy. Everyone passed the exam.

Wes proved himself to be a capable pupil at Combermere, where his best subjects were English and scripture. His upbringing had given him a grounding which was augmented by the emphasis placed on religious study at St Giles' and, by the time Wes entered Combermere, his knowledge of Acts of the Apostles and its teachings was very good. In a scripture exam he scored full marks on a question about Elymas – also known as Bar Jesus the Sorcerer – prompting his classmates to begin calling him 'Bar Jesus'. A couple of years later. Wes finally told his friends that the prefix 'bar' means 'son of', and with the benefit of this information, they decided to change his nickname to Blues, after his father!

All the boys in the First XI with Wes did well academically and went on to achieve success in later life (confounding some of the masters who felt that the cricketers were at Combermere just to play cricket). From that group, there emerged a QC, a doctor and some of Barbados' top entrepreneurs and Cable & Wireless executives: 'All were high achievers, and there were no drop-outs – a special group of people.' Not including Frank King, an established Barbados and West Indies player who was ten years older than the boys, four of the team represented West Indies at cricket; five played for Barbados; four served as members of parliament; and two were knighted. Wes alone achieved all four distinctions.

The other knight was Wilfred Wood, who had been Wes's captain and opening partner in the school's second team before both progressed to the First XI. Wood made history by becoming the first black bishop in the Church of England when he was consecrated as Bishop of Croydon in 1985. He was a leading authority on race relations in London and, after serving on many commissions and councils dedicated to promoting social justice, Bishop Wood was knighted by Queen Elizabeth II in 2002. In 2004 he was placed second (behind Mary Seacole) in a public vote of 100 Great Black Britons. Frequently when preaching, Bishop Wood proudly recalled the occasions 'when I opened with Wes'!

Wes also relates an amusing 'cricket curiosity' regarding Peter Lashley, his fellow Test player from the school team. As a youngster Lashley was small in stature and possessed a sound technique which enabled him to bat for long periods and accumulate runs. After watching 'P. Lashley' compile an impressive innings of 70 in a Combermere match, the sports reporter for the *Barbados Advocate*, O.S. Coppin, asked those present what the 'P' stood for. Nobody knew. Coppin opted for 'Peter' in his match report in that evening's newspaper and, ever since, Patrick Douglas Lashley has been known as Peter Lashley!

Having announced very publicly as a young boy that he was going to Combermere, Wes felt hugely gratified – and vindicated – to find masters there who were even more inspirational than he had imagined. Most of all, he considered it a privilege to have been guided by Ronnie Hughes and Harry Sealy, two wonderful schoolteachers and 'great men'.

Wes and his friends remained loyal to Mr Hughes for the rest of his life, and the enormous affection they felt for him was never more evident than when he lay on his deathbed at his home in 2012. Ronnie's wife Gwyneth arranged for Wes and several others to go to see him and pray with him, and even in those final days Ronnie still displayed his customary spirit and humour. Wes entered the room and got no further than: 'Mr Hughes ...' when he was interrupted: 'Even though I'm on this bed, if you call me "Mr Hughes" again, I'm going to get up, Wes, and give you a good slap!' Although he wanted to be called 'Ronnie', Wes never could, such was his respect for him.

Major Noott is another of his former masters whom Wes holds in extremely high esteem. Their relationship may not have got off to the most auspicious of starts but, over the five years that Wes attended Combermere, the headmaster was so good to him that Wes came to regard him as a father figure. The second beating Wes suffered at the hands of Major Noott on his first day was indeed the last, despite there being a couple of subsequent occasions when – by his own admission – Wes probably deserved one. Instead, the headmaster chose to take Wes aside and admonish him quietly.

The boys realised how fortunate they were to encounter the headmaster and his group of teachers, and years later they were keen to register their appreciation. In 1966 Combermerians Hall, Brancker, Holford and Lashley were members of the West Indies touring party in England, and they organised a celebration in honour of Major Noott at the Waldorf Hotel in London. By then Major Noott was retired and had returned to the UK, but the boys remembered that he was especially partial to Barbados rum. At the function Wes presented his former headmaster with a bottle of the island's finest, from which he proceeded to pour a very generous measure, '80 per cent rum, 20 per cent coke'. Major Noott drank it in one gulp, and his complexion turned bright red. Wes was concerned that something was amiss: 'Sir, are you alright? Was that too much rum?' The reply brought the house down: 'Don't be a jackass, Wes. Too much coke!'

The Combermere experience was life-shaping for Wes. He had known about the school's academic excellence of course, but it provided much more than that: 'On the first day, you walk through that door alone, but you soon come to realise that you will never again be left on your own.' Thus he and his friends developed a sense of belonging to the school and to each other, which has lasted a lifetime.

A major event in the school calendar which continues to this day is Combermere Week, an annual celebration of the school's academic, artistic and sporting prowess. It almost takes the form of a pilgrimage for Combermere *alumni*, including many of those who live overseas. The week is an opportunity for former pupils to renew friendships and to reminisce but is much more than a reunion: they also attend morning assembly and interact with current students during the school day and at the many sporting events. Proceedings are brought to a close on the Friday with a cricket match between the current First XI and a team of old boys, followed in the evening by a lavish social gathering for Combermerians past and present. Wes has played a prominent role in both.

In the annual cricket match Wes captained the old boys several times. He was never on the losing side, although on one occasion in the early 1980s it required all his cricketing and diplomatic skills to preserve his 100 per cent record. Wes's son Sean had warned him not to bat too high up the order as the school team included a bowler called Ricardo Ellcock who was extremely quick. R.M. Ellcock later played first-class cricket for Barbados and in England for Worcestershire and Middlesex before becoming a commercial pilot with Virgin Atlantic Airlines. On this day, he was making the ball fly, and the old boys were reduced to 26 for six when Wes decided to intervene. He strode out to the wicket and demanded to speak to the schoolboys' captain, Clyde Mascoll, a future leader of the Democratic Labour Party (DLP). Wes reminded him that the game was supposed to be a social event played in a friendly spirit and suggested that spinners should be introduced. Dutifully Mascoll brought himself on to bowl spin, and he and the other bowlers were severely punished as the old boys staged a spectacular recovery. Wes scored a century, Sam Wilkinson 72, and by the time Ellcock returned to the attack Wes was seeing the ball so well that he seemed to connect whenever he swung the bat. The old boys won the match, and Wes's unbeaten record remained intact. He jokes: 'I reckon I will have to apologise to Dr Mascoll some day!'

In recognition of his knighthood in 2012, Wes was invited to deliver the feature address at two important events in the Combermere calendar: the annual speech day and prize giving ceremony; and the Combermere Week Friday evening Grand Reunion for old scholars. The latter is considered a particular honour, and Wes was delighted to accept. As always, in 2012 the event was sold out, with Combermerians from the USA, Canada, England and the majority of those living in Barbados attending the celebration, which is held in the school's Major Noott Hall. At the Grand Reunion they socialise, listen to the speeches and join in rousing renditions of the school song, *Up and On*, and the hymn, *To be a Pilgrim*, before disbanding at the end of the evening content in the knowledge that they will be reacquainted in twelve months' time.

The school song is also sung at every Combermerian's funeral, and such traditions have led to some resentment and suspicion of the school. Although it has been co-educational since 1976, its rituals, traditions, and fraternal allegiance remain a source of discomfort to outsiders, who view it as being almost masonic in character. In common with all old scholars, however, Wes passionately believes in the school's positive contribution as a force for good. He is happy to admit that 'if you meet a fellow Combermerian, and say "Up and on", then you both know you have a friend'.

It is undoubtedly the case that the influence of Combermere School pervades Barbadian society on many levels, not least in the field of the arts.

A particularly striking visual example is provided by the Emancipation Statue, more commonly known as the Bussa Statue, which occupies a prominent position on a roundabout on the ABC Highway a few miles inland from Bridgetown. The bronze statue, sculpted by Wes's former art master Karl Broodhagen in 1985, depicts one of the Barbadian National Heroes, Bussa, leader of the 1816 slave revolt, in a powerful symbolic representation of the breaking of the chains of slavery.

Wes is certain that his *alma mater* will have played a part in helping the development of another famous Combermerian. As one of the school's much-loved former pupils, he has been a regular guest at school events, and during a Combermere Week soon after the turn of the century, he was invited to attend the Miss Combermere Talent Show:

> I sat up front and watched as attentively as I could; not exaggeratedly impressed, yet not bored – after all, it was Combermere, my beloved *alma mater*! Then this beautiful teenager walked out in a long white dress and sang. She was so elegant, poised, and confident as she performed. The winner of the contest was that girl: Robyn Rihanna Fenty.

From that humble beginning, Rihanna's meteoric rise is well-documented. Wes counts himself among the legion of admirers of the young lady who is now one of the most successful women in the world and Barbados' leading international superstar:

> During a visit to Atlanta, as I was entering a mall, I stepped aside to make way for a lady with a group of young girls, who were excitedly bobbing and singing: 'Under my umbrella, ella, ella …'. I smiled and asked: 'You girls know Rihanna's song?!' The lady laughed and replied: 'They know the words to all of Rihanna's songs.' I was so proud!
>
> His Excellency Sir Garfield Sobers[3] is Barbados' icon throughout the Commonwealth, but Rihanna has tipped the scales as our global iconic superstar. If success is not an isolated triumph but a sustained level of excellence, Rihanna's achievements will be rewarded at an even higher level. I will just

---

[3] Sir Garfield Sobers became The Right Excellent Sir Garfield after being named as one of the ten National Heroes of Barbados in 1998.

say to this extraordinary young woman: 'Up and on, to the right side of history.'

Wes's words proved prophetic when she was indeed 'rewarded at an even higher level' in November 2021. At the ceremony to mark Barbados' transition to an independent republic with an elected president replacing the British monarch as head of state, Rihanna was announced as the country's eleventh National Hero, joining the original ten named in 1998.

To this day Wes remains in awe of the interventions that shaped his young life, none more unexpected than Mr Hughes' decision to gamble on him becoming a wicketkeeper. As it was, Wes performed well and remained a fixture in that outstanding school team for two years, gaining a reputation as an excellent wicketkeeper/batsman and attracting the attention of the cricket fraternity in Barbados.

3

A Reluctant Fast Bowler

Another master at Combermere who became a mentor to Wes and many of his friends was the mathematics teacher Jack Adams, 'a wonderful man with a quick Irish brogue'. A superb hockey coach, Mr Adams was in charge of the school's formidable team, which was so successful that the entire Barbados national hockey side comprised his Combermere boys. In a fitting tribute, Mr Adams was honoured in 2018 when the school's hockey field was renamed the Jack Adams Ground. Mr Adams and the other masters shared the belief that their responsibility for the boys' welfare extended beyond the classroom and sports field, and he suggested to Mr N.W. Barnes, the assistant manager at Cable & Wireless, that the company should consider recruiting some of the outstanding young men at Combermere. The British telecommunications giant had established a major operations centre in Barbados in the 1940s, and in the early 1950s it had begun employing local boys from the leading high schools as trainees in telegraphy. Many of these recruits were also sent to study engineering at the company's Porthcurno centre in Cornwall. Mr Adams was happy to put in a good word on behalf of 'his boys' – one of whom was Wes in 1955.

In late 1954 at the end of the fifth form, Wes made the decision to leave school to support his mother. Ione had started work at the age of 17; she gave birth to Llewellyn when she was 18, Wes at 19, and had worked twelve-hour days without a break ever since. In the absence of their father, or indeed any other adult male in their household, she had 'mothered and fathered' Llewellyn and Wes for her entire adult life. Major Noott understood the situation, but he wanted Wes to stay on at Combermere to continue his education and play cricket for the school. Wes knew that the headmaster had his best interests at heart and explained that having gained so much from the school – a first-class education, discipline and the ability to analyse and to decipher right from wrong – it was now his responsibility and duty to help his mother.

It was obvious that Wes had given the matter a great deal of thought and that his mind was made up. Disappointed as Major Noott was, he was gratified to see the embodiment of the school's values in this confident, well-adjusted young man, and Wes embarked on the next chapter of his life with his headmaster's blessing.

Selflessness may not be a trait typically associated with teenagers, but Wes had obviously heeded his mother's lessons in integrity and consideration for others. He was so appreciative of the sacrifices that she had made for him and his brother that at the age of 17 he was about to make his own sacrifice in order to help her. Encouraged by Mr Adams, Wes applied for a job at Cable & Wireless, the first and only time in his life that he actively sought a position.

Wes passed the entrance exam and selection process at Cable & Wireless, and the company made him an attractive offer, with basic pay of BWI 88 a month, increasing to BWI 300 once he completed training school. This was an excellent starting salary in 1955, almost doubling what was paid in the Civil Service.

Wes joined Cable & Wireless as a trainee telegraphist. His first year was spent in training school at the company's headquarters in Dover, Christ Church, half a mile from his home in St Lawrence. By this time the family was reunited after his grandmother's home was moved from The Back Ivy so that she could live next to them.

Wes played very little cricket during the first few months of 1955; however, his enthusiasm for the game was as strong as ever, and he recalls with amusement an incident during the Fourth Test of the 1954-55 series between West Indies and Australia in Bridgetown. He was pretending to listen to codes on his headset, when in fact he was tuned in to radio commentary of the cricket. Wes became so engrossed in events at Kensington that he failed to notice the head of the training school standing next to him. As Garry Sobers famously attacked the bowling of Keith Miller, Wes was unable to supress his cries of delight, prompting Mr Cunningham to enquire what he was doing: 'I'm getting in a little audio practice, Sir.' Unfortunately, listening to cricket commentary was not the kind of audio practice expected of trainee telegraphists; fortunately, Mr Cunningham was a reasonable man, and he politely requested that it did not happen again!

Upon completion of his training, Wes became a member of the permanent staff at Cable & Wireless and, although he was required to work on Saturdays, his shifts were flexible, enabling him to resume playing cricket. Cable & Wireless had a thriving cricket club, but the team was in the intermediate division of the BCA. Wes was keen to advance his cricket career by continuing to play in the BCA's elite division – as he had with the Combermere First XI – and so he was pleased to be invited to join Spartan Cricket Club by no less than the club's president Keith Walcott (brother of Clyde). One of the leading clubs on the island, Spartan was established in 1893 for middle-class black men who could not gain admittance to the exclusive white clubs. However, except for Peter Lashley, who joined Cable & Wireless and Spartan, the best of the players from Wes's school team followed the well-trodden path from Combermere to Empire.

On 24 May 1914 (Empire Day) Herman Griffith, a civil servant, formed the Empire Club after being refused entry to Spartan. A fast bowler, he later played first-class cricket for Barbados and 13 Tests for West Indies, including their first-ever Test match in 1928. From 1916, when Empire joined the BCA, they and Spartan developed a strong rivalry. Wes's close friend Rawle Brancker, who joined Empire from school, spoke of his shock when he and several teammates went into the Spartan dressing room after a match to socialise with the opposition. Upon leaving, they were met by a dozen or so hailers – supporters who provided loyal and often rum-fuelled vocal support for their favourite team – who accused them of associating with the enemy. Brancker was taken aback: 'Enemy? We all went to school together!'

The decision to play for Spartan was not one that Wes took lightly. As a Combermerian brought up in a working-class neighbourhood close to the Empire ground, he was considered a natural recruit for Empire. Joining arch-rivals Spartan would not be greeted favourably. However, after much deliberation, he felt that cricketing factors left him with little option: West Indies' wicketkeeper was Empire's Clairmonte Depeiaza, who in the Bridgetown Test match against Australia in May 1955 was involved in a 347-run partnership with Denis Atkinson. At the time this was a record for the seventh wicket in first-class cricket. With such strong competition blocking his path at Empire, Wes made the unpopular but pragmatic choice. Over 60 years later, there are still those who have not forgiven him, even though he played only one season (1959) for Spartan.

In Barbados the start of the cricket season in June coincides with the onset of the rainy season, while football is played from January in the dry season. This is a legacy of the days when the ruling 'plantocracy' of plantation owners, many of whom played cricket, decided that cricket must wait until the end of the crop (known as 'crop over') in late May. In 1955, a few days before Wes was due to make his debut for Spartan in the first game of the season, Mr Barnes approached him at work and congratulated him on being picked to play for Spartan in the first division ... 'But don't you know that we have a team here?'

Wes replied that he did, but he would be unable to achieve his ambition of playing for Barbados unless he played first division cricket. Mr Barnes looked him in the eye and said: 'Yes, I know. That is what worries me.' He then turned and walked away, leaving Wes to ponder his enigmatic comment. In making plain his displeasure, Mr Barnes had sent a message which Wes instinctively knew he should heed; his desire to play first division cricket was outweighed by his need for the job. Reluctantly, he telephoned Keith Walcott to say that he was sorry, but he would be playing for Cable & Wireless in the intermediate division rather than for Spartan. The decision would pave the way for one of the most significant of his calls.

The call from Sonny Gilkes: 'Take the new ball, please Wes'
Wes took his place in the Cable & Wireless team after Ivor Alleyne, the regular wicketkeeper, stood down to make way for him. A few weeks into the season, prior to the home fixture against Wanderers, Wes went to the ground early as usual for some batting and wicketkeeping practice. The captain was an extremely amiable man called Sonny Gilkes who worked as an engineer for Cable & Wireless and later became one of the first locals to be appointed to a management position at the company. He casually walked over to Wes and explained that, due to the absence of opening bowler Robert Mayers[1], he would like Wes to remove his pads and bowl a few overs 'to take the shine off the new ball'.

Wes protested that he had never bowled a ball in a match before, not even at Combermere, and furthermore he had no interest in bowling.

---

[1] One of Mayers' brothers, Anthony, was a fast bowler who played for Barbados. The other, Colin, twice served as the Barbados Consul General in Miami and was one of Wes's best friends until his death in Florida in April 2018.

Although his captain was sympathetic, he remained insistent: he had seen Wes bowl in the nets and felt that he could do a good job as a stop-gap fast bowler. Wes considered himself first and foremost a batsman and secondly a wicketkeeper after his last two years at Combermere. Asking him to bowl made no sense whatsoever. Furthermore, he was concerned that he would let the team and himself down: 'I had never bowled before; he might as well have told me to drive to Bridgetown even though I'd never driven a car!' However, Wes liked and respected Sonny Gilkes and, as he had done for Ronnie Hughes three years earlier, he dutifully answered the call ... and took seven Wanderers wickets for 25 runs!

After Cable & Wireless batted and established a small first-innings lead, Wes proceeded to bowl his side to victory with five more wickets in the second innings. His cricketing destiny had been sealed. His performance was even more astonishing in that it took place at Boarded Hall, the home ground of Cable & Wireless, situated in a valley where the ball frequently swung extravagantly for the faster bowlers. Control was very difficult and required considerable skill, yet Wes bowled with unerring accuracy. He was able to exploit the swing through the air and movement off the pitch to such devastating effect that he single-handedly demolished Wanderers' powerful batting line-up.

For Wes and his teammates, the cricket was just part of the enjoyment of representing Cable & Wireless. There was a strong camaraderie within the side, and after games the players spent many happy hours socialising in the relaxed atmosphere of the small, unpretentious pavilion at Boarded Hall. They were often joined by players from other teams, such as on the evening of Wes's sensational bowling debut. As the players mingled and enjoyed the customary post-match drink, Wes found himself involved in a bizarre conversation with Wanderers' vastly experienced opening batsman, Billy Knowles[2]. After introducing himself, Knowles announced that Wes should be in the West Indies team the following year. He elaborated by saying that in 25 years of playing cricket, he had never faced a bowler swinging the ball as much at such pace.

To Wes the notion that he could be considered a West Indies bowling prospect just hours after bowling his first over in competitive cricket was

---

[2] While Knowles was working as an agronomist for Caymanas Estates in Jamaica, he is credited with discovering another future West Indies fast bowler, C.D. (Chester) Watson.

absurd. Knowles was insistent though, and he promised to bring Wes to the attention of 'the big boys' at Wanderers by taking him to meet them the following Thursday evening. Wanderers was the oldest club in Barbados and, like its rival club Pickwick, had an exclusively white membership drawn from the island's social elite. As such, it wielded enormous influence within Barbadian cricket. Former Barbados captain Noel Peirce, who would be one of two joint-managers on the 1957 West Indies tour of England; West Indies captain Denis Atkinson and his brother Eric, also a Barbados and future West Indies cricketer, were all members of Wanderers. Knowles assured Wes that, having missed his extraordinary bowling debut against Wanderers' second team, Denis Atkinson would be extremely interested in seeing 'the youngster who bowled like lightning'. Wes, however, had serious misgivings about his new role and, when Thursday came, he decided not to go. Failure to honour a commitment was most uncharacteristic of him, and he was extremely remorseful when an embarrassed Knowles rang to ask what had happened. Wes promised to rectify matters the following week.

His first ball on the practice wicket at Wanderers' Dayrells Road ground hit the nets at such speed that it fizzed around the netting for several seconds before dropping to the ground. Once he had overcome his astonishment Denis Atkinson turned to his friend: 'Did you see that?!'

'See it? I heard it!'

Wes did enough in one short spell to impress the Wanderers establishment. After that evening in August and several more impressive performances for Cable & Wireless, word rapidly spread of the young man who bowled at express pace off a short run. Despite having bowled in just a handful of matches in the intermediate division, he was selected to play as a bowler for the BCA against the BCL in the annual trial match for Barbados.

Around this time Wes acquired a very loyal and influential cheerleader. His mother had been extremely appreciative of his selfless decision to leave school to support her, but she missed working, especially the contact with people. Hence, when Ernest Boyce, the owner of a local dry goods and liquor store, offered her a job in his shop for a few months, she gladly accepted. Despite his annoyance, Wes reluctantly agreed, but fortune smiled on him. Everton Weekes regularly visited the shop to meet his friends, Ernest Weir and Billy Donovan, and he was intrigued when he heard that Ione's son was a young fast bowler called Wes Hall, who had just been picked for the trial match. Like most people, he knew Wes as a wicketkeeper and was unaware of his recent conversion to fast bowling. From then on, Weekes took an active interest in Wes, and helped him whenever he could.

The island trial took place each September at Kensington Oval. It was a major event in the cricketing calendar, with players from the respective leagues vying to stake their claim for a place in the Barbados side. The first division of the BCA comprised ten teams. Nine of them were so close to each other in St Michael that it was possible to cycle between the eight BCA grounds (Police and Spartan shared a ground in Queen's Park, Bridgetown) and watch several matches involving Test cricketers in the same afternoon. The remaining club, Lodge School, is situated in the eastern parish of St John, approximately twelve miles from Bridgetown.

By contrast, the BCL comprised country teams from all over the island as well as some city sides, and so the representative match was a showcase for the finest cricketers in Barbados. It gave selectors the opportunity to gauge how players performed under pressure against high-quality opposition, and the careers of some promising cricketers foundered after a disappointing showing in the fixture. In 1955, for example, the BCL team included a talented and highly rated young batsman named Rawle Pinder. He had scored just 20 runs in BCL's first innings when Wes, bowling from the Southern End at Kensington, delivered a stunning ball which pitched on leg-stump and hit the off-bail. Unfortunately, in common with many excellent BCL players who did not succeed in the island trial match, Pinder never played for Barbados. Wes took four more wickets to complete a successful match but was still surprised to be selected as twelfth man for Barbados in the island's next match, the first of two fixtures in March 1956 against a touring team brought from England to the Caribbean by E.W. Swanton, the commentator and cricket correspondent of *The Daily Telegraph*.

Wes was named in the starting XI for the second of these matches, and on 21 March 1956, aged 18, he made his debut in first-class cricket. It was to prove a chastening experience as he struggled to impose himself against a team that included many England Test stars. The Barbados captain,

C.B. 'Boogles' Williams, lost the toss and, shortly before the team took the field, he politely asked Wes to open the bowling from the Southern End and what field he would like to set for Cowdrey.

Wes stopped in his tracks: 'Excuse me. Cowdrey? As in Colin?'

'Yes, didn't you know he was playing?'

'No. I did not!'

Cowdrey opened the innings for Swanton's XI and, as Wes ran towards the wicket to deliver the first ball of the match, his rhythm felt good; seconds later, his timing was perfect as he released the ball. Cowdrey pushed forward to a ball that left him slightly and took the edge of his bat. The ball flew to second slip, where the chance was dropped by Ken Branker. Unfortunately Wes's fortunes did not improve after that disappointment, with Tom Graveney in particular condemning him to a punishing first-class debut.

It was the first of many encounters between Wes and Graveney, and their relationship was always characterised by a healthy mixture of intense on-field rivalry and mutual respect. They ended their careers with honours about even, an outcome few would have predicted after their initial one-sided contest, in which Graveney was especially severe on Wes in scoring 154 in the tourists' first innings. Wes recalls his astonishment when Graveney went onto the front foot and sent a short-of-a-length delivery crashing against the scoreboard; never in his brief bowling career had a batsman advanced down the wicket to attack a short ball, and the experience left him visibly crestfallen. The ever-gracious Graveney promptly walked down the wicket to Wes, put his hand on his shoulder and offered words of reassurance: 'Listen, son, you've got loads of talent, the thing is, I'm on the go, so don't worry about it.' The gesture meant a great deal to Wes, and he smiles when describing how he returned it a few years later. He hit Graveney during a hostile spell at Lord's and, as the batsman picked himself up off the ground, Wes walked up to him and said: 'Oh, Tom, don't worry about it, you're full of talent, you're a great player, but I'm on the go!'

'You remember that?!'

'Every word!'

Wes finished the match with less than spectacular returns: no wicket for 113 runs in 24 overs, four not out in his only innings, and two catches ... by no means a performance to suggest he might be on the verge of making a breakthrough into first-class cricket, let alone the West Indies Test team. Clearly that view was held by the West Indies selectors, who omitted him from the Quadrangular Tournament, a preliminary trial for the 1957 tour of England. The tournament was held in October 1956 and featured the 'big four' territories: Barbados, British Guiana, Jamaica and Trinidad. As it transpired, missing out on selection proved to be a blessing for Wes. The Barbados pace attack comprised his Combermere teammates, the established Frank King and Lionel Williams. Making his first-class debut against British Guiana, Williams bowled eight overs at a cost of 55 runs and was not selected again in the series. From then on, he decided to concentrate instead on batting, although he had to wait until February 1965 before playing his second and final first-class match, for Barbados against an International Cavaliers XI. Wes considered Williams to be a better bowler than he was and is certain that he would have fared even worse if he had played in the 'quad series'. To this day, he remains grateful for his non-selection!

Following the trials, the squad for England was still far from being decided. The selectors had to trim the numbers from the 50-plus players who took part in the tournament to 26 for the final two trial matches to be played between sides led by Clyde Walcott and Everton Weekes in January and February 1957. Wes had played no first-class cricket since his inauspicious debut in March the previous year, but two individuals were largely responsible for his inclusion in the 26: Everton Weekes and E.W. Swanton.

Weekes had taken an interest in Wes since he heard about him on visits to Mr Boyce's shop. Furthermore, having been born little more than a mile from Wes's home in Station Hill, he recognised in Wes the same spirit and determination that he himself had needed in overcoming the struggles of an underprivileged background. He was soon a loyal supporter of young Wesley Hall and pressed for his inclusion in the trial matches.

Swanton could see beyond the difficult start that Wes had experienced against Graveney and recognised his raw talent and potential. Towards the end of their tour of the Caribbean, in a match against a West Indian XI in Trinidad, Swanton's side had faced an unthreatening opening bowling attack of Sylvester Oliver and Clyde Walcottt, who took just two wickets between them in the match. Swanton noted that with the exception of the Jamaican Roy Gilchrist, West Indies were short of genuine pace, especially as King had announced his retirement after the quad series. He made the point that, although Wes was some way from being the finished article, speed was not a quality he lacked. With the backing of these two influential figures, Wes took his place in the trial matches.

The call from the West Indies selectors

The trials were scheduled to be held in Trinidad, meaning two exciting firsts for Wes: his first flight and the first time he would be staying in a hotel. He played for Walcott's side in the opening game but struggled with the demands of the occasion, taking two wickets for 97 and 'bagging a pair' with the bat. Consoled by the knowledge that he had done his best, Wes began to wonder whether he was destined to play at this level.

In the second match Wes played for Weekes' team, and Everton was typically supportive, encouraging him to adopt a positive mindset. Wes responded well: he scored 29 in the first innings, but it was his outstanding second-innings performances which caught the eyes of the selectors as they finalised the squad to tour England in 1957. They concluded their deliberations during Weekes' team's second innings and, with impeccable timing, Wes chose that moment to make by far the most impressive contribution of his senior career to date, scoring 77 in a ninth-wicket partnership of 119 with Gerry Alexander. During his innings Wes struck consecutive fours off the bowling of Roy Gilchrist, who was unamused at being treated with such disdain, especially by a bowler. Gilchrist rushed over to his captain Walcott and demanded the new ball, which Wes promptly dispatched for a huge six over long-leg. The next ball Wes ducked in anticipation of the inevitable follow-up bouncer and watched as it cleared wicketkeeper Rohan Kanhai on its way to the boundary for four byes. As usual, Gilchrist was not slow to offer his opinion but, by standing his ground and refusing to be intimidated, Wes impressed the selectors as they were reaching their decision. He then followed his excellent batting display by bowling with explosive pace and taking three wickets for 63 runs in Walcott's team's second innings.

The selectors had mixed feelings about Wes: he was very raw, but he was fast; he had some talent; he had just made some runs; Everton liked him. This hardly amounted to a compelling case for his selection, and he waited anxiously for the announcement of the squad. The names of the 16 players who would make up the touring party led by John Goddard –

reinstalled as captain after a five-year hiatus during which he had played in only three of West Indies' 15 Test matches – were put up on the scoreboard in alphabetical order:

... Ganteaume A.G.

Gilchrist R.

and then, the momentous third call for Hall W.W.

Among the bowlers Roy Gilchrist had been a certainty; Jamaican pace bowler Tom Dewdney less so, but as a professional player his inclusion was not a great surprise. Selection policy was probably influenced by the spectacular success enjoyed by Ramadhin and Valentine in England in 1950, with a feeling that the two spinners would again win the series for West Indies. With Sobers, Worrell, Denis Atkinson and to a lesser extent Goddard and Collie Smith supplementing the attack, the selectors probably felt that the bowling had sufficient strength in depth, and were willing to take a chance with Wes.

Of those who were omitted, Eric Atkinson was an established Barbados player who Wes felt certain would be picked ahead of him. Similarly, he would have understood if the selectors had preferred Frank Mason, a bowler Wes rated highly. Mason had the misfortune – in cricketing terms – of hailing from St Vincent at a time when players from outside the big four countries tended to be overlooked.

If Wes was the most surprising inclusion in the squad, perhaps the biggest story to emerge from the trials was the omission of the wicketkeeper/batsman, Clairmonte Depeiaza, who in 1955 had scored 122 against Australia in the record partnership with Denis Atkinson. Depeiaza then played two Test matches on West Indies' tour of New Zealand in the early part of 1956, and he was one of six wicketkeepers who took part in the trials. Over the course of the two games, the other five were asked to keep wicket and, in the absence of any communication from the selectors, Depeiaza concluded that his place was in jeopardy. Consequently, before the announcement of the squad, he signed a contract with Forfarshire to play professionally in Scotland, thus ruling himself out of the tour, never to play first-class cricket again. To the surprise of many observers, two more uncapped players were chosen as wicketkeepers: Franz 'Gerry' Alexander, a Jamaican and a Cambridge Blue; and 21-year-old batting prodigy and part-time wicketkeeper Rohan Kanhai from British Guiana.

In the event Kanhai kept wicket in the first three Tests in 1957 before the gloves were passed to Alexander for the remainder of the series and beyond.

The Trinidadian openers Andy Ganteaume and Nyron Asgarali were the most unexpected batting selections. Ganteaume was 36 and had not played Test cricket since his debut against England at Port of Spain in 1948, when he scored a century in his only Test innings (giving him a career Test batting average of 112, which remains the highest in the history of Test cricket). Asgarali was the same age and probably felt that the chance to play Test cricket had passed him by. However, they each scored runs in the Walcott v Weekes trial matches, and both were familiar to Caribbean cricket fans, leaving Wes very much the unknown quantity in the squad. Even large numbers of cricket followers in Barbados were unaware of West Indies new fast bowler: because he played for Cable & Wireless in the BCA intermediate division, those who remembered him from his first division days with Combermere, knew him as a wicketkeeper/batsman.

The twelve-a-side trial matches were not accorded first-class status, and so Wes's first-class record remained no wicket for 113 runs and four not out with the bat. It was therefore particularly bold of Weekes to declare his support for him. Everton had displayed remarkable foresight in looking 'ten years down the road' when he recommended Wes to the selectors, and Wes was determined to repay this faith.

On receiving his third call, Wes felt a combination of astonishment, excitement and pride. Just two years after leaving school, he was about to set sail for England after an extraordinary sequence of events. As a small boy his ambitions may have been limited in number to two – to attend Combermere and play cricket for West Indies – but each was so improbable that achieving both was virtually impossible. Gaining a scholarship to Combermere can be explained by Wes's ability and hard work; however, the path which led to him representing West Indies is far more convoluted. His plan was to be a star batsman, not a bowler who assumed the new ball via the wicketkeeper's gloves. Playing top-level cricket in the school first team as a wicketkeeper was down to a combination of Ronnie Hughes' rare vision and Wes's skill and devotion to practice. His progress from that point to his dream of playing for West Indies appears to be a case of extreme serendipity: joining Cable & Wireless in order to support his mother indirectly gave rise to the bizarre scenario which saw him bowl for the first time; her unexpected return to work brought him to the attention of Everton Weekes; and being overlooked for the Quad Series in which other bowlers fell from contention was his final stroke of good fortune. At the same time, his driving ambition was backed by belief, and he never for a moment accepted that his dreams were unattainable.

People may have considered him an upstart with overblown ideas, but he drew inspiration from David slaying Goliath against seemingly overwhelming odds. True to his strong Christian beliefs, Wes credits God with enabling him to realise his boyhood visions of the future. Furthermore, he believed that the dreams themselves were guided by a higher force; if not, how and why would he have been moved to make such wild prophesies and then invite ridicule by broadcasting them? When reflecting on the twists of fate that worked in his favour, the way events unfolded seems so arbitrary that Wes is convinced it had to be the work of God.

4

England 1957: A Difficult Tour

The 1957 tour of England was a chastening experience for Wes. He had not known what to expect when the team's banana boat, the *Golfito*, set sail, but it very quickly became obvious to him that life as an international cricketer was not going to be straightforward.

Upon arriving in England in April, Wes was shocked by the cold weather, but the players had to acclimatise quickly, with practice sessions beginning the day after the team's welcoming dinner. Another surprise came when he discovered that the players would receive a wage of just £7 a week from the West Indies Cricket Board of Control[1] (WICBC). However, being a new boy, Wes said nothing, especially as Everton told him that on the historic 1950 tour of England, the Three Ws had been paid £5 a week. The situation was not helped by Cable & Wireless company policy, whereby time taken off work for sporting pursuits was treated as unpaid leave. Again Wes did not complain, a decision he took out of respect for a fellow employee, the cyclist Ken Farnum. At the time of the 1952 Olympic Games in Helsinki, the company gave approval for Farnum to take the time off providing he found employees willing to cover his shifts during his absence.

Things took a turn for the better after Wes received a letter from Sir Godfrey Ince, who – to Wes's good fortune – had been appointed chairman of Cable & Wireless eighteen months previously. In his letter Sir Godfrey expressed his pleasure in seeing a member of the company playing cricket in England for West Indies and asked if Wes would pose for a photograph for *Zodiac*, the company's in-house magazine. Over lunch at the company's Holborn headquarters, Sir Godfrey said that he would like Wes to appear on the magazine's front cover to promote the issue's main feature: *Men of the World that we employ*. As the chairman of Cable & Wireless, Sir Godfrey was unprepared for the response. Wes

---

[1] Formed as the West Indies Cricket Board of Control in 1920, the governing body of West Indian cricket changed its name to the West Indies Cricket Board in 1996. It was rebranded as Cricket West Indies in 2017.

agreed on condition that he received payment, explaining that for the six months in England his allowance was just £1 a day.

At this, Sir Godfrey stood up, walked over to a teleprinter and started typing. The reply came promptly and, after reading it, Sir Godfrey smiled at Wes and informed him that he would be on full pay for the duration of the tour. Wes thanked the chairman and told him he was welcome to take 1,000 pictures of him! Sir Godfrey laughed: 'You're going to do well son; you've got guts and a sense of humour.' Wes was so appreciative of Sir Godfrey's intervention that he vowed to repay the gesture by giving a full year's notice when the time came for him to turn professional, a promise he would keep a couple of years later.

This episode provided a positive start to the tour for Wes, and during his time in England he continued to demonstrate his resourcefulness. Despite being thousands of miles from home in unfamiliar surroundings, he displayed the maturity that would stand him in good stead throughout his cricket career and beyond. Following West Indies' groundbreaking success on their previous visit in 1950, the players approached the 1957 tour in an optimistic frame of mind, confident that, with a blend of experienced stars and talented youngsters, they would be able to emulate their predecessors. The optimism was misplaced: disappointing on-field performances and results against a strong England side; injuries and illness; and a less-than-harmonious relationship between the players and management, combined to produce an unhappy tour.

In the Test series, England avenged their defeat of seven years earlier with a convincing 3-0 victory, and the outcome could easily have been worse for the tourists, who battled to hold on for draws at Edgbaston and Trent Bridge. The series was dominated by the heavy scoring of England's batsmen, most notably the celebrated middle-order trio of Peter May, Tom Graveney and Colin Cowdrey. Ably supported by the left-handed opener Peter Richardson, they made runs consistently and completely outshone the West Indian batting stars, Worrell, Weekes and Walcott. Of the great Three Ws, only Worrell's batting performance was anywhere close to expectations, and that was largely due to his magnificent 191 not out at Trent Bridge in the Third Test. The innings boosted his series aggregate runs from 159 to 350, still way fewer than the leading opposition batsmen (May 489, Graveney 472, Cowdrey 435), all of whom played at least three fewer innings.

Walcott and Weekes fared worse although the statistics fail to tell the whole story. Weekes was troubled for the entire tour by sinusitis so severe that Wes was deeply affected by the plight of his mentor and friend: 'I saw Everton Weekes violently sick every morning.' Weekes' suffering was compounded in the Second Test at Lord's in June when he broke a finger, yet typically he returned to score a valiant 90 in West Indies' second innings. That innings is considered by Wes the finest he has ever seen and, by the great Weekes himself, to be the best of his career. Thereafter, Weekes played in pain throughout the rest of the tour. Walcott, too, was seriously handicapped by injury having pulled a muscle in his leg – coincidentally during an innings of 90 – in the First Test at Edgbaston, and, although he would go on to finish fifth in the English first-class batting averages that season, he failed to produce his customary dominant form in the Tests. The Three Ws had scored a prodigious number of runs for West Indies over the previous decade, and the team struggled to cope with the loss of their output.

The West Indies bowlers also failed to match the consistency of their English counterparts: all six of England's frontline bowlers took ten or more wickets in the series, compared to only three West Indians, two of whom took exactly ten. Left-arm spinner Alf Valentine, who along with Sonny Ramadhin had been England's nemesis when both sensationally burst onto the scene in 1950, suffered a calamitous loss of confidence and form. Valentine played in just two of the Tests and failed to take a single wicket in the 26 overs he bowled. Ramadhin was the tourists' leading wicket taker with 14, seven of which came at Edgbaston in the first innings of the First Test. He began the second innings in similar vein, taking the first two wickets to fall as England reached 65, before a change of approach by the England batsmen negated his threat for the rest of the innings and the remainder of the series. England's captain Peter May and Colin Cowdrey came together with the score on 113 for three. Both men adopted the tactic of 'playing' Ramadhin by thrusting their front leg way down the wicket against his bowling and padding the ball away without any attempt to offer a stroke. As the laws then stood, a batsman could not be given out lbw to a ball striking the pad outside the line of off-stump, even when not attempting a shot. Moreover, the ball was striking the pad so far down the wicket that if contact was in line with the stumps, umpires were reluctant to give a batsman out, and none of the numerous appeals by Ramadhin was upheld[2]. When Cowdrey was out for 154, he and May had taken their partnership to 411, which at the time was a fourth wicket record in Test cricket and is still an English record for any wicket in Tests.

Wes was dismayed that England chose to employ tactics that could at best be described as negative; at worst underhand. As a young man brought up in Barbados in the 1940s and '50s, he had been taught to associate the British with values such as honour and fair play. He struggled to reconcile the qualities he had so admired in the likes of Major Noott and Sir Godfrey Ince with the cynical tactics of the English batsmen:

> In the second innings against Ram, those fellas put the pad forward and the bat behind with no attempt to play a shot. They still couldn't pick him; they just pushed their foot forward and then kicked him away. But they made a lot of runs, and Ram was finished.

Ramadhin was indeed 'finished' as a force in the series. He took just five more wickets in the remaining four Tests, and England had succeeded in blunting West Indies' most potent weapon.

The effects of England's strategy should not be underestimated. West Indies' confidence that Ramadhin and Valentine would make a significant impact led to an over-reliance on their star spinners, and they went into the series without a credible backup plan. The pace attack was young and inexperienced: the three fastest bowlers Dewdney, Gilchrist and Hall were 23, 22 and 19 years old respectively, and only Dewdney, with five caps and 13 Test wickets to his name, had previously played Test cricket. By comparison, England's established pace trio of Fred Trueman, Brian Statham and Trevor Bailey had played in 94 Tests and taken 270 wickets between them.

Although the 1957 West Indians' overall win/loss record was similar to that of their 1950 counterparts, the success of a touring side is judged by its record in the Tests. By that yardstick, the summer was one to forget, as West Indies were trounced by England. Their performance prompted a wave of criticism from the Caribbean, often directed at the Three Ws. In the press, Walcott and Weekes were unfairly accused of failing to give their all and of not working to ensure that they were fit for the Tests. Wes completely refutes this: unlike their detractors, he witnessed at first hand their struggles with injury and the efforts they made in extremely trying circumstances.

[2] In his book *A History of West Indies Cricket* (1988), Jamaican Prime Minister Michael Manley (1924-1997) estimates that, during England's second innings, Ramadhin 'must have had at least 50 appeals turned down for lbw'.

Despite their own problems, all three men conducted themselves with their customary dignity, and went out of their way to help the young players.

As the junior member of the party, Wes found that his appearances were limited. Leading up to the First Test at Edgbaston, he featured in just four of the ten tour matches, and failed to convince the selectors that he merited a place in the Test side. Like many bowlers accustomed to the hard pitches of the Caribbean, he struggled to adjust to the soft surfaces in England. He bowled the shorter length that he had always done but, with the lusher grass making the approaches and footholds softer, he struggled with his control and bowled wide a lot of the time: 'Bowling wide in the West Indies with pace is not really a sin, but in England on the slow wickets they make you pay!' Wes had no idea how to adjust to the unfamiliar conditions and, incredibly, he received no coaching on the tour. Weekes and Walcott were particularly supportive – more on a personal than a technical level – by offering their encouragement and making sure he remained in good spirits. He was also grateful for the kindness and encouragement shown to him by his room-mate Roy Gilchrist. 'Gilly' was only a couple of years older than Wes and still relatively inexperienced at first-class level; however, unlike Wes, he had been a fast bowler from a young age and possessed a 'tremendous cricket brain'. He shared his knowledge with Wes, who came to view him as a bowling mentor and – along with Sobers – his best friend within the West Indies team.

Given the meticulous preparation and attention to detail in modern professional sport, it is hard to believe the extent to which Wes was left to his own devices on the 1957 tour. In the softer English conditions he felt far from ready when he arrived at the stumps, but he was loath to lengthen his run up, because he noticed the English pace bowlers running in to bowl from 18 yards and it seemed to work well for them. The problems with his run-up and a general lack of control meant that Wes never felt particularly comfortable when he was bowling, and he was overlooked for all five Tests. Used sparingly throughout the tour, he managed a total of just 27 wickets in 15 first-class matches. In his defence he points out that 22 of his victims had scored a century in first-class cricket, 'which suggested that I wasn't that bad!' It seemed to him that whenever he delivered a good ball, he took a wicket, but unfortunately those good balls were few and far between.

Wes wondered why management did not send him for coaching at Alf Gover's cricket school[3] in south London. As the world's leading bowling coach, Gover would have been able to help Wes with the problems he was experiencing, especially the uncertainty with his run-up. Worrell was saddened by the way Wes and the other young players were treated. In Ernest Eytle's 1963 biography, *Frank Worrell,* he made the following pointed comments:

> The youngsters who had performed so well at home were expected to do the same here, and this resulted in a lack of planning ... There was little tact employed in dealing with the younger members, and it was depressing to see them struggling in unfamiliar conditions without proper advice and assistance.

For Wes the euphoria of his selection could easily – and justifiably – have turned to despair as the unhappy tour lurched on amid a growing chorus of disapproval from home. He was on the receiving end of more than his fair share of criticism, with his first tour of England branded a disaster by cricket 'experts' in the Caribbean. To single out a rookie in this way was unfair, especially as Wes had played no part in West Indies' capitulation in the Tests, three of which were lost by an innings inside three days. Of course, his wicket tally was disappointing but not so dire as to merit the abuse he received. Naturally enough, his initial reaction was to ask why he was being picked on, but very quickly he was able to deal with the situation calmly and logically. He reasoned that, if criticism was being meted out to established stars of West Indian cricket, it was little wonder that he too was a target.

The tour may not have brought Wes the cricketing success he had hoped for but, in terms of his personal development, the experience was invaluable. By filtering out negative influences and concentrating on the positive aspects of his time in England, he was able to make the most of the opportunities that the trip presented. He had to pinch himself sometimes, such as when he entered a West Indies dressing room for the first time and looked around and saw Worrell, Weekes, Walcott, Sobers,

---

[3] A.R. Gover (1908-2001) played first-class cricket as a fast bowler for Surrey between 1928 and 1947; he played four Test matches for England. When his cricket career finished, he devoted himself to coaching at his cricket school in Wandsworth. He is credited with helping to develop the careers of many leading Test players.

and Kanhai. Two weeks later he was at Buckingham Palace meeting the Queen: 'Such a gracious lady, I had seen her so many times, and here I was shaking her hand!'

Prior to the First Test at Edgbaston, Wes was heartened by words of support he received from one of the opposing team's fiercest competitors. He had encountered the England fast bowler Fred Trueman the previous week when the West Indians visited Bramall Lane for the tour match against Yorkshire. Wes bowled well and took four wickets in that match, including that of Trueman in the second innings, and the two men immediately struck up a rapport. At Edgbaston Trueman greeted Wes and asked why he was dressed in his suit. He was most surprised when Wes told him that he had not been selected. Despite Wes's rawness, Trueman felt that a West Indies opening attack of Gilchrist and Hall would have caused more problems for the English top-order batsmen than the chosen new-ball partnership of Gilchrist and the medium-paced Worrell.

At Lord's in the Second Test Wes was again left out of the side, but his spirits were raised by the unexpected appearance of a friendly face. Mr Ivan Smith, his geography teacher from Combermere (whose claims to fame included playing in goal for the Barbados football team), was on a scholarship in Paris, and he flew to England specially to see his former pupil. Like many Barbadians, Mr Smith knew Wes as a wicketkeeper and was completely unfamiliar with Wes Hall the bowler. Although he did not see him in action at Lord's, in true Combermerian tradition he was eager to show support for a member of the Combermere 'family', and Wes was touched that his master should take the trouble to come to London to seek him out.

That first day at Lord's provided a further memorable experience for Wes: 'The gentleman came into the pavilion and he served tea! You didn't serve yourself. I had to tell myself: "Hey, I belong here!" Who would have thought a young boy from The Ivy could say that?'

In addition to the many new and exciting experiences that the tour presented, Wes decided to use his £1 daily allowance to explore the country. The thirst for knowledge from his school days remained undiminished, and now he had the opportunity to witness at first hand places that previously existed for him only in textbooks. Taught by his mentor Ronnie Hughes, history had been his favourite subject at Combermere. For the entire five years the syllabus comprised British history, and Wes was captivated as the subject came to life before his eyes. Each time the tourists visited a new county, he would use any free time to travel to nearby places of interest. In London he took a boat down the Thames to the Tower of London; when they visited Kent he went to Canterbury Cathedral to see where Thomas Becket was murdered; and in Yorkshire he visited battlefields from the Wars of the Roses. It was not just his love of history that motivated Wes to embark on his missions of discovery. He was enthralled by Piccadilly Circus; he rode for hours on the underground; travelled on the top deck of double-decker buses; and took a (short) ride in a taxi! When the team was in Yorkshire, he even made the journey across the Pennines for a day out in the Lake District.

Already Wes was very clearly his own man, and he was able to gain strength from his experiences in England. Perhaps above all, he emerged from the tour with the confidence of knowing that he could cope with adversity and even turn it into something positive: 'The 1957 tour did more for me culturally, and as a man, than it did for me the sportsman. I didn't get 100 wickets, but I found that it was sort of a summer paradise.'

The match against Cambridge University in May was only the third first-class match of Wes's career, and his second appearance of the tour, having played a week earlier against Oxford University. The fact that it was the tourists' seventh match was an early sign that he did not feature prominently in the management's plans. The occasion was significant for Wes: it brought him his first wicket in first-class cricket when he bowled the Cambridge opener G.W. (Geoffrey) Cook. Wes finished the match with five wickets, including in the second innings that of a man with whom he would have many contests over the next decade, E.R. Dexter.

While in Cambridge Wes had a less challenging encounter than those with Ted Dexter on the cricket field. At a social function, a priest came over to talk to him, and asked if he was Wesley Hall from Barbados. He then asked where Wes was christened and, when Wes told him the name of the church was James' Street Methodist Church, the priest's suspicions were confirmed – he had christened him!

'Then you must be Reverend Eweling!'

The two men celebrated this 'million-to-one chance' by spending an enjoyable hour together in a nearby café.

5

Back to Basics

Immediately after the 1957 tour Wes and several other players took part in a friendly match in Jamaica. While there, he took the enterprising step of seeking out George Headley, with the hope of spending some time in the company of the former great batsman. Wes was warmly welcomed by Headley and his wife Rena, who invited him to stay for the weekend as their guest. He sat enthralled as Headley shared farsighted thoughts and theories on cricket. Of all the things he learned that weekend, Wes was most impressed by Headley's mental approach to the game. He advised Wes to adopt a more positive and ambitious mindset when batting and to set himself higher standards when bowling. He encouraged him to follow the example of all truly great players by constantly pushing himself to achieve more and never be satisfied with his performance. This begins on the practice field, for no matter how much natural talent he possesses, a cricketer gives himself the best chance of success only if he works on his fitness and technique. Headley's words convinced Wes that he had much work to do if he was to become a top-class bowler.

During their conversation, Headley told Wes that the most aggressive cricketers were spin bowlers. This observation amused Wes, but over time he would come to agree that spinners are the meanest, most competitive players on a cricket field. Although fast bowlers may glare in anger and curse when the ball goes for four through the slips, they accept that it will happen from time to time. By comparison Headley cited the example of the Australian spinners Bill O'Reilly and Clarrie Grimmett, who took every run scored against them as a personal insult. Hence, against spin bowlers, Headley adopted the tactic of aiming to hit the ball hard straight back to them (to the side of their bowling hand), confident in the knowledge that they would always try to prevent runs at any cost. He found that bowlers had difficulty in spinning the ball after their fingers had been stung by a few well-struck drives! Wes was impressed by Headley's lateral thinking: 'Deliberately playing the ball back to the bowler ... no coach would ever tell a batsman to do that. I have never met a great player who isn't also a great thinker.' Within his own team, Wes later saw the embodiment of the combative spinner in Lance Gibbs, who constantly challenged the opposition batsman: 'He was far more aggressive than me! And I have to agree with Headley. He was right. They didn't call O'Reilly "Tiger" because he was docile!'

The time the two men spent together was precious to Wes. Since he was a young boy, he had revered Headley, and he could recall with ease the details of Headley's Test career which produced ten centuries in just 22 matches and an average of 60.83. Headley was grateful for the genuine interest shown by such a respectful 20-year-old, and he punctuated their conversations with numerous anecdotes, including a story from his Test debut in Bridgetown, against the 1929-30 England team.

Inter-island rivalry was intense and, as a 19-year-old from Jamaica[1] with a big reputation, Headley was regarded with suspicion in Barbados. When he arrived at the wharf in Bridgetown, he was taunted by a man called Flanagan, a well-known hailer for the Pickwick club, which played its matches at Kensington Oval: 'I hear you're the great George Headley! You think you can bat like Master George or Master Tim[2]? We will see.' Headley smiled politely and made his way to greet his hosts before being taken to his hotel. He recalled that at the team's net practice, he saw off the four fast bowlers with an array of spectacular shots, form which he took into the Test as he scored 176 in West Indies' second innings. West Indies were able to draw the match, and Flanagan was converted!

Headley finished the series with four centuries, including two in the same match in the Third Test in Georgetown, and 223 in the Fourth Test in Kingston, the first double-century in Test cricket by a West Indian. He finished the series with 703 runs at an average of 87.87 and, thanks to his majestic batting, West Indies drew the series 1-1.

To conclude his thoughts on Headley, Wes is reminded of a gracious sentiment from Sir Don Bradman. Commentators of the day referred to Headley as 'The Black Bradman'; Sir Don countered that he would be pleased if they called him 'The White Headley'.

---

[1] Headley was born in Panama in 1909 to a Barbadian father and a Jamaican mother. He moved to Kingston with his mother at the age of ten.

[2] George Challenor and P.H. 'Tim' Tarilton were prominent Barbadian batsmen, both of whom played for Pickwick.

In October 1957, when Wes eventually returned to Barbados, the first person to greet him was his mother. Having followed the fortunes of the West Indies team via the radio and newspaper reports, she was aware that Wes had struggled with inconsistent form and had not been selected to play in any of the Tests. She was understandably upset that her son had endured a difficult time, and she worried about the possible effects on him. Her fears were eased when they met, as Wes enthused about all the wonderful things he had seen. He recounted his visit to Buckingham Palace and told her how he had indulged his love of British history. Nevertheless, she suspected that he was putting on a brave face, and she arranged for the two of them to go to a dance together the following evening at the Drill Hall at the Garrison Savannah.

Wes was filled with pride as he set off for the dance with his mother, 'a beautiful 39-year-old lady, who looked so good'. He was aware that as such a handsome couple they were turning heads, but his focus was on his mother and her words of encouragement. This was the fourth of the five occasions when she would offer her support and reassurance at a pivotal juncture in her son's life. She told him to put his experiences in England behind him and concentrate single-mindedly on the future by working to correct his mistakes; she would provide him with all the support and help he needed. Her final words have stayed with him ever since: 'Remember that nobody can make you feel inferior without your permission.'

Wes was at a crossroads. The targets that he had set himself when he was eight – to acquire a good education at Combermere and to play for West Indies – drove him on in his early years, and he had attained both before he was 20 years old. After the disappointments in England though, the reality of playing for West Indies felt a lot less like success than it had in his dreams. Wes realised that achieving targets was not an end in itself but that each one represented a stage in his development; therefore, he needed to redefine his goals and keep pushing himself. The first step on that road was to act on the advice of his mother and George Headley and to work out how to become a better bowler. Teaching the basic skills to youngsters was considered the responsibility of the schools, and as a batsman and wicketkeeper at Combermere he never took part in the bowling sessions. In fact, he had never received any bowling tuition in his life, yet remarkably he had been on an overseas tour as a West Indies fast bowler!

His conversations with Headley had inspired him to further his cricket education, and shortly after returning to Barbados from Jamaica he visited the house of the former West Indies fast bowler Herman Griffith to seek his advice on bowling. Wes explained his good fortune in being selected for the tour and his subsequent difficulties in coming to terms with English conditions. He then listened intently as Griffith put the situation in perspective and offered his advice, paraphrased as follows:

> You were lucky and unlucky to be picked to go to England. You're pacey and, if you had gone somewhere else, you would probably have got wickets, but in England you can't get away with bowling bad balls. England is a place that will teach you what *not* to do. So you need to work on your line and length. Whether you're fast or medium paced, and wherever you bowl, you need to be able to consistently bowl line and length and, to do that, you need to practise and you need to be fit.

It was painfully obvious to Wes that he had neither the strength nor the technical knowledge of a top-class fast bowler. He resolved to devote his free time to practice, split equally between working on his fitness and his bowling technique. In the absence of any coaching or official guidance during the England tour, it was left to his friend Everton Weekes to encourage him to make changes to his training methods, with an emphasis on strengthening the relevant muscles. Wes embarked on a punishing schedule, fitting training around his shifts at Cable & Wireless. His daily routine comprised a five-mile run in the morning, followed by a couple of hours bowling practice and then another five-mile run to end the day. The running required minimal planning but, to help with his bowling, the curators at Spartan and at Cable & Wireless both kindly agreed to prepare a wicket for him at their respective grounds. He bowled at one stump with another placed on the pitch on a good length as he strove to improve his control and accuracy. He had nobody to help him, except on the few occasions when the groundsmen happened to be on hand to return the balls to him. Regular running and swimming were transforming him into a lean, strong athlete, but his bowling was still wayward on the few occasions when he played in matches.

The highest profile of these was the fixture between Barbados and the Pakistani tourists in January 1958. It came early in the tour and, with the

First Test due to start in Bridgetown the following week, players were anxious to stake a claim for a place in the Test side. It was Wes's first match since the England tour, and he struggled with the new ball when the Pakistanis batted towards the end of the second day. It rained overnight, and the following morning he was relishing the chance to bowl on a lively pitch, but captain John Goddard chose to open with the medium-paced seam bowling of the Atkinson brothers, Denis and Eric. Both exploited the conditions, with Eric bowling particularly well and taking four wickets. When the time came for a change of bowling, Wes was expecting to be called, but instead Goddard brought on Sobers to bowl his left-arm spin. Eventually the captain turned to Wes, but by the end of the innings he had bowled 25 expensive overs for the single wicket of Wallis Mathias. He bowled only a handful of overs in the second innings to finish with match figures of one for 126. Adding this to his return of no wickets for 113 on his debut for Barbados against Swanton's XI two years earlier, his two first-class appearances at Kensington Oval had yielded one wicket for 239 runs. The Barbadian cricket public was less than enthusiastic about their latest fast bowler: 'This boy Hall, he can't play' and 'He'll never be a fast bowler, he needs a longer run up' were two of the more complimentary observations that he overheard. He accepted the second of these comments as constructive criticism and took note of it.

Wes was not selected for the first match against Pakistan, nor for any of the other Tests. After a few months of practice, he had become fitter and stronger, and his bowling was quicker, but the problems with his technique persisted. Control and consistency remained elusive. He realised that raw speed could get him only so far; he would need to analyse his game and make changes if he was going to succeed at the highest level.

Again Wes was left to work things out for himself: 'I took note of the opening batsman, Imtiaz Ahmed, who disdainfully hooked every bouncer I bowled to the boundary, and I swore that I would turn that weakness into my strength.' Remembering his difficulties in England and what he had heard after the match against the Pakistanis, it occurred to him that he was arriving at the wicket too early, so instead of bowling from his usual 18 yards, he experimented by doubling the length of his run. The change marked a defining moment in his career as he finally felt he was on the right track. He practised in the nets and found that at the 18-yard mark in his approach, far from being ready to bowl, he was just beginning to feel balanced:

As I walk back to my bowling mark, I will decide what type of ball I wish to bowl. I turn to begin my run-up, starting slowly, gradually increasing my pace so that when I reach the 18-yard mark, I am feeling really good in my run-up. If I am very well balanced at the halfway point, I will usually bowl a quick ball in the six-metre zone short of a length but, if I am unsteady at this point, I will aim to bowl in the four-metre zone on a good length and trust that my action will produce an awayswinger. When I reach the crease, I am at my fastest and transferring the weight of my body at the moment of delivery from my right foot to my left foot. The right hand goes across my body and my momentum takes me off the pitch in my follow-through; otherwise, I will have the tendency to run down the pitch and incur a warning.

Wes was wary of over-complicating matters by becoming too technical. It came naturally to him to bowl side-on with his back facing extra-cover as he leapt into his delivery stride. At this point he concentrated on getting his left foot high in the air, resulting in a classical, high action which allowed him to propel the ball at extreme speed without exerting undue effort.

Not only was Wes able to generate extra pace as a result of these changes, he also noticed significant improvements in his control. He worked for countless hours on grooving an action that he would be able to reproduce under pressure. The more he practised, the fewer were the days when he struggled to find his rhythm. When everything came together, the feeling was almost ethereal:

When I am bowling, and I hit that zone, I feel as if I am soaring like an eagle, it's a feeling so beautiful. I don't sweat when I get into that mood because it's almost effortless, it just comes easily, and everything flows.

Probably uniquely for a bowler of his status and quality, Wes never received any coaching. He remains proud that his self-taught action was admired throughout the cricket world. Several years later he was deeply honoured when the great Australian fast bowler Dennis Lillee said that his action was modelled on Wes Hall's, 'and you can't have a better compliment than that!'

Wes had taken notice of his critics, and his success in devising and perfecting an effective bowling style for himself further demonstrated his drive and will to succeed. 'I suddenly understood that failure is not a single cataclysmic event but a series of little mistakes I was making, culminating in something big.'

He was determined to force his way back into contention for a place in the Barbados and West Indies sides, but for the time being he had to settle for a spectator's role as the West Indies team comprehensively defeated the 1957-58 Pakistani tourists. The most significant feature of the series was the imperious form of the 21-year-old Garfield Sobers, whose maiden Test century was a sensational 365 not out in the Third Test at Sabina Park, a new world record. Sobers' breakthrough heralded the beginning of the reign of the dominant cricketer of his generation: a special player who would be the foundation of West Indies' success and captivate crowds the world over for years to come.

The squad for the next West Indies Test series – a tour of India and Pakistan beginning in November – had been selected as early as April at the conclusion of the final Test against Pakistan, but subsequently Frank Worrell stood down to concentrate on studying for the final exams of his degree at Manchester University. His absence left a major hole which the selectors decided to fill by naming two replacements and, although Wes may have been out of the Test match spotlight, his work and attitude on the practice field had impressed the Barbados selectors. In July 1958 they picked him for the two inter-island matches in Jamaica, where Barbados was due to play for the first time since 1952. Significantly for Wes, a notable name on the Jamaica team sheet was that of former West Indies opening batsman Allan Rae, the captain of the home side, who was now a West Indies selector. Rae had been a hero of the great 1950 team, and he commanded much respect in the Caribbean. Wes opened the bowling for Barbados so, when Jamaica batted, the two of them immediately crossed swords. He took three wickets in a blistering opening spell to reduce Jamaica to 37 for four. One of his victims was Rae, who was beaten for pace and clean bowled, but not before he had been overheard telling his batting partner that Wes's bowling was 'the fastest I have faced since Lindwall [in 1951-52]; this man's shaking my bat!' Wes finished the match with six wickets, and his fine form continued as he took five in the second match, again including Rae, caught by Cammie Smith in the slips.

His timing could not have been better: Rae was so impressed by the rejuvenated Hall that he immediately recommended to the other selectors that Wes should be one of the replacements for Worrell. (The other was the Jamaican batsman J.K. Holt.) For Wes this was a moment of liberation. After almost a year out of the West Indies reckoning, the months of intense work on the practice ground had paid off, dispelling the fears that he may not get another chance.

The arrival of Wes Hall as an international cricketer at the age of 19 had come about as the result of a series of unlikely, haphazard events but, since his return from England, Wes had taken control of the situation by setting his own agenda and making progress on his terms. He approached the 1958-59 West Indies tour to India and Pakistan in a positive frame of mind, confident that he possessed the technical skills and the strength of character to succeed. He is convinced that the adversity he experienced in England was helpful to him:

> If I had played well in England, I wouldn't have done all that work on my bowling and made the improvements to my technique which stood me in good stead for the rest of my career. You do not necessarily learn when you are successful, because there isn't the same motivation to analyse and improve things. I was motivated by my hunger to be successful. I had to get on the bus to go to see Herman Griffith, and then I taught myself how to bowl. I had seen England and it was a wonderful experience, and I knew that if I wanted to see it again I had to learn to bowl. And I did – by working for hours and hours on my own.

6

Taking Test Cricket by Storm

Wes got to know Roy Gilchrist during the 1957 tour of England. The final port of call for the *Golfito* on the tourists' journey from Barbado, was Port Antonio in Jamaica, where a cargo of bananas was loaded and the final passengers embarked. Among them were the Jamaican cricketers, including Gilchrist, Wes's cabin-mate. In private Gilly was far less assured than his on-field persona, so Wes – the more outgoing and talkative of the two – tried to put him at ease during the ten days at sea. From that point their friendship blossomed. As Gilly's closest friend, Wes is convinced that an incident before the West Indians' first county match – against Worcestershire – contributed to Gilchrist's feelings of insecurity and detachment.

The team was taking an evening stroll in Worcester, with the shy Gilchrist typically lingering some distance behind. Two policemen recognised the players in their West Indies blazers; they welcomed them to the city and wished them a successful tour. When one of the officers asked why Gilchrist was detached from the rest of the party, Denis Atkinson decided to play a prank. At Atkinson's request, the officers quizzed Gilchrist and suggested he walk with them to rejoin the others. They caught up and asked Atkinson if he knew Gilchrist. Atkinson said that he had never seen him before in his life. At that point, Wes saw that Gilchrist was overcome with panic:

> Gilly was frozen, in a state of shock ... until the guys started laughing and hugging him; letting him know they were only fooling around. They would never have known how deeply their little joke would affect Gilly. In retrospect, had I been more attuned to behavioural psychology then, as his room-mate, I probably would have reacted differently and been able to help him by sharing some of the things I'd learned. Genuine light-hearted ribbing and malicious aggravation stirred the same reaction, because young Roy never learned how to differentiate between the two.

Although Gilchrist's total of ten wickets from four Test matches in 1957 was a modest return, it was sufficient to establish him as West Indies' leading fast bowler. That status was confirmed in the home series against Pakistan in early 1958. While Wes was working alone for hours on end to resurrect his career, Gilchrist was advancing his by bowling with extreme pace and taking 21 wickets to become the leading West Indian wicket-taker in the series. His ability to unsettle the great Hanif Mohammad was arguably as crucial to West Indies' series victory as Sobers' prodigious run-scoring. Gilchrist dismissed Pakistan's master batsman on five occasions and, at Bridgetown in the First Test, he was responsible for bowling a delivery that went down in local folklore: the first ball he bowled flew high over Hanif and hit the sightscreen so hard that it rebounded all the way back to the wicketkeeper Alexander. Encouraged by his success in the series, Gilchrist gained in confidence and finally began to feel more a part of the team.

Whilst in England in 1957, Gilchrist had signed to play the following season in the Central Lancashire League for Middleton, which he joined after the series against Pakistan. He led the club to their first league title for 20 years, although not without controversy. On West Indies' 1958-59 tour of India, Wes and Gilly were again room-mates, and Wes asked what the bad press from England was about. Gilchrist explained that a batsman who he had struck with a bouncer charged down the wicket towards him wielding his bat. True to form, Gilly did not back down: he pulled up a stump to defend himself and then found himself accused of being the aggressor.

Contrary to Gilchrist's reputation, Wes always found him to be a congenial companion, always willing to give advice and support. He had developed genuine respect for Gilly in England, and this grew during the tour of India. Both were selected to play against Baroda in the tourists' second match and, as a late addition to the squad, Wes was surprised and excited to be in the team so early in the tour, especially as the First Test was due to start in Bombay just 18 days later.

On the evening before the Baroda match, his room-mate had plenty to say: 'Wes, who is the best fast bowler in the world?'

'You are, Gilly.'

'Oh, I like you, College Boy!' (a term he used to describe anyone who had been to senior school!) 'By the end of this tour, I will make *you* number two!'

Wes was taken aback by such fanciful talk, but he was intrigued by Gilly's choice of words. 'I will make you', rather than 'you will be', reassured him that he had found a true ally. Outlandish as Gilly's statement was, his confidence was infectious.

Gilchrist's next comment was equally unexpected: he announced that the following day he would like Wes to bowl around the wicket. Wes was horrified at the prospect. He had never bowled around the wicket and was reluctant to experiment at a time when he was desperate to make a good impression. Unlike Gilly, in cricketing terms, he was playing for his life, for he had yet to justify his place on the tour, let alone stake his claim for a place in the Test side. For a man who was supposed to be making Wes the world's number two bowler, Gilly's plan seemed at best whimsical; at worst reckless. Wes protested, but Gilly was insistent, based on the rationale that batsmen facing Wes would shuffle across the crease towards the off-side, either to get in line with awayswingers, or to sway to avoid short-pitched deliveries bowled from around the wicket. Batsmen in that mindset would then present Gilchrist – bowling fast inswingers from over the wicket – with lbw opportunities from the other end. Reluctantly Wes agreed, and he and Gilchrist proceeded to take seven and five wickets respectively in West Indies' 185-run victory. In the second innings Wes took five for 41 to claim his first five-wicket haul in first-class cricket. The new ball partnership for the First Test in Bombay was decided, and on 28 November 1958 Wes became the 104th Test cricketer to represent West Indies.

The Test series against India marked a decisive point in Wes's career. The home batsmen had no answer to the extreme pace of Hall and Gilchrist, who set the tone for the series by reducing India to 40 for four early in the first innings of the drawn First Test. Wes claimed three of the wickets, including that of Nari Contractor, caught by Eric Atkinson. It was his first wicket in Test cricket and came in his first over, before he had conceded a run.

Gilchrist had been told that the tour of India and Pakistan would be unlike England or Australia where the players could unwind over a drink in a pub so, before leaving London for India, he bought a large record player and 20 long-playing records to provide entertainment for the team. His generous gesture was greatly appreciated by the players, who regularly gathered to enjoy the music in the room he shared with Wes. Such equipment in those days was heavy, and Gilly made the reasonable request that everyone take turns to carry it between the team's accommodation and railway stations. They all agreed, except Basil Butcher. Understandably Butcher's repeated refusal infuriated Gilly; so much so that eventually he found a willing buyer and offloaded the record player and records:

> Of course, the fellows were all disappointed. We had nothing else to do after a game. Gilly did not realise how much the guys looked forward to the music and how much he had taken away from them. He felt that we were all blaming him when the real culprit was Butcher. When some guys said it was Basil's right to refuse his turn to carry the equipment, Gilly countered by saying it was his right to sell it when he wanted.

Another incident occurred during catching practice in Kanpur a couple of days before the Second Test, again involving Butcher. He misjudged a ball and, as it hit the ground, Gilchrist berated him: 'You're always dropping the ball, and you never apologise to the bowler.' When Butcher responded, Gilchrist raised his voice, and was asked by the captain Alexander to stop. As always, Gilchrist insisted on having the last word; he accused Alexander of taking sides by chastising him and not Butcher, and with that he walked off the field.

The management committee became involved and demanded an apology from Gilchrist. When he refused, they decided to send him home, but Conrad Hunte intervened on Gilchrist's behalf and persuaded the committee that he should be given a second chance. Gilchrist was allowed to stay but was dropped for the Second Test in Kanpur.

Even though Gilchrist was a spectator in Kanpur, Wes gives credit to Gilly for the part he played in his own and the team's success. Hall and the Trinidadian Jaswick Taylor opened the bowling and were struggling in the first innings against India's opening batsmen. Wes had taken no wickets for 40 runs as India moved on to 182 for two, just 40 behind West Indies' total. The matting pitch was slow and unresponsive to pace, and both wickets had fallen to the spin of Sobers. At tea Gilchrist offered some advice to Wes: 'Stop pinging the ball, Wes; ease the ball. Slip it, don't ping it.' By this he meant that Wes should roll his fingers across the ball and let it slide out of his hand, allowing it to kiss the surface and skid on without losing too much pace. Wes heeded Gilchrist's words and reaped a spectacular reward. He bowled a fuller length and finished the innings with six wickets for 50 runs in 28.4 overs as India were bowled out for 222, the same as West Indies' first-innings score. Wes finished with match figures of eleven for 126 – the only time he would take ten wickets in a Test match – to help West Indies to a comfortable win, their first on the way to a 3-0 series victory. Like Wes, Gilchrist had never bowled on matting before, yet his cricketing intelligence enabled him to read the situation and advise Wes accordingly.

After the third day of the Kanpur Test Gilly sat next to Wes on the team bus back to the hotel and congratulated him on his first-innings performance. Naturally Wes was feeling upbeat, but his mood was quickly dampened. The team manager, Berkelely Gaskin[1], who was seated in front of them, turned and said: 'Wes, you bowled a beamer and injured a batsman today, and we're not very pleased at all.' Wes protested that he had accidentally hit Manihor Hardikar on the head when the batsman lost sight of a full toss and ducked into it. Thinking that the ball had struck Hardikar's shoulder, he had even appealed for lbw although, as soon as he realised that the batsman was hurt, he was horrified and apologised immediately.

Gilly jumped to Wes's defence; and his response to Gaskin was less diplomatic. After pointing out that Hardikar had accepted the apology, he berated the manager for failing to congratulate Wes on his performance.

Gaskin stood up and, seemingly oblivious to what the two of them had said, simply announced: 'I am banning the bowling of beamers on this tour.'

Gilchrist was already uneasy after being dropped from the Second Test, and the incident further unsettled him. He was picked for the next game – against a combined Indian Universities XI in Nagpur – and shortly before the start of the match, he told Wes that Alexander would instruct Wes to bowl the first over with the wind. Wes dismissed the idea on the basis that the senior bowler would be given the more favourable end, but Gilly was convinced that Alexander had a hidden agenda and was looking for ways to get him sent home.

[1] B.B.M. Gaskin (1908-1979) played two Test matches for West Indies as a medium-pace bowler, against England in 1947-48.

Despite the warning, Wes was still surprised when Alexander handed him the new ball. He glanced over at Gilly, who was smirking as if to say: 'I told you so!'

In the second over of the students' innings, Gilly was at his most menacing and proceeded to unleash an aggressive onslaught, hitting two or three young batsmen with ferocious bouncers. Wes is convinced that some deliveries were bowled at 100mph. After the exertions of bowling 60 overs in Kanpur, Wes had been hoping for an enjoyable, stress-free match; in the event, it turned out to be anything but:

> For me that was the worst match of the tour. It was the most uncompromising bowling I have ever seen. He hit them before they could lift their bats. I told Gilly it was unnecessary: he got six wickets for 16 runs and bowled so fast, that if he had just attacked the wicket, he would have taken all ten.'

Still incensed, Gilchrist was in no mood to listen, claiming that the captain Alexander was not content with dropping him for the Second Test and wanted to embarrass him further. Thankfully Gilly calmed down after the match, and the next few weeks were incident free. He bowled extremely well, taking twenty wickets in the last three Tests, before the players made their way to Amritsar where they would conclude the India leg of their tour with a fixture against North Zone. Unbeknown to Wes, the occasion offered Gilly an opportunity for revenge which he had been looking forward to for some time.

During one of the early Tests, India's leg-spin bowler Subhash Gupte had visited Wes and Gilly in their room and informed them that Swaranjit Singh, the North Zone captain, had complained that they were frightening Indian batsmen. As a Cambridge Blue and member of MCC, Singh was not short of self-esteem, and he went on to boast that he would put a stop to it by dealing with them when the West Indians visited Amritsar. Gilly stored away Singh's words until the fateful match.

In a bizarre contest, both teams' first innings were completed before tea on the first day. The West Indians batted first and were dismissed for 76; in reply North Zone were bowled out for 59. Wes was rested, and in his absence Gilchrist took four wickets, including that of Singh, bowled for a single. Gilly's satisfaction was short-lived.

The tourists' second-innings 228 would be enough for victory, but the result was overshadowed by the sensational events in North Zone's second innings. Gilchrist was still simmering. In Wes's words, 'he was on fire', and he ripped into the top order, taking three quick wickets. Singh fared considerably better the second time around, and after a couple of well-timed boundaries off Gilchrist's bowling, he made a comment to the bowler. Gilly was furious. He walked back almost to the sightscreen, charged in and delivered a fearsome beamer which dislodged Singh's turban. The batsman complained to Alexander, his former Cambridge University teammate; Gilly protested that Singh had provoked him by swearing at him twice, but it was in vain. The damage was done.

Alexander ordered Gilchrist off the field, and after close of play the selection committee met and decided to send him home. On the day of his departure team members came to their hotel room to say goodbye and, after the last of them left, Wes hugged him. Gilly began to cry, not because of his expulsion from the tour – he took a pragmatic view of the disciplinary process and accepted the outcome – but the lack of appreciation for his efforts. It seemed to him that all the hours he had bowled at express pace in the baking heat counted for nothing. He was escorted to the railway station by an Indian official and, after a 36-hour train journey to Bombay, he boarded a plane for London.

Gilchrist never felt comfortable within the West Indies team, and in hindsight Wes suspects this was because he saw himself as a dispensable outsider who was not important to the team and not truly valued – a perception which had probably contributed to his aggressive behaviour.

Roy Gilchrist

Roy Gilchrist was born in 1934, the youngest of 23 children. Jamaica was reeling from the effects of the Great Depression, with the collapse in sugar prices resulting in low wages, unemployment and unrest. Brought up in poverty on a sugar plantation, Gilchrist's childhood was harsh and, by the time he was a teenager, he possessed a quick temper and an aggressive streak. He was conscious of his lack of education, and he resented his father for not sending him to school. In *A History of West Indies Cricket* Michael Manley describes Gilchrist as being 'burdened by those tensions which so often run like scars across the landscape of the personalities of people who come from poverty'.

Wes accepts that Gilly was no paragon of virtue. If someone crossed him, he never backed down, yet the bravado and well-publicised aggression were only one side of Gilchrist's personality. Wes maintains that, in spite of his firebrand reputation, he was essentially an introverted, kind person. In 1961, when the two of them were playing in the Lancashire Leagues, Gilchrist drove all the way down from Bacup to London to pick up Wes's girlfriend from Heathrow Airport, before driving her up to Liverpool, a round-trip of more than 400 miles. Wes has much sympathy for him:

> What the young boy missed in the school room, he made up for by outclassing everyone in the streets where he played cricket. Cricket brought out the best and the worst in him. Gilly knew the game; he really understood cricket, and of course, he excelled at bowling. His cricket knowledge was immense, yet he was rarely heeded; that was difficult for him to accept. Underneath the bravado, Gilchrist hid his insecurity, but he had no knowledge of how to leave his past behind. He was unable to ignore the propaganda and embrace his good fortune in being part of the West Indies cricket team among men of different shades of colour and levels of education.

On the other hand Gerry Alexander, also Jamaican, enjoyed a privileged upbringing; he attended one of the island's leading high schools before progressing to Cambridge University. Wes had great respect for Alexander, a disciplinarian whom he rated as a good cricketer and a decent man but who – having made his Test debut in England in 1957 – was still very inexperienced as an international cricketer and captain. Alexander was aware that having so little in common with Gilchrist was likely to present a challenge, while the latter believed that his lack of education would be used by the captain as a reason to pull rank and talk down to him. An extract from Gilchrist's 1963 autobiography, *Hit Me For Six*, is revealing:

> I always had the feeling that Gilly from the plantation could never be on the same level as Gerry from the varsity. While fellows knew me as Roy Gilchrist, or Gilly, everyone seemed to regard Gerry as Mr F.C.M. Alexander, Cambridge University and West Indies.

Had Worrell captained the team in India, he would almost certainly have handled Gilchrist more tactfully while still retaining discipline. Indeed, in subsequent years, Gilchrist received backing from Worrell, who made representations on his behalf to have him readmitted to the Test side. Despite this, Gilchrist remained *persona non grata* in the eyes of the West Indies cricket hierarchy, and his Test career was over.

For Wes the loss of Gilly was a major blow on a professional and a personal level. He had just begun to feel worthy of his place in the team, and that was due in no small way to Gilchrist's encouragement and the effectiveness of their partnership. Now Wes would have to shoulder the fast-bowling responsibilities on his own and, more than anyone, he was aware of the qualities the team was about to lose:

> Gilly was the fastest bowler I've ever seen, 100mph at times. With all that gladiatorial stuff, people forget how good he was. He got 57 wickets in 13 Test matches. He was so strong: in the Bombay Test, Gilly bowled a total of 64.2 overs in the match – 41 in the second innings – with no let-up in pace.

Hall and Gilchrist were room-mates on two tours but played in only four Tests together, all in India in 1958-59. During that very short time before their partnership was prematurely ended, they formed one of the most explosive and effective bowling pairings ever in Test cricket How they would have performed against stronger batting sides than India will never be known, but they had paved the way for the succession of great West Indian fast bowlers who would dominate world cricket for a generation.

In 2001, at the age of 67, Gilchrist died of Parkinson's disease in St Catherine, Jamaica. Wes was honoured to be asked by the family to deliver the sermon at the funeral. He concluded his heartfelt eulogy by pledging to do everything in his power to support troubled young cricketers:

> I understand that punitive measures are necessary under certain circumstances, but I remain diametrically opposed to any system where there is no rehabilitation process; a system that banned Gilly – for life! A system that allows others to fall through the cracks ... Gilly felt rejected, disqualified, banned and left to his own devices. It was the deepest wound to his soul and, when I

buried him, I made a solemn promise to establish a rehabilitation system. History will absolve him.

History has been less kind to Gilchrist than Wes predicted, but he contends that the more sensitive treatment of present-day cricketers who have been found guilty of misdemeanours is an indirect consequence of the injustice meted out to his friend.

The 1958-59 tour of India was the breakthrough for Wes, as he and Gilchrist dominated the five-Test series. Wes played in all five Tests and took 30 wickets for 530 runs at average of only 17.66. Gilchrist took 26 in the four matches he played. Moreover, Wes found the Indian experience very enjoyable, both on and off the field. After his difficulties in England, he was determined not to take anything for granted. On a tour considered by some players to be a grind, Wes once again gratefully embraced the opportunities offered by a visit to such an exciting country, and he was fascinated by the sights and culture. Teams from England and Australia, wary of eating the local food, were in the habit of taking their own breakfast when they toured India, but Wes had no such qualms: 'I was happy to eat what they gave me! India was tough, but I liked it – and I left with 30 wickets!'

The tour party left India for Pakistan in good spirits, confident that the young squad had the makings of a side to be reckoned with in the post-Three Ws era. However, deprived of the services of Gilchrist, things went less smoothly for them in Pakistan. The first two Test matches, at Karachi and Dacca, were played on matting surfaces much to the liking of the home captain and star bowler Fazal Mahmood, whose 19 wickets effectively won both matches for his side. Gilchrist's pace was indeed missed, both in Karachi, where Hanif scored a century in the absence of his nemesis, and in the low-scoring match in Dacca, where conditions helped the pace bowlers. Wes and the other bowlers were troubled by the mat, which ended level with the stumps, so that bowlers caught the edge with their studs as they neared the end of their run-up. Despite this causing Wes to lose his rhythm, he still managed to take eight wickets in West Indies' 41-run defeat.

The last Test was played at Lahore on grass, and the outcome was very different. West Indies won by the huge margin of an innings and 156 runs in a match notable for Kanhai's brilliant 217 and outstanding bowling in

Pakistan's first innings by Wes, whose five-wicket haul was his third in eight Tests on the tour. In that innings he made history by becoming the first West Indian to take a hat-trick in Test cricket. His victims were Hanif's brother Mushtaq (making his debut at the age of 15 years, 125 days to become the youngest-ever Test player[2]), Fazal Mahmood and Nasim-ul-Ghani.

Wes was wicketless in the second innings as the spinners completed the victory. He finished the series against Pakistan with a highly respectable return of 16 wickets for 287 runs in the three Tests, with another excellent average, 17.93. He shared the new ball with two bowlers, Jaswick Taylor and Eric Atkinson, but neither bowled with anything approaching the speed of Gilchrist, and the attack was less potent as a result. Wes and Gilly had begun to develop an understanding, and Wes missed the positive energy hurtling in from the opposite end. He was required to assume Gilchrist's mantle of West Indies' leading strike bowler, with the extra onus on him to make a breakthrough. Handicapped by the absence of a settled new-ball partner, this would become the norm over the next four years.

By any standards Wes had enjoyed stunning success in India and Pakistan. For a young bowler whose first priority was to justify his place on the tour, the transformation in his fortunes was little short of miraculous. In the eight Tests he took 46 wickets at an average of 17.76, and in all first-class matches on the tour his total was 87 wickets at 15.08. His overriding emotion was one of relief that his hard work had paid off so spectacularly. He had become an established player for his country, far exceeding his objective of proving that he belonged on the tour and in first-class cricket.

The West Indies squad had flown from London to Bombay in early November 1958 and made the return journey the following April. Several of the team were contracted to spend the English summer playing in the northern leagues but, after five months away from home, Wes was looking forward to returning to Barbados. He had been approached the previous year by the Lancashire League club Accrington, and when he arrived in England from India and Pakistan a written offer awaited him.

---

[2] Mushtaq is now the second-youngest Test player, following Hasan Raza's debut for Pakistan at the age of 14 years, 237 days, against Zimbabwe in Faisalabad on 24 October 1996.

Thanks to his excellent start in Test cricket, Accrington were doubling the amount they were prepared to pay him, and Wes would have been tempted had it not been for the promise he had made to Sir Godfrey Ince two years before. For the tour of the subcontinent, Cable & Wireless had again allowed Wes five months leave on full pay, and he wanted to repay their generosity by going back in 1959 and working an extra year before turning professional. Once he had made the grade, the decision to pursue a career as a professional cricketer may have been a straightforward one for Wes, but it gratifies him to know that life would have been good had he stayed at Cable & Wireless. He looks back fondly on his days there:

> It was a wonderful crowd that grew up together. Cable & Wireless was the crucible that transformed the lives of its employees, and those who stayed had a very comfortable life. Others went overseas to further their studies and did very well. Five of us became government ministers – the other four were Branford Taitt[3], Harold Blackman, Clyde Griffith and John Williams. I was lucky to go from such a happy place into the West Indies team which in those days was like a family.

On his return to Barbados, Wes went to live with his mother. She had moved to Grazettes, a government housing area in St Michael about six miles from their former home in St Lawrence. At the same time his grandmother's chattel house had been relocated to a nearby street, so the family remained close; probably too close for Llewellyn and Wes who – aged 22 and 21 respectively – shared a bedroom in their mother's small bungalow!

In 1959 Wes had a couple of interesting encounters with two of his heroes, two thirds of the great Three Ws, both of whom had taken a keen interest in his progress. Frank Worrell had obviously given some thought to how he would greet Wes when the two met following the tour of India and Pakistan, and his quote from a well-known hymn was typically elegant:

> The head that once was crowned with thorns
> Is crowned with glory now.

---

[3] Dr Sir B.M. Taitt (1938-2013) served in parliament from 1971 to 1999, during which time he held the offices of Minister of Trade, Industry and Commerce; Tourism and Industry; Health; and Foreign Affairs.

The second episode involved a meeting for which Everton Weekes was less well-prepared than his fellow 'W' had been. The only cricket to take place on the island that year was inter-club matches, so players had no opportunity to play first-class cricket between the final Test in Pakistan in March and the First Test against England the following January. Therefore, in 1959, Wes played his one and only season for Spartan Cricket Club in the BCA first division. The standard was very high, and the competition was fiercely contested, featuring many Test and first-class cricketers all determined to further their claim for a place in the West Indies team. Wes was at the peak of his fitness, bowling quickly and taking wickets as he prepared for the eagerly anticipated arrival of the 1959-60 MCC touring team.

The most memorable match that season was the first division game against Empire, played at Queen's Park, Spartan's home ground. The park was overflowing as more than 5,000 spectators crammed in to see Test stars do battle in a rivalry as intense as any they would encounter on the international stage. The result was a victory for Spartan, helped in no small measure by a Hall hat-trick, with the second victim being Everton Weekes, bowled first ball. On his return to the pavilion, a Spartan hailer helpfully offered Weekes the benefit of his wisdom: 'You played it all wrong, man', to which Everton drily replied: 'Well, first of all, to play a ball, you have to see it!'

Wes was reminded of his feat many years later, when as an ordained priest he was officiating at a funeral. He shared the pulpit with an old bishop, who recounted the occasion when he had cycled the six miles to St Michael from Ellerton in St George, to watch his hero Everton Weekes bat for Empire against Spartan. Weekes was bowled first ball, 'by a young fella, and I said I didn't want to see that boy again – and lo and behold, he's here this morning, but this time, he's bowling for Jesus!'

The 13-year age gap between them and Weekes' retirement from Test cricket at the age of 33 prevented the two men from playing in a Test together, a cause of considerable regret for Wes. They remained great friends right until Weekes' death in July 2020, and Wes is convinced that 'if it had not been for Sir Everton, you would never have heard of Wes Hall.'

The 1959-60 Test series between West Indies and Peter May's MCC tourists was a disappointment, both in terms of the outcome and as a spectacle. The only victory in the five-match series was claimed by England in the Second Test in Trinidad, a contest marred by crowd disturbances. The trouble started when local debutant Charran Singh was given out – run out – in West Indies' first innings of 112. Bottles and other missiles were thrown, the police fired tear gas to subdue the angry crowd, and the match was delayed as the players were escorted from the field. When order was restored, England continued to dominate and won by 256 runs. The cricket throughout the series was characterised by defensive tactics and slow play, largely from England as they adopted a ruthlessly 'professional' approach. The tactics succeeded in curbing West Indies' scoring rate but were responsible for passages of extremely dreary cricket.

Among the positives for West Indies were the sustained brilliance of Sobers with the bat and Hall's continuing development as a bowler of genuine international quality. With 22 wickets – at an average of 30.86 – he was the leading wicket-taker in the series, and by common consent he was the fastest and most dangerous bowler on either side, despite the presence of Trueman and Statham. Wes posed a consistent threat to England's batsmen, all of whom were troubled by his extreme pace. At Sabina Park in the Third Test he achieved a career-best Test analysis of seven for 69 in the first innings, and in the second innings he was responsible for a moment which has gone down in West Indian cricket folklore.

Bowling to the England captain Peter May, Wes delivered a thunderbolt which flew off the lightning-fast wicket and crashed into the off-stump with such force that it snapped the timber clean in two. That dramatic moment was captured on camera, and the image was transmitted around the world as evidence of Hall's destructive speed. Less well known is that the incident happened more by chance than by design: in his delivery stride Wes had got into his side-on position as close to the stumps as he could, with the intention of producing some late outswing from a ball pitching on off-stump and finding the outside edge of May's bat. The ball pitched in the perfect spot, but it came back in off the pitch to beat the *inside* edge of May's bat and crash into the off-stump. May had noted from Wes's delivery position that he was attempting to angle and move the ball away from him, and he concentrated on covering the away-movement, leaving him unprepared for the in-cutter. To Wes the incident demonstrated the fine line between success and failure: 'The commentators and experts all over the world were telling me that it was a great ball, that I bowled the perfect ball. But I knew, and May knew, it just happened, and I got lucky!'

Wes also excelled in the Fourth Test at Georgetown, where he returned figures of six for 90 in England's first innings, a performance he rates above his seven wickets in Jamaica. Whereas Sabina Park had been typically lively and helpful to fast bowlers, at Bourda the pitch was innocuous and the smaller playing area meant that whenever the ball beat a fielder in the inner circle it went to the boundary.

Success continued to elude Wes at his home ground, however. The First Test was played at Bridgetown, and match figures of one wicket for 107 runs took his career aggregate at Kensington Oval to two for 346 in three first-class matches. Such were his struggles there that he began to despair of ever performing well in front of his home spectators.

That match marked the first time Wes had played Test cricket in the Caribbean and also the Test match debut of Chester Watson from Jamaica, his new opening bowling partner. Watson was a year younger than Wes, and he bowled with genuine pace at Bridgetown, showing sufficient promise to retain his place for the remaining four Tests in the series. Bowling with venom and a great deal of heart, Watson took 16 England wickets, yet he was not given the opportunity to become the long-term replacement for Gilchrist that West Indies and Wes urgently needed. Worrell shared the new ball with Wes in the second innings in British Guiana and, at Port of Spain in the Fifth Test, a young tearaway fast bowler from Barbados called Charlie Griffith made his debut. In a taste of things to come, Griffith became Wes's fifth new ball partner in eight matches in the 'post-Gilchrist era', although it would be more than three years before he would play his second Test match.

Another unresolved issue remained a source of debate. Following Goddard's unhappy tour of England in 1957, Alexander was appointed West Indies' captain for the 1957-58 home series against Pakistan despite having only two Test appearances to his name. To most observers, Worrell's claims to the job far outweighed those of Alexander, although contrary to popular belief Worrell had not been overlooked. He had, in fact, been offered the captaincy for the Pakistan series but had opted instead to stay in England for the middle year of his economics degree at Manchester University. However, the board's failure to exploit the experience and wisdom of other worthy alternatives to Alexander – most notably Weekes and Walcott – reinforces the perception that the choice of the West Indies captain was based less on merit than other factors.

In a move that caused exasperation and anger, the WICBC chose to retain Alexander for the 1959-60 series against England, even though Worrell was available following the completion of his studies. Throughout this saga, both men had displayed tact and maturity and emerged with great credit. Alexander recognised the obvious claims of Worrell and informed the selectors that it was time for a change. The board resisted on the basis that the team was making excellent progress under Alexander's leadership and persuaded him to continue for one more year. It is a measure of Worrell's poise that he accepted the vice-captaincy for the 1959-60 series with good grace, for at the age of 35 time was not on his side and Alexander's extension could have put paid to his chances of ever realising the cherished prize. At the time, Wes was not fully aware of the drama unfolding around the issue of the captaincy, but he had clear opinions on the subject nonetheless: 'Alexander was a good man, a really nice fella. I don't want to say a word against him, but let's face it, we knew Worrell should have been captain since 1953.'

7

Life in the Leagues

The series against Peter May's England team ended on the last day of March 1960, in time for the start of the cricket season in England. Having agreed terms the previous year with Accrington, the time had come for Wes to turn professional and sample Lancashire League cricket. It was to prove hard work but a valuable experience. The life of the club professional in the northern leagues was one of modest bed and breakfast accommodation; coaching commitments; playing with numb hands on cold, wet days; and above all, a requirement to produce a match-winning performance every Saturday afternoon. All of this was a world away from the glamour of international cricket, yet the leagues boasted numerous overseas Test stars, attracted by lucrative contracts and the opportunity to improve their skills in unfamiliar conditions. Accrington in April provided Wes with a typically rainy welcome to Lancashire, but a welcome of a different sort made a greater impression on him.

A young boy saw him in the street and went running to his mother, shouting: 'Mummy, there's a black man coming down the road!' She ushered her son inside and closed the door. At 22 years of age and the only black person in a strange town, Wes could have been forgiven for beating a hasty retreat to his digs, but instead he walked up to the house and knocked on the door. When the woman answered, Wes introduced himself as Wes Hall, not 'Blackman' (a common surname in Barbados). As the new professional at Accrington, he was keen to make friends with her little boy and looked forward to taking him to practise in the nets. In the meantime, he would be grateful if the youngster could help by carrying some of his gear to his digs!

In his three years at Accrington, this was as close as Wes came to being made to feel like an outsider. His friendly, outgoing personality undoubtedly played a part in him being warmly accepted, and he felt at home in the town:

I had many white people who I'd grown up with and who I loved. When I went to Accrington, I lived a decent life and was treated with dignity. If not, I wouldn't have spent five years in the leagues; I'd have left after one year and gone home.

Wes had been away from home for months at a time before, but on those occasions he travelled as part of a touring team, stayed in hotels and had not been required to interact with the local community. At Accrington he was on his own:

It was a case of 'sink or swim', and fortunately as a loquacious person, I got to know a lot of people who became good friends, and they made me feel very welcome. I settled in well and felt part of the community. I was happy there.

Wes recalls taking another youngster under his wing: David Lloyd was a very promising 13-year-old left-arm spinner when the two first met. Lloyd remembers with fondness the way Wes looked after him, taking him to Trent Bridge to see his first Test match and giving him his first proper bat. As a condition of his contract, the club professional was required to run coaching sessions for club members every Tuesday and Thursday evening and, although Wes was able to coach to a good level on all aspects of the game, the young Lloyd had reached a stage where he would benefit from specialist spin bowling tuition. Fortunately Wes was able to call on the services of an expert: his friend Garry Sobers, who was spending the summer as the professional at nearby Radcliffe, drove to Accrington to help out. Wes felt Lloyd should be playing in Accrington's first team even at the age of 13 but, as was customary in the leagues, he was held back until he was 15. On his debut against Rishton in 1962, Lloyd's bowling figures of three for 24 suggest Wes had a point.

Convention was a major part of life in the leagues; frequently matches became contests between the two respective professionals, with each expected by his club to get the better of his opposite number and deliver a victory. Professional bowlers were routinely required to bowl unchanged for the entire innings and were under added pressure from the other players to qualify for a collection from the spectators, since by tradition the professional would treat his teammates to a drink (or two) in the bar from the proceeds. Bowlers earned a collection by taking six wickets for

30 runs or fewer[1]: 'They wanted you to average less than five [runs per wicket], they weren't giving it away!' Wes used to employ unconventional tactics to achieve it: if he had taken four or five wickets, he moved his slips back to the boundary, based on the logic that they would then be useful in saving precious runs! Even when he finished an innings with five wickets, Wes would always buy the first round of drinks for his teammates, and his selfless commitment to the team confirmed him as one of the most popular overseas professionals ever to have played in the leagues. From the committee room to the spectators' benches, he was admired for his wholehearted effort, cheerful demeanour and above all, his immense on-field contributions.

As a non-drinker throughout his cricket career, he developed a taste for the soft drink Vimto and, after a long, tiring bowling spell, the cry: 'Two Vimtos for Wes!' became familiar in the bars of Lancashire League cricket clubs!

Wes took 100 wickets in each of the three years he played at Accrington. During this time the club enjoyed an upturn in its fortunes, spectacularly so in 1961 when Wes led the team to a first League Championship since 1916. Success in the leagues ranks highly among his cricketing achievements: it may have been amateur cricket, but the standard was high and very competitive and he was vying with 13 other professionals to win the championship for his club. He enjoyed being part of a young, developing team which included several outstanding cricketers, in particular the wicketkeeper Jack Collier who, in Wes's estimation, was up to county standard and could have had a career in first-class cricket: 'I was very surprised he didn't play for Lancashire. In three years I don't think he dropped one chance off me.'

Twice Wes took all ten wickets in an innings. Both occasions were in 1962, the first against Burnley and the second against Bacup and his erstwhile bowling partner Roy Gilchrist. Gilly enjoyed a ferocious reputation in the leagues and, before the game, he caused quite a stir as he warmed up theatrically in a bright red tracksuit. Many of Accrington's batsmen were intimidated, so the captain Frank Rushton asked Wes if he would open the innings. He agreed, and Gilchrist's reaction was typical:

[1] A bowler qualified for a collection by taking: six wickets for 30 or fewer; seven wickets for 35 or fewer; eight wickets for 40 or fewer; nine or ten wickets at any cost; a hat-trick. Qualification for a batsman was 50 runs: for a wicketkeeper, five victims.

'Hey, College Boy, what you doin' with the pads on?'

'I'm opening.'

'You're a hero?'

'Yes.'

'All heroes are dead!'

With that, Gilly laughed, hugged his friend and walked back to his mark.

Wes remembers 'smelling leather the entire innings'. Although he made only 26, he stayed at the crease and took the strike against Gilchrist for most of Accrington's innings of 94 all out. Gilchrist became increasingly frustrated that Wes was preventing him from bowling at the amateurs, and he unleashed a barrage of bouncers. Despite being struck repeatedly on the body, Wes held firm and Gilchrist finished with only one wicket. Battered and bruised, but with his job done, a fired-up Wes responded with a devastating return of ten wickets for 28 runs which blew away the Bacup innings for just 64. Four points for his team, a collection and winning the honours in his individual battle all added up to a highly satisfactory if painful day, made all the sweeter as he walked off the field. Gilchrist was waiting for him at the boundary; he smiled, shook his hand, and said: 'Dinner's on me, mate!' This gracious side of Gilchrist was rarely seen but, as far as Wes is concerned: 'That was the Gilly I knew!'

Unquestionably Wes was a tremendous acquisition for Accrington, and he also benefited enormously from the arrangement in terms of both his professional and personal development. He passed all tests with flying colours. The cricket was hard, and his on-field responsibilities far exceeded those he had experienced previously. He may not have been the captain, but, as the professional, he was required to be the *de facto* leader of his team, even at the age of 22. He learned that producing outstanding performances would count for little unless he could encourage his teammates and carry them with him. As his confidence increased, he found himself more able to exert his influence on the team, as he developed the leadership qualities which have been in evidence throughout his life.

Happy memories came flooding back when Wes made a return visit to Accrington in November 2017. After a stroll around the cricket field, he enjoyed an evening of fun and nostalgia with David Lloyd and other club members past and present. He was delighted to be reunited with his teammates, including a visit to the nursing home of Jim Eland, his opening bowling partner from 55 years previously. Jim was suffering from advanced dementia, but seeing Wes stimulated him and he responded in a way that amazed and delighted his wife and family. His parting words when Wes promised to return to see him the following year were: 'I'll be here, champ!' Sadly Jim died a few weeks later. During a telephone call to Mrs Eland on Christmas Day, Wes was able to share memories of his old friend with the whole of Jim's family: 'It meant so much to her that a tear came to my eye. That is what cricket is about – how it can bring people together. People and friendships and memories.'

Wes's relationship with Accrington is beautifully summed up by David Lloyd in his 2018 book, '*Around the World in 80 Pints*':

> Seeing one of the sport's great physical specimens competing alongside the blokes of your town against a neighbouring one, slotting seamlessly into the community, striving to do the best he could for both himself and those he represented, taught me something of the way cricket was meant to be and how the values could be applied outside of the boundary as well as inside. The way Wes conducted himself provided a real life lesson.

The international cricket calendar now features countless overseas tours and global tournaments across multiple formats. One of Wes's long-standing laments has been the failure of cricket's authorities to address cultural differences between countries. His thoughts on the subject date back to his time at Accrington. As Barbados was a British colony, all aspects of its society – from education to the system of government – were modelled on the 'Mother Country'. Wes was surprised, therefore, to be caught out by matters of etiquette from time to time, such as when he visited Blackpool with some of his Accrington teammates. They stopped at a fish and chip shop, and Wes's shock when he saw people leaving with their food wrapped in newspaper instead of eating at a table turned to horror when his friends opened the paper and started eating in the street:

> If my grandmother saw me eating in the road, she would have given me such a hiding! I could not believe what I was seeing! I could not force myself to do it, it was so alien to my culture, but I felt like a fool because everybody else was doing it. And then when I sat down and opened my meal, it was full of newspaper. Nonetheless, I became a great lover of fish and chips after that!

This and other trivial examples turned his thoughts to more serious questions. If similar cultures could produce such misunderstandings, Wes questioned how contrasting ones could be expected to coordinate smoothly. He began to ponder the need for cricket to recognise cultural differences and then accommodate them. Such thinking was ahead of its time and shaped policies which Wes would later pursue as a cricket administrator.

In 1960, for the second successive year, Wes played no first-class cricket other than matches representing West Indies. Following the success of his first season with Accrington, he and the five other league cricketers in the West Indies squad sailed directly from Tilbury to join the rest of the 1960-61 tour party in Australia. After the rigours of the season, the month at sea offered some much-needed rest in preparation for the momentous series which was about to unfold.

8

Australia 1960-61: The Series that Saved Cricket

The 1960-61 Test series between Australia and West Indies is still considered by many to be the greatest ever, characterised by positive cricket from both sides, brilliant individual performances and thrilling finishes.

Preceding years had seen an increase in negative tactics in Test cricket, with teams intent more on avoiding defeat by stifling the threat of the opposition than taking the initiative themselves. Slow over rates and scoring were commonplace, and the game's image and popularity were suffering as a result. The previous Test series in Australia featuring the 1958-59 MCC tourists was a case in point, with some astoundingly dull cricket. In Brisbane in the opening Test match, England batted for 119 eight-ball overs[1] while making 198 runs. Trevor Bailey's 68 occupied over seven and a half hours, matched by Australian opener Jim Burke who took more than four hours to score 28 runs. A few weeks later, on the second day of the Fourth Test in Adelaide, England managed to bowl just 51 overs. The following year marked MCC's dismal and negative tour of the Caribbean, so that when West Indies went to Australia in 1960-61, cricket was 'on death row'.

Both teams resolved to remedy matters. They were united in their desire to entertain the crowds by playing aggressive cricket, and the tone was set by the two like-minded captains, Richie Benaud and Frank Worrell.

Richie Benaud was a dashing cricketer whose instinct was to attack whenever possible, whether as a pugnacious middle-order batsman, aggressive leg-spinner or imaginative captain. Following his appointment as captain for the 1958-59 series against England, he had won his first three series, gaining widespread respect and a reputation as a shrewd cricket tactician.

If Benaud captured the imagination of the cricket public in Australia, the excitement that accompanied the appointment of West Indies' new captain, Frank Worrell, bordered on hysteria. Gerry Alexander was

---

[1] Eight-ball over were the norm in Australia until 1978-79 when six-ball overs were adopted.

an intelligent, honourable man, and for some time he had recognised Worrell's superior claims to the captaincy. In fact, Wes suspected that Alexander was embarrassed to captain Worrell and, before the squad was selected, he again expressed his reluctance to lead the team. This time the selectors relented. They accepted Alexander's 'resignation', and he was made vice-captain. The change paid immediate, unexpected dividends: relieved of the responsibilities of captaincy, Alexander enjoyed his best-ever series. He scored 484 runs, and his average of 60.50 was the best by any batsman on either side.

At last, aged 36, Frank Worrell became the first black professional cricketer to be appointed captain of West Indies[2]. In the eyes of all but a few he was also the first to be chosen on merit rather than on considerations of race and social status. This was a defining moment in the history of West Indian cricket, transcending the boundaries of sport, and the long crusade against colonialism could claim a tangible triumph. It provided vindication for the Trinidadian author and political activist C.L.R. James, who for years had been at the vanguard of the campaign demanding Worrell's appointment as captain. James saw the issue as a metaphor for black people's struggle for equality, and his objection to Alexander's captaincy had drawn widespread backing throughout the West Indies. For James the historic occasion of Worrell being made captain was one step on a long road. He issued a rallying call in the form of a letter of support, in which he congratulated Worrell and wished him success in moulding West Indies' group of talented young players into a strong unit. Demonstrating his faith in Worrell, James predicted that if the team acquitted itself well in Australia, it would be a major step towards independence for the Caribbean colonies. Quite a claim, and ostensibly a colossal burden to place on the shoulders of the new captain, but James had absolute confidence in Worrell's ability.

The Australian Chairman of Selectors was Sir Donald Bradman, and he asked Benaud for permission to address the Australian players to outline what was expected of them in the series. Bradman's message was short and to the point: 'Gentlemen, I'd like to congratulate you on your selection

[2] George Headley, as an amateur, captained the side for just one Test, against England in Barbados in 1948.

for this First Test match. I just want you to know that the selectors will be looking very favourably on those who play attractive cricket. Good luck.'

For Worrell the series was hugely significant on many levels. He was mindful of his and the team's responsibilities, both to the people of the Caribbean and also to the wider game of cricket, yet he remained unaffected by the weight of expectation as he calmly set about his task. Some of his methods were unorthodox. For example, in the entire four months of the tour, he held just three team meetings, instead encouraging players who needed help or advice to come to him for a one-to-one conversation. He considered this far more effective than delivering general comments to a group.

For their part the players were expected to behave responsibly and with common sense. Outside the Test matches, they were free to go out and socialise in the evenings, but Worrell made it clear that during the Tests late-night drinking in the hotel bar would not be tolerated: 'I pick fit teams' was an innocuous-sounding statement, but it subtly implied that those who disobeyed him would be dropped if they ignored his curfew and reported for duty the following morning the worse for wear. It followed that if they were not selected they would then be at serious risk of not being picked for the next series. Quiet but firm discipline such as this helped Worrell unite the players while, beyond the dressing room, his decency and charm commanded a degree of respect rarely accorded to a cricketer.

Again Wes did not have the benefit of a regular new-ball partner, with Worrell, Watson and Sobers[3] all tried at various times. Unfortunately, Worrell's request for the readmission of Gilchrist into the West Indies side had been rejected by the WICBC, and Griffith, the other bowler of genuine pace, was also overlooked. Griffith had made his Test debut against England in Trinidad in March 1960 – West Indies' last Test match – and was unlucky to be discarded after the three West Indies fast bowlers took only four wickets between them on a batsman-friendly pitch. Wes and Watson were selected for the Australia tour, while Griffith was left out in favour of Eric Atkinson, and when Atkinson was unable

---

[3] The 1960-61 series marked the first time in Test cricket that Sobers bowled left-arm fast-medium seamers, complementing his existing bowling variations: slow left-arm orthodox (finger spin), and wrist spin.

to take time off work Tom Dewdney was recalled to the squad for the first time since the 1958 Pakistan series. Dewdney did not play in any of the Tests, and once again it fell to Wes to shoulder the bulk of the fast-bowling responsibilities. It is hard to disagree with Wes's assertion that 'if Charlie Griffith – and/or Gilchrist – had gone on that tour, we would have won the series.'

Another area where Wes found himself in need of more robust support was in the footwear department. In the early part of the tour his cricket boots regularly split, causing him great pain. During the match against New South Wales in Sydney, just a week before the start of the First Test, blood from blisters on the soles of his feet was seeping through the leather as he bowled. The problem was remedied by the Melbourne master-shoemaker Hope Sweeney, who supplied Wes with two pairs of his kangaroo-skin bowling boots. They were so supple and comfortable that Wes wore boots made by Sweeney throughout the rest of his career.

To widespread delight, the cricket in the 1960-61 Test series more than lived up to the brave words that preceded it. Fortunes ebbed and flowed within and between matches, with both teams looking to take the initiative throughout. In Brisbane the First Test ended sensationally in the first tie in Test cricket. Fast-moving Second and Third Tests ended in straightforward wins for Australia and West Indies respectively. In the Fourth Test at Adelaide Australia somehow clung on to claim an unlikely draw, albeit in controversial circumstances; and they won the Fifth and final Test at the Melbourne Cricket Ground (MCG) in another thrilling finish, again somewhat contentiously. The result of the series – 2-1 to Australia – was in doubt until the penultimate ball of the series.

Many players made telling contributions in the Tests, including Wes, who finished the series with 21 wickets at an average of 29.33, making him West Indies' leading wicket-taker again. He took centre stage as the drama of the series unfolded, and it fell to him to deliver the final overs in both the tied Test and the Fourth Test in Adelaide, where West Indies came tantalisingly close to pulling off a victory which would have guaranteed them at least a drawn series.

In Adelaide, in only his second Test, off-spinner Lance Gibbs became the second West Indian bowler – following Wes in Lahore two years previously – to take a Test hat-trick when he dismissed Ken Mackay, Wally Grout and Frank Misson in Australia's first innings. After Worrell's second-innings declaration set Australia 460 to win, West Indies seemed certain to move into a 2-1 series lead when the hosts slumped to 207 for nine with 109 minutes remaining in the last day. Shortly after the last-wicket pair of Ken 'Slasher' Mackay and Lindsay Kline came together, Mackay played a ball from Worrell to Sobers who was fielding at silly mid-off. The West Indian players celebrated the catch and began to walk off, but Mackay stood his ground. Umpire Colin Egar ruled that it had been a 'bump-ball' and motioned for the game to continue. Despite West Indies' best efforts, Mackay and Kline continued to defy their bowlers for the next hour and a half.

Wes was entrusted with the final over and, although he bowled with every ounce of effort, Mackay resisted, opting simply to stand and take the last ball in the stomach rather than attempt a shot and risk offering a catch. He let out a gasp and his knees buckled, but he recovered his composure, chewed hard on his gum and walked off triumphantly having achieved his objective of saving the match. Wes and his teammates remained convinced that the ball from Worrell had carried on the full to Sobers; moreover, it was universally acknowledged that Sobers would never resort to claiming a false catch. However, the West Indian players recognised the difficult job faced by the umpires and did not to make an issue of the incident. Their obvious disappointment was eased by the knowledge that they had played their full part in an enthralling game of cricket, and they approached the final Test in Melbourne with optimism. From a personal perspective Wes is proud that in the heat of battle he was never tempted to try to win the match for his team by directing a short, fast ball at the tail-ender Kline.

The match at the MCG followed a familiar pattern, with Australia again batting last in pursuit of a challenging target. They needed just six runs with three wickets left and appeared to be on course for victory, with Mackay and fellow Queenslander, wicketkeeper Wally Grout at the crease. Facing Alf Valentine, Grout cut a ball which cannoned into the ground and rolled into the outfield behind the stumps. The batsmen completed two runs seemingly unaware that a bail had been dislodged. Wicketkeeper Alexander appealed to the umpire Egar, who consulted with the square-leg umpire, Colin Hoy. Hoy confirmed that Alexander had not disturbed the wicket with his gloves, yet Egar decided to give the benefit of doubt to the batsman. The runs stood, leaving four more required for victory and still three wickets in hand. In the context of the series, six runs with two wickets remaining would have been significantly more challenging and, despite Grout's dismissal next ball, Australia managed to scramble home by two wickets.

For the second successive match West Indies could feel justifiably aggrieved that a crucial decision had gone against them, but again they refused to make excuses and apportion blame. To have done so would have been out of character for Worrell and his team and would have contravened the spirit of the series. There were bigger issues at stake, and West Indies were delighted to have contributed to a series that did so much to restore cricket's reputation and popularity. Wes offers the generous, if rueful, assessment that 'those two umpires [Egar and Hoy] were two of the best I have seen. I thought they only made two mistakes, and both went against us.'

The West Indians' attitude and the style of their cricket gained them unprecedented popularity for a touring side, and many Australians acclaimed them as the moral winners of the series. A hastily arranged farewell parade was held in their honour and, despite the very short notice, half a million people thronged Collins Street in Melbourne as the West Indies players made their way in open-topped cars to the town-hall for the farewell banquet. Each player has his own memories of that emotionally charged occasion; Wes recalls:

> The crowd was shouting: 'We love you! You won it! We know you won it! Come back soon!' The great Australian all-rounder Keith Miller said it was the most spectacular reception for any team in cricket history. Frank Worrell made a great speech, Richie Benaud made a great speech. Big men cried.

Cricket-lovers all over the world breathed a collective sigh of relief that the game had been brought back from the brink by such a wonderful series. Wherever West Indies played, they drew large crowds eager to watch their flamboyant cricket. They played hard but always with a smile; none more so than Wes. Many words have been written about the series, and one book in particular, *The Greatest Test of All*, written by the former Australian batsman Jack Fingleton in 1961, appealed to Wes: 'The only thing he wrote that I didn't like was that "Hall was the darling of the women at all grounds." When I came back to Barbados, I had a lot of explaining to do!'

After the final Test, Sir Donald Bradman approached Wes and asked if he had read *Beyond a Boundary* by C.L.R. James: 'Yes, Sir.'
   'But do you own the book?'
   'No.'
   Three months after that conversation, a parcel arrived at the Post Office for Wes, sent by Bradman, and containing a copy of *Beyond a Boundary*. Bearing in mind the letter James had written to Worrell at the beginning of the tour, this gesture rounded off the series perfectly.

The 1960-61 series was the only occasion that Wes and Richie Benaud faced each other on the cricket field, but the two men remained great friends. The last time they met was when Benaud and his wife Daphne visited Barbados shortly before Benaud's death in April 2015. Tony Cozier organised a lunch for them and the Barbadian players who had participated in the tied Test: Wes, Cammie Smith, Peter Lashley and twelfth man Seymour Nurse. Also present were Sir Everton Weekes, who had played for West Indies on Benaud's Test debut in Sydney in January 1952, and Michelle Kennedy-Green and Pat Constant, sisters from Trinidad who had settled in Australia and were close friends of the Benauds. The event was such a success that everyone agreed to Benaud's request for a repeat before he and Daphne left the island. However, in the meantime, Benaud fell in his hotel room and injured himself. Wes and the others were fully expecting him to cancel the second lunch but, to their delight, he defied the pain, and the lunch went ahead. To be enjoying the company of friends from the other side of the world, brought together by cricket, was a life-affirming occasion for Wes: 'That was one of my big moments, to see everybody there that day. Sadly it was the last time Richie and I would see each other.'

9

The Tied Test

Such was the drama of the First Test in Brisbane, and the role played in it by Wes, that it merits a chapter of its own.

The first four days were packed with captivating cricket as the initiative fluctuated between the teams, setting the scene for the unforgettable final innings. West Indies batted first after Worrell won the toss, and their total of 453 included Sobers' dazzling 132 and an entertaining 50 by Wes. He was involved in a crucial ninth-wicket partnership of 86 with Alexander, who made 60. Australia replied with 505, the highlights of which were Norman O'Neill's epic, battling 181 (the only century by an Australian in the series) and Bobby Simpson's 92. After tea on the third day, with Australia's score on 469 for five, Wes had figures of no wicket for 122, but he persevered magnificently to finish with four for 140 as Australia were bowled out for the addition of just 36 runs.

Facing a first-innings deficit of 52 runs, West Indies made a disappointing 284 in their second innings, in which Worrell top-scored with his second 65 of the match. Wes again batted well in scoring 18, and he shared a vital last-wicket partnership of 21 with Valentine before becoming Alan Davidson's sixth wicket of the innings and 11th of the match, leaving Australia with a victory target of 233 runs in 312 minutes.

In Australia's first innings Wes had bowled 30 eight-ball overs, yet he shrugged off his tiredness and tore into Australia's top order. He took the first three wickets to fall – including that of the first-innings hero O'Neill – as Australia were reduced to 49 for four. West Indies were still in a strong position when Benaud joined Davidson at the wicket with Australia on 92 for six, 140 runs behind with 150 minutes left in the day. Over the course of the next 140 minutes, these two batted with skill, bravery and some good fortune to change the course of the match.

Just a few minutes remained as Sobers began what would be the penultimate over. Nine runs were required for victory with four wickets in hand; Benaud and Davidson stood on the verge of completing a memorable recovery. Two runs came from the first three deliveries, and Benaud played the next into the leg side before setting off for another quick single. Joe Solomon, fielding at mid-wicket, picked up and hit the stumps with a direct hit to run out Davidson for a magnificent 80. With 44 runs in Australia's first innings, and his eleven wickets in the match, Davidson became the first cricketer in Test cricket – in the 498th match – to score 100 runs and take ten wickets in a match. More importantly West Indies had finally broken the 134-run partnership, and the new batsman Grout arrived in the middle with the score on 226 for seven and seven runs needed from twelve balls. A scrambled single from the seventh ball of Sobers' over left Benaud on strike for the eighth, anxious for the one run that would get him to the other end to face the last over. Benaud failed to connect, the run was prevented, and Grout was left to negotiate the final over, to be bowled by Wes.

Wes looks at that final tumultuous over in terms of the *feelings* experienced by the central characters and the extent to which players were influenced by those feelings as the pressure 'swung backwards and forwards like a pendulum'.

Ball 1

Needing six runs for victory from eight balls with three wickets in hand, the odds were in Australia's favour, especially if Benaud, on 52 and batting confidently, could relieve Grout of the strike against the pace of Hall. From his fielding position at mid-on, Worrell offered advice and encouragement to his bowlers, and he and Wes conferred at length before Wes walked back to his mark at the start of the final over. Obviously, Grout's intention would be to get Benaud on strike, and Worrell's words to his fast bowler were designed to calm Wes rather than offer advice: 'I want you to keep it tight, Wes, Benaud is going to try to get a single.' Wes replied: 'Keep your eyes on me, skipper, and you will see something special this over!' This was not arrogance or bravado, but an expression of his feelings; he was relishing being at the centre of the action. He had already bowled 17 overs in the innings, but he was desperate to be involved in 'something exciting'. He would not be disappointed!

The first delivery of the over was 'very fast' and slightly short of a length; Grout went back and shaped to swing to leg, but the ball was onto him too quickly and struck him in the groin before dropping at his feet. He ignored the pain and set off for a laboured run. Benaud, running to the danger end, had already sprinted halfway down the pitch with Grout still in his crease and, with the fielders in a state of confusion, the batsmen were able to scramble the leg-bye for the single they had so desperately wanted.

Ball 2

With five needed to win from seven balls, and Benaud on strike, Australia were now firm favourites. The pressure was on the West Indians, and Wes in particular. Earlier, Worrell had instructed Wes not to bowl bouncers to Benaud, and again he called him over to emphasise the point: 'Benaud will be looking to finish this quickly, he'll try to attack you and hit a four early in the over, so do not bowl a bumper.'

'Skipper, I will not bowl a bumper.'

Subsequent events are best explained by Wes himself:

> Any time I am in the middle of my run, and I feel good, that means I am going to be quick. I had decided I was going to pitch the ball up, and I don't know what happened to me. When my right foot hit the 18-yard marker, I have never felt so great, so full of grace like I was floating, and I decided then that I was going to go short. If I'm not feeling right at half-way, and I bowl short, then I am fodder, but I felt so good I was going to let this one fly and put it up around the ribs. Rhythm and flow, and balance. Bam! I bowled a bumper; the same bumper that I was *not* going to bowl!

Wes did indeed let it fly, and Benaud was only part way into his shot when the ball came off the top edge of his bat and Alexander took the catch. Wes and his teammates were ecstatic. He went over to Worrell and exclaimed: 'Skipper, we've got him, we've got him!'

Worrell was not amused: 'What did I tell you?!'

'But, Skipper, we've got him!'

'If that ball had taken a thicker edge, what would have happened? Where would it have gone? Over Alexander for four, maybe even six.'

Ball 3

Five runs were required from six balls, with two wickets left. Wes felt deflated that in his moment of triumph he had been reprimanded by his captain. He could understand Worrell's logic, if not the sophistication of his man-management skills: Worrell knew enough of Hall to have confidence in his strength of character and calculated that, rather than dishearten him, the telling-off would focus his concentration and make him more determined. It certainly deterred Wes from bowling another short ball. The next ball to new batsman Ian Meckiff was fast and on a good length just outside off-stump. Meckiff attempted a drive but Wes followed through and fielded the ball at short mid-off, for no run.

Ball 4

Australia required five runs to win from five balls. Wes describes the next delivery:

> I decided to aim at leg-stump because he's not a star bat. It just missed, but Grout was obviously feeling the pressure and went for a risky bye to the 'keeper to get back on strike. Alexander threw it to me, and I tried to run Meckiff out and missed the stumps from about four yards. Big mistake ... all three stumps to aim at, and I missed by a mile. Valentine wasn't the greatest fielder, but I will always be grateful for him backing up. If I'd given away four overthrows ... That was what the pressure did, and now it was all back on me.

Ball 5

Four balls remained; Australia's victory target was four runs and, with the senior batsman Grout now on strike, the pressure certainly was back on Wes. With Worrell's words echoing in his ears, the bouncer was not an option, and he bowled another good length delivery. Anticipating a short ball, Grout moved onto his back foot and attempted to play the ball to leg. A leading edge sent it spiralling in the air toward square-leg, where Kanhai fixed his eyes on the ball and set himself to take the catch. Suddenly his field of vision was filled with Wes charging towards him. Wes took the 'catch', but as his elbow made contact with Kanhai's head, the ball bounced out of his hands and onto the ground, and the batsmen completed a run:

> I was bowling under a lot of pressure, but still thinking about what I was doing. Grout was back, expecting a bouncer, and so when I pitched it up he scooped it up in the air. Kanhai was waiting under it, and I didn't even see him. That's what pressure can do to you. People don't realise how hard it is for a fast bowler. Every ball, you put in the effort with six or seven times your body weight going through your left knee, and then I had to twist

and change direction from my follow-through on the off-side, suddenly to go for the ball at square-leg. There's so much going on that it's easy to make a mistake, but I am not excusing it, not at all. Anyway, I said: 'The good Lord has left us', and Kanhai laughed! His comments were not exactly complimentary – not to make me feel bad, but just because he was so disappointed. I felt so bad too, and I had to agree with him!

The collective cry of anguish from the spectators as the ball looped off Grout's bat towards Kanhai was replaced by disbelieving cheers when Wes dropped the catch. For the Australian players in the dressing room, the excitement was unbearable as fortunes swung to and fro. Benaud himself observed: 'They couldn't take any more!' It seemed likely that the dropped catch was the final turning-point in the game: if it had been taken, the last pair – both tail-enders – would have been at the crease requiring four runs from three deliveries and, with one wicket required for victory, West Indies would surely have been favourites.

Ball 6
Australia had two wickets in hand and needed three runs from three balls. At least the number ten batsman Meckiff would be on strike, although this was scant consolation to Wes, for whom the previous two balls had been a personal disaster. Missing a relatively easy run-out chance was dispiriting enough, but then to drop a catch that a teammate would surely have caught was potentially devastating. Wes could have been excused for wanting to hide but, as the man entrusted with the last over, hiding was not an option. Instead, he was able to summon the necessary resolve and, far from feeling crushed, he took pride in the responsibility he had been given. The inspiration for this positive frame of mind was his captain. Worrell strolled up to Wes between deliveries and spoke to him encouragingly. His presence and reassurance were comforting: 'Winfield, take it easy, take it easy, you will be ok.' These words could have been said by anyone, but the calm manner in which Worrell spoke convinced Wes that everything would turn out well.

Wes planned to bowl the sixth ball full and at the stumps, but he pitched his intended yorker slightly short: 'Somehow Meckiff swung and connected – wonderful shot – and the ball went almost all the way to the square-leg boundary'. Conjecture has it that the ball slowed down short of the fence because the grass had not been cut that morning. Whether or not that was the case, Conrad Hunte was able to sprint round to square-leg and cut it off a foot inside the rope as the batsmen completed their second run. The scores were then tied, and Grout turned for the third and match-winning run with the ball still in Hunte's hands 80 yards from the wicket. The throw was fast and accurate. Alexander gathered the ball a few inches from the stumps and ran out his opposite number as Grout dived in a vain attempt to make his ground.

Ball 7

With the scores level, Australia's last man Lindsay Kline came in to take strike. Two balls of Hall's over remained. The tension that had been building throughout the day around the Wooloongabba ground reached fever-pitch as the drama of the final over unfolded. Somehow Wes had to find a way to summon the composure to bowl. If ever there was a moment when a cool head was needed, this was it. Thankfully for Wes, that cool head was near at hand:

> Worrell was a master. Before the seventh ball he came to me –
> they needed one run to win – and he said: 'Winfield, don't worry,
> everything will be alright, just whatever you do, don't bowl a no-ball, because if you bowl a no-ball you won't ever be going back to
> Barbados! Those people won't let you land!' That made me smile.
> He knew the right thing to say; it diffused the tension.

Introducing humour and humanity at that stage helped Wes to settle before the crucial next delivery. Even amid the mayhem, Worrell kept to his tried and trusted plans, calling out to Solomon at square-leg to move finer. As was his custom, he then subtly motioned the fielder back to his original position without the batsman's knowledge. This was effective only if the fielders were disciplined in following Worrell's instruction to keep their eyes on him at all times. Solomon was, and he took up a position just backward of square to the left-handed Kline. Back at his mark, Wes began his run up and the crowd fell silent. He felt in control and at ease, his balance was good, and he concentrated on producing a full and straight fast ball – and avoiding a no-ball!

The delivery was on a good line and length, but well short of Wes's quickest 'because I put my right foot[1] down very deliberately to make sure

---

[1] At that time, the no-ball rule related to a bowler's back foot. The 'front-foot rule' was introduced in 1963.

it wasn't a no-ball'. Kline got behind the line and was able to work the ball towards square-leg. Meckiff set off for the winning run in the mistaken belief that Solomon was fielding at fine leg and, as the spectators erupted to cheer an Australia victory, Solomon swooped forward to pick up the ball and shy at the single stump he could see. His direct hit left Meckiff inches short of his ground, Australia were all out, and Test cricket had produced its first tie. Under the most intense pressure imaginable, the discipline of Worrell, Solomon and Hall in sticking to their plans was matched by their ability to produce their skills at such a critical moment.

The 4,000 spectators roared their appreciation. They had witnessed history in the most thrilling circumstances imaginable, by two teams straining every sinew in pursuit of victory, yet without losing sight of the higher objectives of sportsmanship, respect for the opposition and the integrity of the game. In the confusion of the frantic finale, players from both sides were initially unsure whether they had won or lost, but all were exhilarated by the unifying power of cricket. That suffocating last over brought to a conclusion a wonderful Test match and set the tone for a series which would produce three of the most exciting finishes ever

The cricket, and particularly the West Indies players, captured the imagination of the Australian public, who took Worrell, Sobers, Kanhai, Hall and the rest of the team to their hearts. The West Indians' contribution to the series led to them receiving unprecedented recognition, with a motorcade through Melbourne followed by the creation of the Frank Worrell Trophy, to be contested in all future Test series between Australia and West Indies. It is difficult to imagine how West Indies could have left a more positive impression during the 1960-61 tour of Australia, and Wes remains immensely proud to have played such a major part.

The tour ended after the Melbourne Test in February 1961, and Wes continued on the routine of non-stop round-the-calendar cricket that had begun with the MCC tour of the Caribbean the previous year. Together with five of his colleagues, he took a boat from Perth to England, as he again headed straight from West Indies duty to a season at Accrington. The next Test series was due to begin the following February with West Indies hosting the touring Indians but, before then, not only did Wes face another arduous Lancashire League season but an altogether new challenge awaited him.

10

The Influence of Worrell: Planning a Career Path

Wes's cricket career ran concurrently with a development plan devised for him by Frank Worrell. These are dealt with separately, beginning with Wes's career path.

Upon assuming the West Indies captaincy, Frank Worrell was determined to make a positive impact. One of his objectives was to use his position to oversee the advancement of West Indian cricket and cricketers. He saw the potential for a great West Indies team built around Wes and his contemporaries, and he did everything in his power to turn his vision into reality.

Worrell was conscious that, at the age of 36, his days of 'hands on' leadership were limited. He was more than ten years the senior of many of the young stars and realised that he would probably not be around as captain long enough to lead the team to its peak, so he took the unprecedented step of putting in place a player development plan which he could continue to monitor after his playing days. Leading Caribbean cricketers were in demand to play and coach overseas, particularly in England and Australia, and Worrell took the opportunity to capitalise on their profile for the benefit of West Indian cricket. His intention was to expose players to new experiences which would help them to improve and progress; they in turn would bring back to the Caribbean the new thinking and methods they had learned on their travels.

Wes fitted Worrell's plans perfectly and, following the 1960-61 tour of Australia, he approached him in the role of mentor. He congratulated Wes on his performance on the tour and thanked him for being such a positive influence on the team, describing him as 'the greatest one-man entertainment band, with a proclivity for comedic inspiration.' Wes explains his light-hearted demeanour: 'I was just so happy to play for my country. I was a jovial fella, and I did not think that a spirit of jocularity should be outlawed!' Of course, Worrell recognised that there was far more to Wes than his good humour: intelligence, maturity, confidence and excellent communication skills marked him out as having exceptional potential, and he created a demanding career path designed to push Wes to achieve that potential. The programme of personal development would run parallel to his cricket commitments for the rest of his career.

Having played several seasons of league cricket in Lancashire, Worrell was aware of the benefits that Wes was reaping from his association with Accrington, and he encouraged him to continue. Furthermore, he recognised that, for the first time, West Indians could take their skills beyond the Lancashire Leagues. The West Indies team had captured the imagination of the Australian cricket public, and so Australia was the obvious starting point. Playing in Australia would help their development – and hence benefit West Indian cricket – more than a season of sporadic inter-island matches in the Caribbean. To the prospective employer in Australia, the timing was perfect: the recently departed West Indies team had enjoyed unprecedented popularity, and the state sides stood to benefit enormously, not just from the players' on-field contributions but also commercially. The dashing West Indians would bring fresh excitement to the Sheffield Shield competition, and their box-office appeal would attract spectators. Several Australian states were hoping to recruit West Indian players, and the ever-astute Worrell was more than willing to act as a go-between. He sounded out the relevant parties in Australia and then put their proposals to the principal targets: Hall, Sobers and Kanhai. All three were delighted to accept the exciting new challenge, and in late 1961, they joined Queensland, South Australia and Western Australia respectively.

The Australian season ran from October to March so, with his Accrington commitments, Wes would be playing tough, competitive cricket the whole year round. If he had been unprepared for the 'rock-star welcome' that he and Sobers received when they arrived at Brisbane Airport, he would be even more taken aback by the standard and intensity of 'the hardest cricket I have ever played'. For instance, in the 1961-62 Sheffield Shield match at the Sydney Cricket Ground, his Queensland team faced a New South Wales side featuring no fewer than ten Australian Test cricketers[1] past, present, and future. Notwithstanding the quality of the opposition, Wes excelled in his two seasons in Australia. In 1961-62 he

---

[1] The only NSW player who did not represent Australia in Test cricket was the wicketkeeper, D.A. (Doug) Ford.

took 43 wickets at an average of 20.25, breaking the previous Queensland season record of 39 set by L.S. (Len) Johnson in 1949-50.

Just as at Accrington Wes's performances were matched by his attitude and commitment, and he impressed everyone with the way he applied himself to all aspects of life in his new environment. While in Australia he was sponsored by Esso, in return for which he was required to coach children throughout the state of Queensland. Wes was involved in Esso's 'tiger in your tank' advertising campaign, and he was charged with spreading the word on behalf of the company as he travelled around the state accompanied by a senior sales executive. The Managing Director of Esso Australia, Mr Frank Kelly, provided Wes with a car, gave him his schedule of coaching assignments, and Wes did the rest.

The coaching was hard work. Sometimes the clinics would be attended by hundreds of eager children, a potentially nerve-wracking situation for a young man without any teaching experience. However, the ordeal of addressing such a large crowd held no fears for Wes. As a voracious reader, he had full confidence in his powers of expression, and his natural loquaciousness ensured he was seldom lost for words, so that he was never afraid of speaking. The children he coached were not in need of advanced tuition, so Ronnie Hughes' excellent grounding in the basics of the game had furnished him with the technical know-how he needed.

Wes gained enormous satisfaction from the pleasure he was able to bring to the children, particularly the less fortunate ones – such as disadvantaged aboriginal children or those suffering handicaps – for whom his visit was a rare highlight. He embraced the challenge and threw himself wholeheartedly into his task: 'I coached in virtually every town that you could call a town in Queensland ... and Queensland is a very big place!'

Although his two years in Australia were exhausting, he was richly rewarded by the experience. He thoroughly enjoyed the camaraderie of the young players, and stalwarts like Slasher Mackay, Peter Burge and Wally Grout became good friends, always on hand to offer advice. In those two years, he learned a great deal about cricket and himself.

As far as Worrell was concerned, the arrangement could not have worked out better. Hall, Sobers and Kanhai were so successful for their respective teams that they all received invitations to return. Also, for the first time, people in the Caribbean could see that their players were good enough to thrive in top-level cricket outside the region. This was vital to Worrell's vision: if West Indian cricket was to be taken seriously on the world stage, it needed first to take itself seriously. Only then could its cricketers go forward with the confidence to become the best team in the world.

While in Australia, Wes indulged his love of horses and horse racing, and he became a familiar figure with the bookmakers and at racetracks. On one occasion, when Sobers was in Brisbane for South Australia's fixture against Queensland, the two of them went to the races with a couple of friends. Esso used to upgrade Wes's company car regularly, and he drove to the track in his latest model, a green Holden which they left in the car park. Wes used to pride himself on his knowledge of the runners and racing form, and he jokingly boasted of his expertise. It was good-natured fun but annoying to the others when he backed the first three winners and announced that he would prove his self-discipline by walking away and going home: 'I have no further hunches, the odds are now against me, so I will leave you amateurs to it.'

Sobers left with him and, when they reached the car park, Wes suddenly became aware that 50 per cent of cars on the road in Australia were Holdens – 'and a lot of them were green!' The attendant at the entrance had spotted them leaving early, and he watched with interest as the two men moved from car to car trying the locks. The man was becoming increasingly suspicious, and Wes thought it was just a matter of time before he called the police. He therefore decided not to try to open any more cars. That was at 3.30. The last race was at 5pm, and by six o'clock there were just two cars left in the car park – both green Holdens! Wes waited with his friends for the owner of the other one to leave: 'To the puzzlement of the car park attendant, I opened my car with the key, and we were gone before he could ask any questions!'

The younger players' fondness of racing did not meet with Worrell's approval. Cricketers' earnings were modest, and he felt that betting on horses was foolish. Wes argued that it was important to have outside interests as a release from the pressures of cricket. He tried to explain that gambling in small amounts provided entertainment and excitement, but Worrell remained adamant that they were merely squandering money they could ill afford to lose. In 1961 a few of the West Indians who were playing in the northern leagues got together to watch television coverage of the Epsom Derby, and Worrell joined them. In the sweepstake both

Wes and Sobers were feeling pleased with themselves after pulling fancied horses, and they teased Worrell when he drew Psidium, a 66/1 outsider. They were less chirpy an hour later when Psidium had become the longest-odds Derby winner since 1913! Worrell capitalised on his moment of triumph. His renowned generosity of spirit deserted him as he drove home his point that betting is a mugs' game and that he would not be buying the others a single drink with his winnings!

> And he was true to his word; he did not buy one drink for the guys that night! We didn't see him get vexed often, but he disliked us gambling. I think though he was only trying to protect us and stop us getting into trouble.

Following Wes's two successful seasons in the Sheffield Shield, Worrell decided that he was ready to take on a coaching assignment in Jamaica in the 1963-64 and 1964-65 seasons. Wes was sponsored by the Jamaica Manufacturers Association (JMA) to coach on the sugar production estates, and in that role he worked alongside a senior manager at JMA called Arthur Bonitto, one of two brothers[2] who had played first-class cricket for Jamaica. Again Wes gave his total commitment to the new role and, after his experience of coaching youngsters in Queensland, he found it enjoyable and rewarding to coach adults as well.

Worrell then turned his attentions to English league cricket. Accrington had become a second home for Wes: he thrived on the involvement, he loved the people, and they loved him. The cricket was tough, and he learned a great deal. He accepted his coaching commitments as part of the job, carrying out his duties with typical good humour, but he and Worrell felt that a less taxing role would allow him to concentrate more on developing his own game. Worrell therefore arranged a meeting with officials of the North Staffordshire League team Great Chell.

The meeting took place during the 1963 Oval Test. Worrell insisted that when in London the players must be well-dressed, and Wes sat in the room at the Oval – in his smart suit – while Worrell negotiated with the Great Chell contingent. He drew their attention to Wes's impeccable appearance and did such a good promotional job on his behalf that

[2] A.R. Bonitto was a leg-spinner who played nine times for Jamaica between 1946 and 1952, taking 24 wickets at 34.79. His brother N.L. (Neville) Bonitto made 17 appearances between 1947 and 1957 and scored 1,413 runs at an average of 58.87.

Wes was offered a better contract than he had expected. Hence, in the 1964 English season, the Staffordshire club became the latest part of the development programme organised for him by Worrell.

Test series were relatively infrequent in the 1960s: after the Oval Test in August 1963 – Worrell's last – West Indies' next Test was against Australia in Port of Spain in March 1965. Worrell aimed to ensure that the gaps in the calendar were filled with experiences that would advance Wes's cricketing education and broaden his horizons. Although Worrell retired completely from first-class cricket in 1964, he took it upon himself to continue to direct the career of his *protégé*, and Wes's two seasons in Jamaica were each followed by an English summer at Great Chell.

Life as the professional at Great Chell was very different from Accrington, where for three summers he had immersed himself in the life of the town and become part of the community. Having grown up in close-knit villages in Barbados, Wes had felt comfortable in Accrington, where everyone knew one another. By contrast, in 1964, he lived in Liverpool and drove to Great Chell on matchdays. Relieved of coaching duties, his sole responsibility was to play cricket for the team on Saturday afternoons, and he was happy to make the 120-mile round-trip to Stoke-on-Trent once a week in return for the extra freedom:

> The people were very friendly and welcoming. If I'd been there as a 22-year-old growing up with the team like I was at Accrington, it would have been the same for me at Great Chell. But I started playing for Great Chell when I was at a different stage in my life: I was 26 and about to get married.

Although they did not win the league, Wes took wickets and enjoyed playing at Great Chell. The standard of cricket was good; Sobers was the professional at Norton in the same league. After a defeat against Norton, when Wes was asked what had gone wrong, he quipped: 'Well, we've only got one pro, I was playing against two!' Wes was referring to Garry's brother Gerald, who also played for Norton. He was an amateur but was such a good batsman that many felt he could have become a professional cricketer.

During the 1964 season, Wes married Shurla, his girlfriend from Barbados. The wedding took place in Liverpool with 13 West Indian Test players and officials from both Accrington and Great Chell in attendance. Worrell officiated as best man, although 'The Skipper' was a far more effective calming influence on the cricket field than in the church: 'Waiting at the church, he was more nervous than I was!'

Back on more familiar ground, Sir Frank (Worrell was knighted in 1964) organised a return to Australia for Wes in 1965-66 after his two stints in Jamaica and at Great Chell. When Wes was told of his destination, he assumed he would be going back to the rigours of state cricket, and he objected in no uncertain terms. The placements in Jamaica and Staffordshire had exposed him to new experiences while keeping him fit between Test series but, as far as Wes was concerned, another season of Sheffield Shield cricket was more likely to leave him physically drained than in prime condition. He was therefore hugely relieved to learn that Worrell had arranged for him to play in Sydney grade cricket as captain of the Randwick club before the West Indians' five-month tour of England began in April 1966.

While at Randwick, Wes was tasked with observing the structure of the club and identifying the strengths of the Australian system; he was then expected to bring back ideas which would benefit cricket in the Caribbean. This indicated a significant shift in Worrell's thinking. He had always known that Wes was a very bright man, and latterly he had also been impressed by his success in overcoming challenges in unfamiliar situations. The Randwick appointment gave Wes extra responsibility beyond focusing on his own development; hence Worrell became the first person to formally recognise Hall's potential as an innovator and leader.

Shurla joined Wes in Sydney, and the couple had a marvellous time there, thanks largely to the friendliness of the people they met. George Wintle, the manager of the South Sydney Juniors League Club, was especially welcoming; Ian Davis, one of the players, and his girlfriend became great friends of the Halls and took them to race meetings and exhibitions and showed them the local sights. Wes particularly appreciated the fact that everybody treated his wife so well.

Wes enjoyed the cricket, too. Compared to the seasons at Queensland when he combined playing and coaching, Randwick was relatively undemanding even though he was team captain. Matches in grade cricket were played over two days on consecutive Saturdays. In between, Wes found time to relax – his favourite haunt was Bondi beach – and concentrate on training, so that by the end of the season he was extremely fit. He loved life at Randwick: 'a very good club and wonderful people.'

As well as making the most of the lifestyle, Wes warmed to the task that Worrell had set him. He studied how the club operated and was particularly struck by its status as the focal point of the local community. It was inconceivable that a boy from Randwick would play for any other club, and the system was driven by parents who did everything they could to support their sons. In Randwick and districts throughout Sydney, a day at the cricket was the social event of the week, with entire families watching their sons play in the junior leagues. Virtually every boy was encouraged to play the game, with the result that talented cricketers were unlikely to slip through the net.

The standard was very high, and Wes was extremely impressed by the number of outstanding young cricketers playing in the Under-19 Poidevin-Gray Shield and the Under-16 A.W. Green Shield. He soon concluded that the system compared favourably to that in the West Indies, where school cricket was pre-eminent, resulting in lower levels of engagement by parents, who typically left the responsibility for developing young talent to the schools. Although cricket was the leading sport in the Caribbean, it did not enjoy the profile it had in Australia. Wes spent many hours discussing these differences with Wintle and, having gained a thorough understanding of the Australian model, the second part of his brief was to use his findings to effect changes back home. This led to the fourth of his calls.

The call from WITCO
Wes learned of the final assignment of his career path while in London during West Indies' 1966 tour of England. The tour manager, former West Indies captain Jeffrey Stollmeyer, asked him to come to the captain's room at the Waldorf Hotel. Worrell was present and revealed his most ambitious proposal yet for Wes. He wanted Wes to apply the methods he had witnessed at Randwick to the development of youth cricket in Trinidad. Unlike previous assignments this would be a long-term project, lasting four years from 1967 to 1970, giving Wes the opportunity to settle down in Trinidad and see the job through to completion. In an arrangement brokered by Stollmeyer – himself a Trinidadian – Wes would be employed in a marketing and public

relations role by The West Indian Tobacco Company Limited (WITCO), who would sponsor his work with young cricketers. Hugh Henderson, WITCO's Marketing Manager, had been the driving force behind this initiative, and he was eager to engage Wes. Worrell was then living in Trinidad and serving as dean at The University of the West Indies' (The UWI) St Augustine campus, and both he and Wes welcomed the prospect of spending time together.

There was, however, an obstacle to overcome before Wes could embark on this new challenge: he had signed a contract to play for Haslingden in the Lancashire League in the 1967 English season, and that would clash with his role in Trinidad. Worrell was adamant that Wes should go to Trinidad and persuaded him to ask Haslingden to release him from his contract. The club generously agreed to the request, on the proviso that Wes found a 'good' West Indian replacement. They would not be disappointed.

The player who occurred to Wes was an exciting young Guyanese[3] batsman who had been selected for the tour of India. Clive Lloyd had burst onto the scene in the previous Shell Shield season, and many people felt he was unfortunate to be overlooked for the 1966 tour of England. Lloyd's omission dismayed several influential figures, including the West Indies captain Garry Sobers and the Prime Minister of British Guiana, Forbes Burnham, who was so upset that he launched a withering attack on the selectors.

Notwithstanding Lloyd's reputation in the Caribbean, he had yet to make his Test debut. Wes consulted Lloyd's cousin Lance Gibbs, and they decided that, before putting him forward as a possible replacement for Wes at Haslingden, they would see how the youngster fared in India on his first tour. Lloyd duly obliged with scores of 82 and 78 not out in Bombay on his Test debut and a series batting average in excess of 56. Wes informed Haslingden that Lloyd was keen, a deal was struck, and neither party looked back. Lloyd's leadership credentials were established at Haslingden, where he took on the captaincy before going on to captain Lancashire and, famously, the celebrated West Indies teams of the 1970s and 1980s. His place as one of the game's most important and influential leaders is beyond question.

---

[3] British Guiana formally achieved independence from Britain and became Guyana in May 1966.

Wes answered Worrell's call and began work in Trinidad in early 1967. He was happy at the prospect of living in the same place for four years and was immediately made to feel at home at WITCO. The company's management was extremely pro-cricket and supportive of the initiative. Hugh Henderson took the lead, and Wes soon realised that he could not have had a more helpful ally. Henderson outlined the company's vision and how Wes fitted into the plan. He would be supported by a team drawn from senior managers at WITCO and also including the Trinidad and future Test batsman Charlie Davis. In Barbados, club cricket was established across the island, with the leading schools and the BCA bearing the responsibility for spotting and nurturing talent. Trinidad was a much larger island crossed by mountain ranges, and cricket was concentrated in the more developed north, particularly in and around the capital Port of Spain. Mr Henderson and his team wanted to tap into the talent elsewhere, and so Wes would have to be able to coach all around the island. He was given a car and the promise of all the material support he needed.

Wes's first assignment was to oversee a training session for promising youngsters at the WITCO cricket ground in Champs Fleurs, a few miles east of Port of Spain. Approximately 60 boys turned up, and Wes was looking to trim that to around 15 players who would receive special coaching. One encounter sticks in his memory. Early in the day, a small, curly-haired boy from nearby Arima came out to bat. Batting left-handed, he put his right foot down the wicket to his first delivery, and in one flowing movement he crashed the ball past point. Wes had seen enough; he called the next boy forward and Larry Gomes had become his first 'discovery'.

His second was soon to follow. The following day he went to Point Fortin, near the south-western tip of the island and saw a 14-year-old batsman who outshone boys several years his senior. Richard Gabriel would go on to become a long-serving opening batsman for Trinidad and Tobago and to represent West Indies in eleven one-day internationals (ODIs) in 1983 and 1984. Wes was left to reflect on his good fortune:

God had been good to me, that in my first two days I was given two future West Indies players. I knew there and then, even though Larry was 13, that he was going to be a star. Richard too: he was good enough to play first-class cricket at 14.

Wes was also grateful for the staunch backing he received from everyone at WITCO, especially Hugh Henderson, whose commitment was reflected in his handling of Gomes. He recognised the youngster's special ability and took personal responsibility for his welfare by acting as his mentor and ensuring that Larry had whatever he needed to make it as a professional cricketer.

Wes made it a priority to address the regional disparity within Trinidadian cricket. The Beaumont Cup was contested annually between North Trinidad and South Trinidad and, apart from the few occasions when the match was drawn, the result was victory for the north. Such was the imbalance that only three people from the south had played for West Indies and virtually all Test cricketers were from Port of Spain. Travelling around Trinidad, Wes soon realised that much of the island's vast talent went unfulfilled, particularly in the central sugar-cane belt, where families of labourers were less likely to have time and money to devote to their sons' cricket. Based on his findings, the management team decided to establish an island-wide youth league. Wes wanted to call it the Frank Worrell League, in honour of the man who was responsible for coordinating the plan; Mr Henderson thought otherwise. He had no objection to naming the new league after Worrell, but on the basis that Wes was the person doing the work, he felt that calling it the Wes Hall Youth Cricket League (commonly shortened to the 'Wes Hall League') was more appropriate. Furthermore, naming it after the person directly involved would appeal to the local volunteers whose engagement was crucial.

Having signed a four-year contract with WITCO, Wes was committed to living in Trinidad when not on Test match duty. In order to maintain match-fitness and sharpness, he needed to find a cricket club on the island, and he opted to join Harvard Cricket Club, one of the many clubs in the first division which played on the sprawling Savannah racecourse in Port of Spain. His choice was unique in that every other overseas West Indian cricketer who had played club cricket in Trinidad, had been a member of Queen's Park Cricket Club. As the most illustrious and wealthy club in Trinidad, Queen's Park attracted the best players, and their home ground, the Queen's Park Oval, boasted a beautiful playing surface befitting a Test-match venue. By contrast, the Savannah had a sand track, used for horse gallops which Wes had to negotiate in the middle of his run-up! His reasoning in choosing Harvard shows how seriously he was taking his responsibilities. He wanted to examine the infrastructure of cricket in Trinidad and thought it more likely that Harvard would give him a feel for the state of the game at grass-roots level:

> I didn't feel that Queen's Park needed any more help. As I saw it, making the other clubs stronger would improve the standard overall in the competition. I was impressed with Harvard Cricket Club which, like Queen's Park, had the three elements that I identified as being fundamental to the development of the Wes Hall League: talented players, good coaching and a flourishing membership. Young Brian Lara was one of those who started at Harvard before moving on to Queen's Park.

The burden of paperwork was undertaken at the WITCO offices, allowing Wes to concentrate solely on organising the cricket. He paid regular visits to the coaches in the island's various cricketing outposts, so that everyone was moving in the same direction in terms of methods and coaching techniques. Teams would compete against one another in the Wes Hall League and, by promoting the cricket as a regular Sunday day out, he was successful in increasing family involvement. Influenced by what he had seen in Randwick, Wes 'wanted to coach the whole person, not just tell them about batting or bowling'. The government had already appointed top coaches, such as former Test cricketer Andy Ganteaume, to work in the schools, and Wes set about augmenting the programme, supported by a network of administrators to help overcome the logistical challenges. Wes acknowledges that he could not have succeeded without these dedicated coaches and organisers: 'Thanks to them, this thing worked like clockwork. It was a beautiful thing!'

Within a matter of months, there were sufficient teams for the Wes Hall Youth League to begin. Matches started at nine o'clock on Sundays, therefore players travelling long distances would need to set off very early to arrive on time. WITCO recognised this and hired a caterer, Robina Robinson, whose company was to provide a snack for the boys when they arrived as well as a full lunch between innings. The infrastructure of the league cost a great deal of money and, thanks to WITCO, Wes was able to put everything in place without relying on charity.

The Wes Hall League quickly became a success. Within a year of its inception, the Trinidad Under-19 and Under-15 teams were made up exclusively of boys from its ranks. In Wes's youth, although the best young players were exposed to the rigours of men's cricket, the only inter-island youth cricket he had seen was when Queen's Royal College from Port of Spain visited to play Harrison College. That changed when he was in Trinidad: Barbados boys toured Trinidad, Trinidad went to play Jamaica, and a triangular tournament involving Barbados, Guyana and Trinidad was held to pick a junior West Indies team for the 1970 tour of England. They performed brilliantly in England. Larry Gomes, Richard Gabriel, Boya Sahadeo, Dudnath Ramkisson and Nirmal Nanan were all products of the Wes Hall League in Trinidad. Four of the junior players – Gomes, Gabriel, David Murray from Barbados, and Herbert Chang of Jamaica – went on to play for West Indies.

Wes feels that the importance of establishing pan-Caribbean youth cricket on an organised footing cannot be an overestimated in terms of the development of West Indies cricket. He considers the youngsters who toured England in 1970 to be pioneers just as much as the first West Indian party to do so seventy years previously[4] and the players who became West Indies' first Test cricketers on the historic 1928 tour of England.

The selection meeting to finalise the Trinidad squad for the triangular series was memorable for Wes for the wrong reasons. It took place in June 1969 at Presentation College, San Fernando, 35 miles south of Port of Spain. As Wes was driving home afterwards, a driver overtaking him misjudged the oncoming traffic and swerved back towards Wes, clipping his car and sending it careering down the bank into a vegetable patch. Wes was pinned in the driver's seat and, with his car engine still hissing, it took two people to pull him out. As he flitted in and out of consciousness in hospital, his only memory is of listening to commentary of Sobers being run out at Lord's in the second Test of the 1969 tour of England!

By the time Wes left Trinidad in 1970, promising young cricketers were emerging from all over the island. The Wes Hall League *per se* was disbanded, but the basis of the system that Wes established – the provision

---

[4] In 1900 a West Indian team captained by R.S.A. Warner became the first from the Caribbean to tour England. The 17 matches, against county and representative sides, were not accorded first-class status.

of equal opportunities for players irrespective of their background – still operates. He is gratified that a region such as Preysal in central Trinidad is now a thriving hub for professional cricket. Before being part of the Wes Hall League, very few cricketers had come from Preysal, but it has since produced many players, and several Barbadians have played there professionally.

The Randwick experience had been an eye-opener for Wes, and he admits to having copied much of what he learned there, particularly in his attempts to make cricket the centre of the community. This was exactly as Worrell had envisaged, although even he would have been surprised by the speed with which the Wes Hall League produced results. Its success confirmed Worrell's vision for the development of West Indies cricket, which was matched by his inspired choice of Wes to execute it. In his first foray into the world of management and administration, Wes had established a structure, and coordinated all aspects of the operation. Incredibly this was all accomplished while he was still an active international sportsman. He is rightly proud of his work and what it achieved:

> In the four years I was in Trinidad, we actually got something started, we brought on some talent, and by getting the youngsters coming out to play in the league, we got somewhere near to the Australian system of developing young players.

Sadly, Worrell's untimely death in 1967 meant that he did not see the fruition of his plan.

The demands of his career path guaranteed that a hectic schedule was the norm for Wes during most of his career. His first season for Queensland ended in February 1962, and just ten days later he was in Trinidad for the first of five Test matches against India. The exciting young West Indies team under Worrell continued to show progress, beating India 5-0 to record their first series whitewash. Wes cemented his reputation as their leading bowler with 27 wickets at an average of 15.74 in the series. Remarkably, for the fifth time in his five Test series to date, Wes was the leading West Indian wicket-taker, an indication of the quality and consistency of his bowling and also the extent to which the team had come to rely on him.

During the Second Test, the first of the two played at Sabina Park, Wes achieved a notable milestone on his way to figures of six for 49 in India's second innings. When R.F. Surti was out lbw, he became Wes's 100th Test wicket, in only his 20th Test match. He also flourished with the bat, averaging 40 in the series.

Not everything went to plan though: an incident at Port of Spain during the Fourth Test left an unpleasant taste and may even have prevented him from achieving a rare bowling feat. The first two days went exceptionally well. West Indies batted first, and Wes shared an unbroken last-wicket partnership of 98 with Worrell before the captain declared with Wes on 50 not out, his second Test half-century. In the final session of the second day, Wes tore through the Indian batting line-up, claiming the top five batsmen for just 20 runs as India slumped to 61 for five. At the close of play, he left the field tired, thirsty and hungry; by the time he got to the restaurant in the team's hotel that evening, he was ravenous. He ordered a well-deserved steak with roast potatoes, only to be informed by hotel staff that the players' twelve-dollar meal allowance would not stretch to such 'expensive food'. Wes was furious; he paid for the meal himself and was still seething when he arrived at the Queen's Park Oval ground the next morning.

Worrell was unaware of what had happened at dinner and greeted Wes cheerily: 'Winfield, you can get all ten wickets today.' Wes informed his captain that taking ten wickets was not a possibility because he would not be bowling. After hearing Wes's explanation, Worrell agreed with his stance: he had long campaigned for the fair treatment of players, and this was another example of a player suffering a raw deal at the hands of management.

Wes had not gone to the stadium with the intention of making a stand, but at that moment it seemed like the right thing to do. He decided on principle not to bowl, even though he might have taken ten wickets. His point made, he resumed his place in the attack in the second innings: 'You've got to move on, I didn't want to let my teammates down, and the management knew how I felt.'

When questioned, the waiter at the hotel claimed that he was acting under the instructions of the secretary at Queen's Park, Sonny Murray, the uncle of future West Indies wicketkeeper Deryck Murray. Worrell remonstrated with Murray, who assured him that he had issued no such directive. Responsibility lay with board officials who apparently prioritised cost-cutting over the well-being of professional sportsmen representing their country. Several years later when he spent time in Trinidad, Wes again encountered Murray and found him to be extremely kind and helpful.

In the 1961-62 Test series against India, Hall had opened the bowling with three different partners. Chester Watson from Jamaica played in the First Test before being discarded for the rest of the series; Sven 'Charlie' Stayers from British Guiana was given the new ball in the next three Tests; and the 21-year-old Jamaican Lester King made his debut in the final Test at Sabina Park. King bowled very well, with match figures of seven for 64, and was deservedly selected to tour England in 1963.

In such a one-sided contest, the absence of a new-ball partner to ease the pace-bowling burden had not been a particular problem, but Wes was concerned that this was the issue most likely to prevent the team from achieving greatness. While Lance Gibbs had come to the fore as a world-class spinner to succeed Ramadhin and Valentine, Wes had been without a regular partner in four series and 18 Test matches spanning the three years since Gilchrist's final Test in February 1959. In that time he had opened the bowling with no fewer than eight different bowlers, one of whom, Charlie Griffith, was about to make a dramatic return and would become the bowling soulmate Wes craved. Griffith was a fearsome fast bowler who complemented Wes, the final piece in the jigsaw as the West Indians continued their drive to become cricket's world champions.

11

England 1963: Hall and Griffith Unleashed

For West Indies' next challenge – the tour of England in 1963 – the team would need to be strong in every department. Like all his colleagues Wes was relishing the prospect, and he was particularly enthusiastic about the inclusion in the party of the 24-year-old Barbadian fast bowler Charlie Griffith. Griffith's only first-class cricket since his Test debut at Port of Spain against England in 1960 had been a few matches for Barbados, including an infamous encounter with the Indians in Bridgetown in 1962. Prior to that match Wes had taken 14 wickets in the first two Tests of the series but, when it was announced that Griffith would be playing for Barbados against the Indians, Wes warned the tourists that Griffith was bowling quicker even than him. Griffith lived up to his billing: in the first innings the Indian captain Nari Contractor was struck by a delivery from Griffith which caused a hairline fracture of the batsman's skull. Contractor was taken to hospital where an emergency operation saved his life. Worrell was one of those who gave blood.

Wes's intervention probably played a part in unsettling the Indian batsman; Contractor had misjudged the bounce and was so quick in taking evasive action that he ducked into a ball which rose barely above bail height. These facts were largely ignored after the situation had been inflamed in the second innings. Local umpire Cortez Jordan called Griffith for throwing, prompting widespread controversy and allegations that he was a 'chucker'. The accusations haunted him throughout his career, although Wes believes passionately that Griffith operated within the laws of the game, as did the selectors: early in 1963 Griffith took 13 wickets in two island matches for Barbados to force his way into the West Indies squad bound for England.

Between West Indies' series against India in 1961/62 and England in 1963, Wes embarked on the same gruelling schedule as the previous year.

Accrington was followed by Queensland, which led straight into the tour of England. He was weary from playing so much hard cricket, but he was in peak fitness and his game was in great shape. Six years after his previous tour of England, he was now one of the stars of the team, a fact formally recognised in 1962 when he became the first West Indian to be named by the Imperial Cricket Conference[1] (ICC) as the world's number one-ranked bowler.

Wes reflected on the progress he had made since 1957 and remembered what he had learned on that dismal, fractious tour. Now, with Worrell as the elder statesman of a group of players who had grown up together, every member of the squad was treated fairly. Worrell had broken down the old inter-island cliques and, finally, a West Indies team was pulling in the same direction: 'We were all equals in that team – even Sobers, who was a genius! We enjoyed spending time in each other's company, and before every tour we looked forward to meeting up with our friends again.'

The 1963 series in England was a seminal moment in the development of the team. After coming so close to beating Australia two years previously, and subsequently thrashing the Indians, West Indies had never had a better-balanced side. The blend of youth and experience was perfect; they possessed enormous flair, yet could play with restraint when the situation required; and within their ranks they had a cricketing superstar and their greatest-ever captain. Equally importantly the side was confident and happy, and it was no surprise when West Indies won the series convincingly 3-1, and Worrell picked up the inaugural Wisden Trophy. Everywhere Worrell and his men played, they attracted large, appreciative crowds, including many from the Caribbean who had settled in the UK.

The tour represented a glorious finale for the captain, who turned 39 during the summer and retired from Test cricket at the end of the series. There were numerous fine individual performances, with Hunte, Kanhai, Butcher, and Sobers all scoring heavily. Griffith, Gibbs, and Sobers all took 20 or more wickets. Hall's tally of 16 wickets was just half the number of his new-ball partner, and he was grateful to Griffith for sharing

---

[1] The Imperial Cricket Conference was founded in 1909 as world cricket's governing body. It changed name in 1965 to the International Cricket Conference. In 1989, it adopted its current name, the International Cricket Council.

the fast-bowling burden that he had borne alone for the previous four years. Most commentators on the tour agreed that Wes was unfortunate not to take more Test wickets and to exceed his total of 74 in 20 first-class matches. He was consistently hostile and threatening and bowled far better than his Test-match average of 33.37 suggests. Without doubt he was crucial to the team's success.

An unexpected triumph for Wes came in May against Cambridge University at Fenner's. Batting at number nine, he struck his first – and only – century in first-class cricket. His 65-minute hundred was the fastest first-class century of the summer and especially pleasing as he claimed the accolade ahead of his old friend and sparring partner Fred Trueman. Victory in that match contributed to the tourists' first-class record of 15 wins, two losses and 13 draws, almost identical to that of the great team of 1950 (16-2-12).

The highlight of the tour was the extraordinary last day of the Second Test at Lord's. Once again Wes played a central role in a breathless finale which was filled with every bit as much tension and drama as the tied Test in Brisbane.

West Indies had won the First Test at Old Trafford by ten wickets and, following a routine victory against Sussex at Hove, the players were in confident mood when they arrived at Lord's for the Second Test. Worrell won the toss, and West Indies batted first. They established a first-innings lead of just four runs and were then bowled out for 229 in their second innings. Highlights up to that point included an attractive 73 by Kanhai, an entertaining 25 not out from Wes and six wickets for Trueman in West Indies' first innings; and scores of 80 by Barrington, 70 by Dexter and five wickets for Griffith in England's reply. West Indies' second innings produced more high-quality fast bowling by Trueman who took another five wickets and helped cause West Indies' collapse from 214 for five to 229 all out. Only a wonderful batting display by Basil Butcher, whose marvellous 133 took the score from 15 for two to 228 for nine, saved West Indies from almost certain defeat. His score was exactly 100 runs more than the next highest, made by Worrell.

England's victory target was a manageable 234, but two wickets for Wes in a hostile opening spell helped reduce them to 31 for three midway through the fourth day. It seemed that West Indies were on course for another victory, but by close of play England had recovered to a far healthier 116 for three, with Ken Barrington and Brian Close the not-out batsmen. However, the score told only part of the story: Colin Cowdrey had been forced to retire hurt on 19 with a broken wrist after being struck by a delivery from Wes when the score was on 72.

On the team coach on the way to the ground the following morning, Worrell approached his two fast bowlers. As always, they were sitting together, and he asked them what they would do if they were captain. Wes confidently informed his skipper that he would bowl as usual from his preferred Nursery End and use the Lord's slope to shape the ball away from the batsmen. With Griffith tearing in to bowl his inswingers from the Pavilion End, they would build pressure and take wickets. Unfortunately Wes's plans were scuppered by Worrell's reply: Griffith was suffering from a slight groin strain, and Worrell thought it would be easier for him to bowl from the Nursery End where the slope would take him naturally away from the wicket on his follow through. Reluctantly Wes accepted his captain's logical reasoning but was left feeling apprehensive at the prospect of operating from the Pavilion End.

Entering the final day, England were favourites to win the match. They needed a further 118 runs with seven wickets in hand – effectively six given Cowdrey's injury – but, with plenty of time remaining, there was no need for them to take risks. Encouragingly for West Indies, though, the morning was damp and overcast, and the loss of the morning session to the weather suited Worrell perfectly. When play began at 2.20pm, there were exactly 200 minutes left in the match, putting England under time pressure. It also allowed Worrell to implement his favoured strategy of subjecting England to an all-out pace barrage from Hall and Griffith. He had warned the pair that they would 'have a long trek today' and was true to his word as Wes bowled unchanged for the entire day's play, and Griffith delivered all but three of the overs from the opposite end. Wes was most displeased that those three were bowled by off-spinner Gibbs: 'Lance bowled his overs so quickly, I got less than two minutes' rest!'

With the score on 130, Griffith eventually ended Barrington's resistance and, when he dismissed Jim Parks, England were 158 for five and struggling to save the match. Close and Fred Titmus staged another recovery and, as the match entered the final hour, England had reached 186 for five, 48 runs short of victory.

By this time Wes had been bowling for nearly two and a half hours with just a 20-minute rest at tea. He actually felt the tea-break was a hindrance: his muscles became stiff, and he had to re-establish his bowling rhythm when play resumed. Nevertheless, he summoned the energy to run in with the same fire and menace as at the start of play and, just as the game appeared to be swinging back in England's favour, with 31 runs required in 40 minutes and five wickets remaining, he struck twice in successive deliveries to dismiss Titmus and Trueman. With England reduced to 203 for seven, the general expectation was that, having done his job, an exhausted Wes would make way for Sobers to be brought into the attack to take the second new ball with Griffith. However, it was not Sobers but Hall who took the new ball.

As the match reached its climax, Wes was also required to make a couple of crucial stops at fine-leg to prevent boundaries: 'After bowling for all that time, to run around and pick up the ball and throw it back over the stumps, it was tough!' He was extremely fit, of course, but he was also helped in his marathon effort by his captain's gentle coaxing: 'Thank you, Winfield, just another one [over] please, and we'll see how things go. Just keep it there, you're doing a great job, don't let them get runs, just keep it there ...' However tense he himself may have been, Worrell was always on hand to offer calm words of encouragement, sharing the responsibility of managing the situation with the bowler. Just as in Brisbane two years earlier, Wes was immensely grateful for Worrell's support:

> He would never throw you the ball and just leave you to it; he
> was always fielding at mid-on, and when the ball was hit into the
> field or thrown to the wicketkeeper he would run to the stumps
> at my end.

Close carried England to within 15 runs of an unlikely victory but, with 20 minutes remaining and the score on 219, he was finally dismissed by Griffith for 70. This brought together the last two fit batsmen, with the number eleven Derek Shackleton joining David Allen at the crease. Over the next few minutes, leg-byes and scrambled singles took the score to 226 for eight and, with enough time left for one more over, all four results were possible. Just as Worrell had entrusted Wes with the crucial final overs in Australia two years previously, he turned to him again. As in Brisbane and Adelaide, the tension on the field and in the stands was unbearable as Worrell and Hall attempted to keep their emotions in check and impose some order on proceedings. The nation was so engrossed in events at Lord's that when television coverage of the cricket was interrupted to accommodate the news summary the BBC was inundated with complaints from cricket fans and hastily returned to Lord's. The viewers were not disappointed.

Ball 1

England required eight runs for victory and, with word emerging from the England dressing room that Cowdrey would come out to bat if required, West Indies needed to take two wickets. Wes's first ball was fast and full, just outside the off-stump; Shackleton took a wild swing and missed, and the ball went through to wicketkeeper Murray for no run.

Ball 2

Needing eight runs from five balls, Shackleton played defensively to the next delivery and set off for a single as the ball dropped at his feet. Remarkably for a man bowling his 24th consecutive over, Wes changed direction in his follow-through and sprinted towards the ball to attempt a run-out. He failed to pick up the ball cleanly however, and Allen was able to make his ground.

Ball 3

With England requiring seven runs from four balls, Worrell had positioned himself at short-leg to prevent any more quick singles. The third ball of the over was flicked off his legs behind square by Allen for one run, leaving England one stroke from victory.

Ball 4

Worrell had to tread a precarious line between defence and attack as he strove to take the final two wickets while defending a five-run lead. He positioned five fielders on the boundary, four of them protecting the leg side typically favoured by lower-order batsmen. Wes knew that Shackleton was likely to go in search of the runs and that he struggled to connect with anything fast and wide of the off-stump. He produced the perfect delivery. The ball narrowly missed the edge of Shackleton's flailing bat on its way through to Murray. While Shackleton stood looking at the ball, Allen took it upon himself to run a bye and had almost made his ground with the ball still in the wicketkeeper's hands. There followed a display of wonderful cricket awareness and composure under intense pressure by Murray and Worrell. Standing back 20 yards behind the wickets, Murray threw the ball underarm to his captain at short-leg. Spotting that Shackleton was slow in setting off for the run, Worrell turned down the option of throwing the ball to Wes who was positioned at the stumps. Instead, he raced the batsman to the non-striker's end and completed the run-out.

Ball 5

The previous ball had returned the advantage to West Indies: the dismissal of Shackleton left his team one wicket from defeat, while the six runs needed for victory looked a tall order as Cowdrey took the field with his broken left wrist in plaster. If required to bat, he would adopt a left hander's stance holding the bat in his right hand. The saving grace for Allen was that he, and not Cowdrey, was on strike. Wes had mixed feelings: he felt if that Cowdrey was prepared to come out to bat and take the hero's plaudits, he could expect no favours, yet he felt uneasy at the prospect of bowling to him. He was relieved therefore when Cowdrey went down the wicket to Allen and told him to play out the remaining two deliveries for the draw:

> The worst thing would be if a man is showing such courage and determination batting with a broken hand, and something else had happened to him. So I was very glad that he did not get down to the striker's end. I would have bowled a 'proper' ball, fast and straight at the stumps. Of course, I would never bowl a bouncer, but I wasn't going to bowl underarm either! Colin was such a good player that even with one hand, he easily could have hit a four.

Against the tail-ender Allen, Wes needed to summon one last effort to produce a couple of fast, straight deliveries. The fifth ball was just that, and Allen got behind the line and pushed into the covers for no run.

Ball 6

Five days of intense battle and fluctuating fortunes had come down to the final ball of the final over. England could still win in the unlikely event that Allen hit a six or Wes bowled no-balls or wides. In a moment of *déjà vu*, Worrell warned him against doing so! More realistically, one wicket would give West Indies a 2-0 lead in the series, so Worrell brought in his fielders. Wes charged in to complete his 40th over of the innings; and even though a bouncer may well have induced panic and a false shot, he did not consider bowling short: 'A bouncer could have won the Test, but was I going to risk knocking down a tail-ender just to win a Test match? I would never consider doing that.' The ball arrowed towards middle stump, and again Allen courageously got his body in line and played into the on-side, safely out of reach of the two short-legs. Despite his disappointment, Wes's first reaction was to turn to Allen and applaud the man who had just thwarted him. However, before the players could exchange the customary handshakes, they became aware that hundreds of spectators were rushing across the outfield towards them. Players and umpires made a dash for the pavilion to avoid the crush, none faster than Wes, who managed to coax one final effort from his weary legs!

The match was drawn and, as in the tied Test, both teams emerged from the drama with great credit:

> Neither Brisbane nor Lord's resulted in a win, one was tied, and the other was drawn, but that is the beautiful thing about cricket; you do not need a winner for a match to be spectacular. I got more wickets on other occasions than I got on those days, and in matches that we won, but I am looking at what it did for cricket. To be the person who was trusted to bowl the last over on both days, that's a special thing. In my view those Tests should have equal billing, because both were fantastic sporting performances by every player who took part.

When pushed to rank one performance over the other, he veers towards Lord's:

> Bowling on the last day at Lord's in '63 is probably my single best performance, even better than the tied Test, where I did well [nine wickets and a half-century]. I bowled unchanged from 20 past two until six o'clock with just a 20-minute break for tea. I was uncomfortable bowling from the Pavilion End, but I bowled 40 overs and got four for 93 – just missed the honours board! I do not know if others saw it as a big thing but, believe me, three hours 20 minutes bowling 24 straight overs ... it was a hell of a thing! I'm not sure that people saw the beauty of that,

the beauty of human endeavour – but that has to be my greatest day in cricket. It was such an effort that in the Third and Fourth Tests, I was a passenger. I didn't come back and bowl fast and take wickets until the Fifth. Thank God Charlie was so fit and strong. At Leeds and the Oval in the last two Tests, he took 18 wickets and bowled us to victory.

That last afternoon at Lord's took an enormous toll on Wes's body. He was so exhausted that he could barely move, and he was unable to travel with his teammates after the match for the fixture against Hampshire commencing the following day. Instead, Frank Worrell arranged for him to have the luxury of a chauffeur-driven ride to Southampton in the back seat of the 'very big car' belonging to Jamaican commentator Roy Lawrence. After sitting out the game in Southampton, Wes returned to action in spectacular fashion in the next county match at Southend-on-Sea, taking six for 22 as he and Griffith routed Essex for 56. This success was a false dawn, for it was a further month before Wes felt completely recovered from his Lord's exertions.

Griffith's magnificent form in the latter part of the series followed an incident which occurred during the Lord's Test. His sister-in-law, who lived in London, prepared some West Indian food for him and a few of his teammates and, after close of play, she took it to The Waldorf Hotel where the team was staying. Charlie was out when it arrived, and Wes – Charlie's roommate – told Sobers that a feast had been delivered to the room. Sobers arrived, followed by several other players and, although Wes encouraged them to leave enough for Charlie, he probably could have been more assertive: 'I must admit I didn't keep a sharp eye on it and, when Charlie came back, there were just a few scraps left! I apologised, of course, but he was very upset.' At the end of the tour Charlie's astonishing performance levels prompted Wes to announce mischievously that it was a good thing that they ate all his food because it fired him up for the rest of the series!

The special relationship between Wes and Worrell was based on mutual respect and understanding and a genuine affection for each other. The only occasion when things became strained between them occurred during the 1963 tour, when Wes reacted to a perceived injustice. Like most of his colleagues Wes had a strong sense of the history of the game, and a highlight of a tour to England was the opportunity to play at Lord's. He recalled how thrilled he had been to play there against Middlesex in 1957, and it disappointed him that in 1963 his friend Seymour Nurse, who was on his first tour of England, was omitted from all three of the West Indians' matches at Lord's despite playing in 17 matches that summer. Wes gave vent to his feelings, describing the treatment of Nurse as 'unreasonable'. That was too much for Worrell. He acknowledged that Wes had a valid point but made it clear that expressing it in such terms in front of the whole team was unacceptable:

> Worrell was a man of Christian faith and strong principles, and when he told me that I couldn't talk like that, I knew I had overstepped the mark. He wasn't angry, just quite stern. It was a lesson in propriety that has served me well. I was discombobulated when he said to me: 'The best, with a bad attitude, is no longer the best.' It was the first time I had heard him use those words; they hit me hard and made me think. I apologised and assured him it would not happen in future.

Both men dealt with the matter in a mature, civilised way; common sense prevailed, and the disagreement was diffused.

12

Behind the Celebrations

Sport occasionally provides a showcase for acts of heroism. Cowdrey walking out to bat with a broken arm was such an occasion; his advance down the pavilion steps and across the Lord's outfield to the middle remains one of cricket's enduring images. His bravery cast him as the hero, while Wes – the man who had inflicted the injury and who stood between Cowdrey and glory – found himself in the role of villain. In the context of the match, such a billing was understandable, and Wes took the barracking of the crowd in his stride. What he found more sinister, however, was the campaign waged against West Indies' fast bowlers and the effect it had on public perception and behaviour. Hall and Griffith had played together just twice before the 1963 tour of England: in Trinidad in the last Test of the 1959-60 series against England; and for Barbados against the Indians in 1962. Events in that match at Kensington Oval, where Griffith terrorised India's batsmen, influenced the attitude of the English press, with many openly questioning the legality of his action.

Wes viewed the short-pitched delivery as an essential part of a fast bowler's armoury. The psychological edge it gave him was essential in keeping a batsman guessing and, whether directly or indirectly, bouncers brought him many wickets. Contrary to lazy assumptions which went unchallenged, his intention was never to hit anyone, either in England in 1963 or indeed throughout his career. Critics ignored the fact that, far from being a bouncer-happy tearaway, Wes adhered to the prevailing common practice of not bowling short at tail-enders. Just as in the closely-fought Tests in Australia in 1961, a couple of fast bouncers may well have resulted in a West Indies victory at Lord's, but the risk of hitting and injuring lower-order batsmen dictated that he never considered this an option.

During his superb 70 in the first innings Dexter was struck several times by Griffith bouncers, and in the second innings Wes hit Barrington with a short ball before the fateful blow to Cowdrey. Events then threatened to turn ugly during Hall's long battle with Close. Rather than taking a risk by playing a shot at short deliveries, Close adopted the tactic of standing and allowing the ball to hit him on the body. The spectators winced as the ball repeatedly thudded into Close's chest. They began to voice their displeasure at Wes's bowling, ignoring the fact that Close was electing not to take evasive action. Wes did not enjoy the spectacle either but, with runs at a premium, his options were limited. He faced a conundrum: he was having difficulty finding his bowling rhythm from the 'wrong' end at Lord's, with the result that 'every time I pitched it up it went for four, and every time I pulled back my length, he got hit!' As far as Wes is concerned, he was perfectly entitled to try to unsettle Close, a seasoned campaigner who had first played for England in 1949 and who would make the last of his 22 Test appearances in 1976:

> Close knew what he was doing. He captained Yorkshire, and if you captained Yorkshire in those days you had to be a fantastic tactician. He was very tough and very smart. I was bowling for my country; Close was trying his heart out for his country too, and his personality was such that he would not back down.

Close then raised the stakes in a further attempt to unsettle Wes:

> On my run, I was looking at my mark at halfway, and when I got to the crease I looked up and saw that he had come two yards down the wicket. I felt that I couldn't bowl the ball because he had probably come to remove something from the pitch. I pulled up sharply and hurt my back. And he laughed! That got me mad. I said to him: 'Are you from England? And that's what you do?' He just looked at me and gave me a wicked smile and went back to his crease.

Close used this ploy several times, forcing both Hall and Griffith to abort their run-ups. Such tactics may be commonplace in the modern game, but in 1963 stricter codes of sporting honour prevailed – especially in cricket – and gamesmanship was frowned upon. The crowd was under the misapprehension that Wes was the guilty party, and he was heckled from the stands for much of the afternoon. Comments by Close after the match showed that he had deliberately tried to disrupt the bowlers' rhythm and that he felt this was legitimate: 'It wasn't unthinking bravado. Far from it. I made Hall lose his cool. His line and length suffered.' Close thus absolved Wes of indulging in gamesmanship, but Worrell went a step further by pointing an accusing finger at Close to show where he felt the fault lay. He acknowledged Close's courage, but he said that the tactics he had used were 'wrong'.

Several years later, Close sent Wes a photograph showing his upper body covered in bruises from that afternoon, with the message: 'Wes, it's a good thing the balls were soft in those days!' With good reason Wes feels that he was unfairly adjudged the guilty party. He certainly suffered the repercussions:

> That's how Brian Close saw it. It was a battle that he was happy with and happy to be a part of; he was a friend of mine, a very decent man, and he took it as a joke, but everybody else was sending me hate letters.

Furthermore, Wes was vindicated for his part in the injury to Cowdrey. In the batsman's own words, 'It was a good length ball from Hall which flew, unaccountably, and broke my arm just above the wrist. It made the most awful noise!' Cowdrey's intervention undermined the accusations of improper conduct levelled at Wes, although there remained those who were unhappy with the tactics of West Indies' pace attack. Playing for Queensland, he had encountered some hostility on the occasions when he had struck batsmen with a short ball, but nothing in Australia prepared him for the reaction awaiting him in England in 1963. England won the Third Test at Edgbaston to square the series, but after losing at Headingley in the Fourth Test their captain Ted Dexter wrote a scathing newspaper column condemning the West Indies tactics. He went on to declare the Test series 'meaningless'. Several high-profile batsmen – notably Barrington – spoke out in support of Dexter, and the issue became a major controversy in the cricket world. Commentators and the press questioned the ethics of the West Indies team and continued to demonise Hall and Griffith. It felt to Wes as if open season had been declared on them.

In his 1963 book *The West Indies at Lord's*, the English author Alan Ross was particularly forthright. He paid tribute to Hall's marathon spell of high-intensity bowling on the final day: 'His final over was as ferocious as his first', but questioned West Indies' approach. He referred to 'the unpleasantness of the bowling', which he attributed to 'Worrell's cold-hearted strategy'. As Wes points out, this is a grossly inaccurate and unfair portrayal of a great man whom the author obviously did not know. Moreover, the assumption that Wes was acting on his captain's instructions is patronising in the extreme. The implication that Hall and Griffith were merely weapons deployed by Worrell invokes the stereotype of the fast bowler as a willing workhorse relying on others for direction; in the context of the Worrell/ Hall relationship, nothing could be further from the truth.

In fact, the only comment the captain made to his two fast bowlers regarding strategy was that he saw them as West Indies' best chance of victory; hence, they should be prepared to bowl long spells on the last afternoon. Worrell took the view that intelligent, experienced cricketers like Wes and Charlie knew the game – and their own games – well enough to make their own decisions. He trusted them implicitly, and on no occasion did he incite them to bowl short: 'Frank Worrell never told me to bowl bouncers but, whenever I pitched that ball up to Close, he hit it. I worked that out for myself.'

Another thing Wes was able to work out for himself was the effect of the negative press on the public's attitude to the West Indian fast bowlers. It is widely accepted that the 1963 tourists were among the most popular ever to visit English shores and that Wes was held in great affection by the overwhelming majority of cricket fans up and down the country; less well-known is the abuse endured by Hall and Griffith. Wes states: 'I could bowl two bouncers at somebody, and I'd get hate-mail' and relates one of many shocking examples. The letter, received a few days after the Lord's Test, was from a woman who wrote:

Dear Mr Hall,
You big, black, ugly baboon. Why don't you go back home to the West Indies on the next banana boat?

This disgusting message was typical of the depths to which many people stooped.

I used to receive a lot of bad stuff. People don't know it, but I got a lot of hate-mail in England and some in Australia. I tried to block it out in the sense that I did not get upset about it, but it was difficult, knowing that people thought these things about you.

Of course, expressing a distaste for his bowling in civilised terms was completely legitimate, but so often it was delivered as a racist insult. The fact that Wes had to find his own way of dealing with such outrageous abuse indicates the extent to which racism was an accepted feature of society. Learning to live with it by 'blocking it out' is not something that any human being should need to do. Shamefully, that is how it was for Wes and his teammates.

As far as criticism of Wes's tactics is concerned, those responsible did not realise that he never had a personal quarrel with a batsman, let alone tried to inflict injury. He remains proud that no batsman 'ever heard a bad word out of my mouth towards them. They were never threatened by me, and they knew that I never hit anyone on purpose. I would rather hit the stumps. My conscience was clear.'

A clear conscience helped Wes to cope with this occupational hazard when playing for Queensland against Victoria in Melbourne in December 1961. He took five wickets in the first innings, but the main talking-point was the fast bouncer which Bob Cowper mis-hooked. The ball crashed into Cowper's head and ballooned to mid-wicket, where it was caught by Ken Mackay. On his way back to the MCG pavilion Cowper collapsed on the outfield. Wes was horrified by the injury and extremely frightened but, in the absence of malicious intent on his part, he had no feelings of guilt and was able to ignore the hostile reaction of the Melbourne crowd: 'I carried on doing my job.' He took four more Victoria wickets in the second innings, and Queensland won the match.

Wes also feels that the element of fear when facing a genuinely fast bowler provides a rush of adrenaline and a thrill that are unique in cricket. He urges people to consider that many batsmen relish a contest that challenges their ability and courage:

> Let's face it, a batsman knew if I was bowling at 95mph and he got hit he would be in trouble. I hit Colin McDonald with a ball in the tied Test. He was in real pain, and I was very sorry for him, but I knew that if the next ball was up there in the slot, he was going to drive it for four. He was up for the contest, a very courageous man.

At the end of the 1960-61 series, McDonald came up to Wes, carrying his 'baggy green' Australian cap. He told Wes that he was retiring from Test cricket and that it had been a pleasure to share the field with him. He handed the cap to Wes, a gift from a respected opponent and friend:

> I'd like to impress on bowlers, 'that one can succeed in this department without displaying open hatred and general abuse'.

Those were the words Frank Worrell used in 1965 to describe my attitude, and it meant a lot to me then. It is a hell of a statement nowadays! I always had time to have a laugh with the opposition. A bit of fun between two men who knew the rules and respected each other made it more enjoyable; it did not mean we were trying any less. I've hit some men, and it's made me sick, and the men who got hit are all going to say that I would never intentionally do that. Everyone knew I was just playing hard and fair cricket, and I could take it as well as give it out.

He gave and took when batting against Ted Dexter in Trinidad in 1960. Wes ducked to avoid a bouncer and landed in an ungainly heap on the ground. Dexter came down the wicket to him and said: 'Wes, get up. I've got another one for you, because I know you're going to give me ten!'

'Make that twenty, Ted!'

During the match between Queensland and the 1962-63 MCC tourists in Brisbane, Wes bowled a bouncer that the Warwickshire batsman Alan Smith attempted to hook. The ball was too quick for Smith and struck him on the ear. To everyone's relief, despite bleeding profusely, the injury was not serious. Wes was less fortunate later in that same innings when a delivery pitched in the bowlers' footmarks, took off and flew down the leg side. The Queensland wicketkeeper Wally Grout – 'the best wicketkeeper I have ever seen and a hilarious character' – dived to collect the ball but was deceived as it swung late and hit him full in the face, breaking his jaw in two places.

Wes was mortified to see his good friend so badly hurt, although Grout was forgiving when his teammate visited him in hospital later that evening armed with cans of beer as a peace offering. Wes was extremely appreciative of Grout's attitude: 'Don't worry, Big Man, bring the beer, bring the beer! Everything's alright!'

Unfortunately, others were less understanding. After the Grout incident Wes again received hate-mail for injuring 'an opponent': people who obviously had no idea that Grout was the wicketkeeper standing 40 yards away were only too keen to seize the opportunity to berate Wes.

Wes had many on-field battles with another Australian batsman, his good friend Bobby Simpson. He rates Simpson one of the best opening batsmen he played against; such a fine player of fast bowling that it was pointless bowling bouncers to him. The only incident between them occurred during a match between Queensland and New South Wales in Brisbane, when Wes bowled a fast, good-length delivery which struck and injured Simpson. It made Wes aware of another consequence of hitting a batsman: he was also friendly with Simpson's wife, Meg, and was as sorry for the indirect pain he had inflicted on her as the damage done to her husband. She appreciated that Wes was doing his job and bore no hard feelings:

> Allan Davidson's wife, Betty, was also very cordial: she greeted me with a smile and enquired about my family ... unlike some wives who were very distant, and I understand that. Their husbands go home with big bruises on their bodies, and I'm the man who has been hurling down 95mph projectiles at them, so the wives are not going to love me!

As a final word on his relationship with batsmen, Wes refers to a letter sent to him by Colin Cowdrey some years later. In a gracious double-compliment, Cowdrey states that Wes was the fastest bowler he ever faced and was by some distance the more upset of the two men when Cowdrey's arm was broken at Lord's in 1963.

Hailed as one of the great Test matches, the 1963 Lord's Test has assumed a special place in cricket folklore. However, it also exposed inconvenient issues surrounding reactions to the tactics used by Hall and Griffith. Historical perspective offers some insight.

The Three Georges: Challenor, John and Francis; the great George Headley; Constantine and Martindale; the Three Ws; and Ramadhin and Valentine ... over the years West Indies had produced these and many other fine individual cricketers, but a lack of strength in depth had prevented them from mounting a sustained challenge to the game's superpowers, Australia and England. Finally a team from the Caribbean with the ingredients to be the best in the world was poised to upset the established order. Great batting was combined with blistering pace in a team packed with star players. In Sobers West Indies had the best cricketer on the planet; Worrell was a once-in-a-generation captain; Kanhai a magnificent batsman; and Gibbs the world's leading spinner. Hall and Griffith formed the most devastating fast-bowling combination in the world.

Since the sensational 1932-33 'Bodyline' series in Australia, the ethics of fast bowling had not been the subject of serious debate, even though fearsome, aggressive bowlers were commonplace during the intervening 30 years. Australia's Lindwall and Miller wrought havoc throughout the 1940s and 1950s; and English fast bowlers, including Trueman and Tyson, intimidated batsmen with their extreme pace and hostility. In what appeared to be a case of double standards, tactics that had been tolerated became unacceptable when employed by Hall and Griffith. The following extract from *Pace Like Fire* reveals Wes's thoughts at the time:

> The critics slammed me unmercifully and accused us of going back to the Bodyline days. Maybe we were bowling as though we wanted to win, but when Trueman, Statham, and Bailey throttled us in a similar way on the same strip [Lord's] six years previously they had drooled their admiration. Now the shoe was on the other foot and some people were not quite so pleased.

While double standards and jealousy were perhaps understandable in response to West Indies' advance in cricketing terms, there was a feeling in the Caribbean that vilification of its bowlers had its roots beyond the cricket world. Amongst others C.L.R. James put forward radical – though plausible – explanations. He had identified the link between cricket and independence, and it is a matter of fact that the colonies' drive towards independence was reaching its conclusion at the same time as the West Indian cricketers were pushing to become the world's number one team. Worrell and his men embodied the optimism and confidence of the region, and it is not a huge leap to view criticism of Hall and Griffith as a racially motivated expression of resentment of the cricket team's place at world cricket's top table.

'The Iniquitous Front-Foot Rule'
In 1963 changes to the laws governing no-balls not only made Wes's job more difficult, but he is also adamant that they precipitated the end of his career. Years later, mention of the 'front-foot rule' still provokes an uncharacteristically vigorous and hostile reaction.

Ostensibly the new law was introduced to put a stop to fast bowlers exploiting the existing law, which stated that the whole of the bowler's back-foot (the right foot of a right-arm bowler) must land behind the bowling crease. The position of the front foot had no bearing on the legality of the delivery, and consequently some fast bowlers became adept at planting the back foot behind the bowling crease and dragging it forward in the delivery stride. In some cases the front foot was then planted as far as two feet in front of the popping crease, giving the bowler an advantage by effectively shortening the length of the wicket. The new law required part of the front foot to be behind the popping crease (and the back foot inside the return crease).

The change was instigated by 'Gubby' Allen, the Chairman of MCC's Cricket Committee, supposedly to curtail the practice of dragging the back foot. However, even though neither Hall nor Griffith were 'draggers', Wes suspected that the real intention was to negate their threat on the 1963 tour of England. The new law was introduced into English domestic cricket in the summer of 1963, but West Indies refused to accept it on the tour, granting the bowlers a temporary stay.

Opponents of the front-foot rule – including esteemed Australian captains Sir Donald Bradman, Richie Benaud and Ian Chappell – have argued persuasively that its success in eliminating back-foot draggers came at a heavy price. It made the difficult job of the umpire even harder. It is far easier to judge a no-ball along the line of the bowling crease than checking whether part of the bowler's foot has clipped the batting crease. Also there is less time to look up and refocus on the batsman after concentrating on the front foot rather than the back foot. Batsmen, too, are disadvantaged by having less time to respond to the umpire's 'no-ball' call.

The most serious objection, though, is the physical damage to fast bowlers. The Australian author Doug Ackerly researched the subject, and his findings were published in his 2017 book *Front Foot! The Law That Changed Cricket*. With up to seven times the bowler's body weight passing through the front foot on landing, the incidence of lumbar and front-foot stress fractures among pace bowlers increased significantly after the introduction of the new law.

Wes is convinced that 'the front-foot rule is the most iniquitous rule in cricket'. His was a smooth transition from run-up to delivery and, like other bowlers of the time, the delivery stride was an exaggerated stretching out of the front leg at the end of the run-up. In order to veer away to the off-side and avoid running down the pitch, he then pivoted on his planted left foot and changed direction in one movement. With the change in the laws, bowlers adopted a far more violent action, transferring their forward momentum into a leap in the air and bringing their front foot down forcefully onto the popping crease to avoid overstepping. The impact upon landing was enormous as energy was unleashed through the front leg. In addition deep holes created by the repeated planting of the bowlers' feet in the same spot were an obvious danger. As a result coaches began to encourage bowlers to bowl more 'front-on' to lessen the risks as they twisted on their knee at the moment of impact with the ground:

> I don't know if the authorities studied what real fast bowling is ... if you are bowling side-on, bowling 25 overs in a day, you could bowl 15 of those on rhythm alone, and you're not losing pace. Nowadays coaches teach bowlers to go front-on because they think that's safer, but if you are bowling front-on you are always straining and so you tire far more quickly ... and when you're tired you get injuries. At the end of my run I was at my fastest, with a much longer stride than a medium-pacer or spinner. Spinners used to bowl from the bowling crease; now they can jump way over the back line and their front foot lands on the batting crease. So their job got easier, they were able to bowl from a yard closer to the batsman. The people who changed the law were not fast bowlers, and they did not understand the pain it was causing.

Wes deplores the damage the front-foot rule did to the art of fast bowling, and his impassioned opposition to it is fuelled by personal grievance. He is convinced that the change in the law was the direct cause of his career-ending injury: in Auckland in 1969 he seriously hurt his back when he fell badly after his front foot landed in the large hole created by the bowlers. At the age of 31 he had bowled his last ball in Test cricket. In his opinion, the negative effects of the rule cannot be overestimated:

> I find it sad that you hardly ever see a bowler with a beautiful side-on action like Trueman, Lillee or Snow – or even Hall! I have seen other fast bowlers who are six feet nine inches tall and show no appreciable increase in speed between the start of their run-up and delivery stride. There is no attempt to get the left foot high in delivery. They are merely tiptoeing through the tulips and bowl at 80mph. I don't think it should be too hard to get this dreadful rule rescinded. It will help cricket, and stop young people being permanently injured.

Charlie Griffith

Notwithstanding the feats of Hunte, Kanhai, Sobers, Gibbs and Hall, the story of the 1963 tour was the emergence of Charlie Griffith. Before West Indies went to England, Wes was established as the number one bowler in the world rankings, with 116 wickets at an average of 21.87 in 23 Test matches. By contrast Griffith had taken only two wickets in one Test and was relatively unknown. That was about to change. His 1963 statistics are astonishing: 32 Test wickets at 16.21 and 119 wickets at 12.83 in first-class cricket. Moreover, he finally provided Wes with a reliable, long-term new-ball partner. Their professional relationship lasted for the remainder of their careers, and their friendship has continued throughout their lives.

Born in the quaintly named Pie Corner in the parish of St Lucy at the north-eastern tip of Barbados, Charlie moved down to Bridgetown as a young man. He joined Empire, thus beginning a lifelong association which would see him serve the club as captain and later president. When he and Wes met, they immediately struck up a rapport, and Charlie became one of the three roommates – along with Gilchrist and Nurse – Wes had during his Test career.

Wes was impressed by Charlie's ambition and resilience, not to mention his physical strength, which was never more apparent than after the 1963 Lord's Test. Whereas Wes struggled for weeks to recover fully from his monumental effort and took just three wickets in the next two Tests, Griffith – who bowled only three fewer overs than Wes on the last day at Lord's – took 14 wickets in those matches. He followed that with nine more at the Oval in the final Test: 'The English batsmen couldn't handle him. He was the star of the series.'

The doubts surrounding Griffith's action persisted, however. As his roommate Wes saw the pain it caused him and marvelled at how he coped. Charlie possessed exceptional mental fortitude and resilience, qualities which would help him achieve success in business after he finished playing cricket. Wes is adamant that Griffith got a raw deal, largely because his open-chested action was different. He insists it was 'different but legal', in the way that many bowlers' actions have been, from Jeff Thomson to Lasith Malinga. The issue will probably never be conclusively settled either way but, over the years, Wes has witnessed a softening of attitudes towards Griffith, with many people wanting to apologise to him.

Griffith's immense contribution to West Indies cricket is beyond doubt, and his introduction in 1963 completed West Indies' transformation from an exciting collection of individual talents into a great, world-beating team. From 1963 to 1965, when the West Indies Test side was at its peak, he was probably the most effective fast bowler in the world. His success was based on formidable natural attributes: his physique, strength and stamina were matched by no other cricketer; and his work ethic drove him to maximise those assets. He pursued a rigorous fitness regime and practised for hours to perfect his devastating bouncer and yorker. In its review of the 1963 series, *Wisden* declared that 'his command of the yorker has not been equalled in this century.'

A quiet man off the field, Charlie was a kind and supportive friend to Wes when they played cricket together and in later life. As roommates the two bowlers spent hours discussing cricket and comparing notes on opposition batsmen. They were inseparable, to the extent that Clyde Walcott likened them to 'an old married couple!' Even nowadays, the two are just as close: 'I don't think of Charlie Griffith as my friend, I think of him – along with Sobers and the late Rawle Brancker – as my family. My children know them all as "Uncle"!'

Charlie has led a full and successful life since his playing days. He pursued a career in sales and management and became a senior executive at the Barbados Lumber Company, where in his 80s he still works as a consultant. In addition to serving as president of Empire for twelve years, he was a renowned coach, employed by the Barbados Government to teach cricket in schools and by the BCL as its head coach. He later became a member of the BCA board (and a life vice-president) and a member of the West Indies Cricket Board (WICB). Such was the strength of the bond between the two men that Wes was as delighted when Griffith received a knighthood in 2017 as he had been when he himself had been knighted in 2012: 'It felt as if they were honouring Hall and Griffith, and it brought completion to the partnership. We were a team, a combination that was so devastating.'

The admiration was mutual. In his 1970 autobiography, *Chucked Around*, Griffith frequently speaks glowingly of his friend: 'For me to have the honour to bowl at the other end to Wes – even though I could never match his unforgettably rhythmic and poetic approach to the wicket – was a great privilege.'

13

World Champions and the Tragedy of Worrell

After their success in England West Indies faced a frustrating hiatus from Test cricket between the Oval Test in August 1963 and the First Test of the series against Australia in Jamaica in March 1965. At that time, beating India, England and Australia in consecutive series would confirm West Indies as world champions and, with Wes and many of the other players in their mid-20s and in their prime, they were impatient to take on the Australians and assume their place at the pinnacle of world cricket.

West Indies had been tantalisingly close before. They had beaten England at home in 1948; they won in India a year later; and in 1950 the famous victory at Lord's on the way to their first series win in England had led to optimism that West Indian cricket had reached a turning point. The team of the Three Ws, Rae, Ramadhin and Valentine had delivered ground-breaking success, and there was talk of the world championship when they set sail for Australia in 1951. Unfortunately, the team fell short and lost that series 4-1.

Circumstances were remarkably similar ahead of Australia's visit in 1965: after thrashing India, an exciting young team which had beaten England in England was preparing to take on Australia for the title of best team in the world.

This time West Indies would have the benefit of home advantage and, crucially, they had in place an effective and inspirational leadership structure. When Worrell retired from Test cricket at the age of 39 after the 1963 series, he assumed the role of West Indies team manager. Under his guidance the team had developed a unity and sense of purpose and, to ensure continuity, he wanted Sobers to succeed him as captain. Sobers was widely respected for his intuitive cricket brain, and his phenomenal ability would enable him to lead from the front. Initially he was reluctant. Whereas seniority, status and universal consensus had made Worrell the obvious choice to lead the team in 1960, Sobers felt that promotion from the ranks would make it difficult for him to impose his authority on the team. His eventual decision to accept was based on his sense of duty to West Indian cricket. Wes, for one, was delighted: 'It had to be Garry. Not only was he a brilliant cricketer, he had an exceptional cricket mind. For anyone else to captain Garry would not have been right.'

Had Sobers decided against taking on the captaincy, Charlie Griffith was in little doubt who should have been given the job. In *Chucked Around*, he states:

> If his career had not coincided with that of the incomparable Sobers, Wes would have made, in my view, an outstanding captain of the West Indies ... It is a mistake only to consider the funny side of Wes, for when he wants to be serious no judge can better him. His opinions and views were always sought by other players when business was important – and his opinions were always respected.

The 1964-65 Test series against Australia in the Caribbean followed Wes's first season with Great Chell and his coaching duties in Jamaica. He was, therefore, well prepared for the First Test match at Kingston. After Sobers won the toss and chose to bat on a fast Sabina Park wicket, West Indies were dismissed for a disappointing total of 239. In reply Australia were all out for 217, as Hall and Griffith bowled with unrelenting pace to bring their side back into the game. Wes, in particular, was lethal, as confirmed by Griffith in *Chucked Around*: 'I have never seen Wes bowl so well. He was devastatingly quick and persistently hostile.' Wes took five for 60 and followed it up with four for 45 in the second innings, to inspire his team to a 179-run victory. He bowled 43 overs in the match, but thereafter in the series he was used relatively sparingly, bowling just 103 overs in the remaining four Tests, with off-spinner Lance Gibbs taking on a huge workload. Wes finished the series at the top of the West Indies bowling averages with 16 wickets at 28.37 and was a major contributor to his team's 2-1 series victory, West Indies' first over Australia. The slender margin was somewhat misleading, as West Indies had led 2-0 after winning the Third Test in British Guiana, and their only defeat was in the 'dead' Test in Port of Spain.

In his letter to Worrell in 1960, C.L.R. James had maintained that a good showing by West Indies in Australia later that year would help to hasten the end to colonialism. History records that Trinidad and Jamaica gained independence in 1962; Barbados and Guyana in 1966. Cricket was so important in West Indian culture that it would be fitting if James' prophecy could be validated; although Wes stops short of agreeing completely, he takes pride in the knowledge that he and his colleagues played their part in a region-wide movement:

> It may be a coincidence, but it certainly helped. Frank Worrell was not the most powerful man from the point of view of political office. Prime ministers and other senior politicians obviously wielded more power, but he was the most beloved and, with the impending collapse of the West Indies Federation[1], he was the most important West Indian in the world. He was 'only' a cricket captain, but James wanted him to know that this was an opportunity for him and his men to show the world that the West Indies were ready for independence. When the Federation eventually folded in 1962, Worrell was the man who everyone in the West Indies was looking to for leadership.

Wes gives credit to the people of the Caribbean for the part they played in the process:

> When we became world champions, the indomitable spirit of the West Indian people was so great that it fuelled the genius of the great players like captains Worrell and Sobers, and it encouraged the lesser mortals. Everyone was inspired knowing they were playing for their people.

The players may not have realised it at the time, but they were part of a greater movement in the Caribbean, articulated by Wes in a 2012 speech (featured in a later chapter) exploring the link between cricket, citizenship and independence.

Irrespective of the cricket team's role in the ongoing social and political upheaval, there was no doubt that West Indies occupied the game's summit after victory over Australia. The players were eager to consolidate their status, and their next challenge was the 1966 tour of England. The

---

[1] The West Indies Federation was a political union of ten British colonies, formed in 1958 with the aim of becoming a single independent state. Internal disagreements led to its collapse in 1962.

series, just three years after the previous visit, was organised with the aim of cashing in – literally – on the team's popularity, not least with the many West Indians living in England who turned out to support them. West Indies' reputation for playing exciting cricket had long since established their box-office appeal, yet player remuneration remained completely incommensurate with the revenue they generated. The issue was a recurring theme for most of Wes's Test career and, to make matters worse, the inconsistent scheduling of Test cricket meant the players could not rely on a regular income, however meagre. Some, including Wes, were able to make a living playing cricket around the world but, in the absence of an organised domestic competition (the inter-island Shell Shield competition was not introduced until the 1965-66 season), many players had no guarantee of financial security.

> When you have recipients on one side and paymasters on the other, there is a natural lack of trust, and dialogue is important. In all the time I played for West Indies, we were never involved in a discussion over our salary. We played for what was offered, and I believe that they probably offered us what they could afford, but there was no discussion. The board members were often men who had put in their own money to keep West Indies cricket viable, and they were responsible for managing all administrative matters, including team selection. Unlike today there was no income from television rights or the ICC; the only significant income was from gate receipts. I'm not saying they should have paid us large sums of money, but in hindsight I feel that, if they'd understood the importance of sharing information, perhaps greater transparency would have led to trust and a better relationship between us and them.

Wes's moderate attitude owed much to the pride he took in representing West Indies. He also recognised the players' good fortune in having a spokesman as astute as Worrell campaigning on their behalf. Following the 1950 tour of England when all players received weekly expenses of £5, Worrell succeeded in negotiating contracts for the leading players. Hence, on the 1951-52 tour to Australia and New Zealand, the Three Ws, Ramadhin and Valentine became the first West Indies cricketers to be engaged on a professional basis.

Professional players were paid £800 for the 1963 tour of England, and the amateurs received £100. For Sobers, Kanhai and Hall, £800 was less generous than it appeared, as they were required to travel to England before they had completed their contractual obligations in Australia, resulting in a £300 loss of earnings from their respective state sides. Despite requests from the players, the board refused to make up the shortfall. Even more unfair in Wes's mind was the situation whereby Charlie Griffith could take 32 Test wickets and 119 in all matches on the tour, yet receive only £100 for his efforts. Such discrepancies were eliminated on the 1966 tour, when every player, irrespective of seniority or status, received £1,100. The new system created its own anomalies: little-used squad members were paid the same as the senior players and, following inevitable criticism, the board decided to adopt a pay scale based on players' Test appearances. Wes observed the way in which the board operated; he began to develop an interest in industrial relations and to form his own ideas on how the situation could have been better managed.

With the nucleus of the 1963 side in its prime, and with Sobers as captain, West Indies embarked on the 1966 tour of England with high expectations. Their confidence was justified: they beat England in the Test series by a 3-1 margin to retain the Wisden Trophy and, apart from defeat in the final 'dead' Test at the Oval, they comprehensively outplayed their hosts.

Sobers was in majestic all-round form: he was the leading batsman in the series with 722 runs at an average of 103.14; he took 20 wickets at 27.25 to finish second to Gibbs in the West Indies bowling averages; and he held 10 catches, the most by any player on either side.

In terms of tour matches won, West Indies were slightly less successful than their 1963 predecessors, and some argued that they were over-reliant on the brilliance of Sobers, but they confirmed beyond doubt their standing as the best team in the world. As with many successful sides, this great West Indies team benefitted from continuity, twelve members of the 17-strong squad having toured in 1963. With few injuries, and most players retaining their form over several years, the side was very settled and presented the selectors with few headaches.

Wes had a satisfactory tour. He took 18 Test wickets, behind Gibbs and Sobers who took 21 and 20 respectively. His bowling average was a respectable 30.83. With echoes of 1957, he points out the quality of his wickets and argues that the bare statistics failed to do him justice:

> Those 18 wickets were worth 24. Except for John Snow there isn't one tail-ender[2] amongst them. I know I bowled much better in 1966 than in 1963, because after my spell at Lord's in 1963 I was done for the rest of the series.

During the 1966 series, Wes became West Indies' leading Test wicket-taker, overtaking Ramadhin's record of 158 when he had Colin Milburn caught by Griffith in the Third Test at Trent Bridge. It was a spectacular achievement: Wes was playing in only his 36th Test, seven fewer than Ramadhin. By the end of the series he had extended his total to 166.

The tour was a triumph for an unsung member of the team, Seymour Nurse, the second-highest run-scorer in the series with 501 at an average of 68.62. Wes felt he never received the recognition he deserved:

> He batted with such artistry that he was Man of the Match at Trent Bridge for scoring 93 and 53 when Basil Butcher made 209 not out in the same match. They were always quick to drop him. I don't know why, he never let us down.

For Wes an enjoyable aspect of being a successful cricketer was having the opportunity to meet interesting people from other walks of life, including celebrities and other famous sportsmen. One such encounter took place in the away changing room during the 1966 Lord's Test, when the players received a visit from the world heavyweight boxing champion, Muhammad Ali. It would be inaccurate to describe Ali as a cricket fan but, as a vehement campaigner in the American civil rights movement, he wanted to meet this team of black athletes who stood at the pinnacle of their sport. Ali spent some time speaking to Sobers, the superstar of the team, before meeting the other players. He reserved special praise for Wes, whose 36 overs in England's first innings (in which he took four for 106) maintained his record of bowling long spells at Lord's. Wes recalls their meeting with amusement:

> He said that he's never seen anyone with stamina like that, and that if he had my stamina he would fight three men in a night: knock the first two out in two rounds and then have some fun

---

[2] In the Lord's Test match Wes dismissed number nine F.J. Titmus, who was an able batsman generally considered a bowling all-rounder.

with the other one for six or seven rounds! I was bowling from my favourite end, the Nursery End, and in good flight. Goodness knows what he would have said if he'd seen me in 1963, bowling non-stop from the Pavilion End for over three hours!

Mike Marqusee's 1999 biography of Ali, *Redemption Song: Muhammad Ali and the Spirit of the Sixties*, confirms that Ali 'was particularly impressed with the master pace-bowler Wes Hall. "[Cricket] too slow? I don't think so. Running up as fast as Wes Hall would be good training for me."'

Victory in England confirmed West Indies' status and, by common consent, marked the high point in their fortunes up to that point. Sir Hilary Beckles[3], the Barbadian historian and academic, has since used a biblical analogy to describe the journey made by West Indian cricket. In his 2017 book, *Cricket Without a Cause: Fall and Rise of the Mighty West Indian Test Cricketers*, he referred to Worrell as Moses, in recognition of his years of dedicated toil; and Sobers, the man who finally led West Indies into the promised land, as Joshua.

Most of the West Indies players left England in mid-September 1966, just two months before the start of their three-Test match tour of India. Wes stayed in England for the birth of his son Sean on 22 September and flew straight to India from London, confidently looking forward to adding to the 57 wickets he had taken in ten Tests against the Indians. He arrived in India raring to go, feeling as fit as he ever had and bowling well in the early-tour net sessions. In Bombay during one of those practices, tour manager Prior Jones, a former Trinidad and West Indies fast bowler, called Wes out of the nets. He asked him to bowl a ball in the outfield so that a photographer could take a promotional picture for the forthcoming series. The outfield was damp and, against his better judgement, Wes began his run-up. His misgivings were justified:

> After my delivery, I slipped on the wet grass and landed heavily on my right knee ... I've fallen before, but when I fell I could feel my knee go. I was in so much pain; I knew straightaway that I was in trouble. Bowling was a real struggle, and I limped through those three Test matches.

[3] A former member of the West Indies Cricket Board, Professor Sir Hilary McDonald Beckles has served as The UWI's vice-chancellor since 2015.

The series marked the beginning of Wes's decline as a Test bowler. Hindered by his injury, he was unable to bowl with his usual sustained hostility, and he took only eight wickets in the three Tests at an average of 33.25, relatively expensive for a bowler whose career Test average was 24.97. In a striking parallel, the West Indies team was beginning to show signs that it too was a waning force. Griffith, with nine Test wickets, was less effective than he had been, and opening batsman Conrad Hunte retired from Test cricket at the age of 35 after the Third Test in Madras. They won the three-match series 2-0, but Sobers' customary brilliance and consistently high levels of performance from Kanhai and Gibbs papered over cracks elsewhere in the team. Other than the emergence of Clive Lloyd, there was a lack of young talent challenging the established players. This was especially true in the pace bowling department, where the back-up for Hall and Griffith, 27-year-old Lester King, was not selected for any of the Tests.

The tour passed relatively smoothly for West Indies, although it was not without its difficulties, most obviously during the Second Test in Calcutta. The authorities had sold more tickets than the ground could accommodate and, with too many people in the stadium, those unable to find seats in the stands moved onto the grass around the boundary edge. The police used batons and tear-gas to force them back, prompting a counter-attack which developed into a major riot. Seats were ripped out and burned; a stand and the pavilion were set alight. Fearing for their safety, several of the West Indies contingent wanted to abort the match; others, notably Wes and Worrell (who was in India as a guest of the Indian Government and spent time accompanying the team), thought otherwise. Wes had witnessed the riot in Trinidad in 1960 during the Second Test against England, and he was aware also of the crowd disorder which halted the Test against England at Sabina Park in 1954, after Jamaican batsman J.K. Holt was given out LBW with his score on 94. On those occasions play had resumed, and Wes felt that the team should avoid making a hasty decision. If they refused to play, there would be a strong risk that India would call an immediate end to the tour. Obviously this would be in nobody's interests, and he was particularly anxious not to disappoint the cricket-mad supporters in India. The situation was resolved when West Indies received assurances that order would be restored and maintained. After the loss of a day's play while the debris was being cleared, West Indies won by an innings to seal victory in the series following their triumph in the First Test in Bombay.

During that Calcutta Test, events unfolded which were to prove far more significant for West Indian cricket than bonfires in the stands. Frank Worrell had been feeling tired and generally unwell for much of his time in India. He said nothing to anyone, and Wes recalls him fulfilling a speaking engagement at a dinner organised by the Indian Cricket Board: 'He gave a wonderful speech, such a brilliant speech ... His last speech ...' The players had no inkling that anything was amiss until a couple of weeks later. Worrell had intended to fly to his home in Trinidad after his commitments in India, but instead he went to Jamaica where he made straight for the University Hospital of the West Indies at Mona for a check-up. His condition deteriorated rapidly in Jamaica, and he was diagnosed with leukaemia.

The squad left India at the end of January. Wes travelled to Trinidad to begin work with WITCO and the Wes Hall League. While there, he would play first-class cricket for Trinidad and Tobago, and remarkably his appearance a week later in the Shell Shield was his debut in the competition at the age of 29. Also he was playing not for his native Barbados but for his adopted island, emulating Frank Worrell and Clyde Walcott, who played for Jamaica and British Guiana respectively. That season Trinidad and Tobago's fixture against Jamaica took place in Kingston in early February, presenting Wes with an opportunity to visit Worrell. Beforehand, he spoke to his friend Dr Eugene Ward, who explained the gravity of the situation – Worrell had six weeks to live: 'That hit me like a hammer blow'. Frank's wife, Lady Velda, called Wes to say that she needed to speak to him. Wes could not say he already knew of her husband's terminal illness through Dr Ward, and he felt extremely awkward at the prospect of pretending he was hearing the news for the first time:

> I found that very hard. I sat there with her, feeling that I had sinned, and all the time I was aching because one of the greatest men in the world and one of the most important people in my life was dying at the age of 42. That had me in real trouble. When I went in to see him, he was sitting up in bed. He was as regal as ever. He was so dignified there on that bed. I greeted him as I always did: 'Hi, Skip, how are you?' I have never forgotten his reply: 'Winfield, I've got everything in life, except good health.'

And my spirit sank, it tore me apart knowing that he realised the gravity of the situation. Every now and again you have the privilege of meeting people like Frank Worrell.

With the permission of Lady Worrell, Wes was accompanied by the Trinidad and West Indies wicketkeeper Deryck Murray, a member of the West Indies team that toured England under Worrell in 1963. Worrell was friends with Deryck's father Lance Murray and his uncle Sonny Murray, the secretary at Queen's Park Oval. Given these various connections, Wes thought it appropriate that the youngster should accompany him:

Frank had always taken a particular interest in Deryck. He was a good young man, very clever, and Frank liked that. He was only 23, and I warned him in advance that it would be difficult. But he was very good, and very respectful, and I am glad he was there with me.

As Wes was about to leave, Worrell described how his nurse was always so cheerful and upbeat, but that morning, when she turned away from him, her smile gave way to a look of deep sadness. That was the last conversation between Worrell and Wes. On that poignant note, the two men parted. Sir Frank died on 13 March 1967.

To celebrate Barbados gaining independence in 1966, two matches were played at Kensington Oval in March 1967 between Barbados and a Rest of the World team. As the players were leaving the field at the end of the second of these, the plane carrying Sir Frank's body from Jamaica for burial in his home island flew directly over the ground. The pilot slowed the aircraft and tipped its wings in salute, and the players raised their bats and caps in a silent farewell salute to the captain.

The loss of Worrell was felt worldwide; obviously for those close to him, it was an especially difficult time. Fortunately for Wes, his many commitments kept his mind busy and, although he missed Worrell terribly, he was determined to continue giving his best in everything he did: 'It was the least I could do for Frank, carrying on the work that he had started me on.'

In the 1966-67 domestic season Wes made four appearances for Trinidad and Tobago in the Shell Shield, including one against Barbados. He also played for Barbados in the matches against the Rest of the World XI.

Discomfort from his knee prevented him from running to the wicket at his usual speed, and his pace was significantly reduced, leading the West Indies management to lazily (and incorrectly) conclude that the problem was his lack of fitness. Wes knew it was more serious: 'It was ludicrous to say I was unfit. Just a few months earlier, I had been praised for my fitness by Muhammad Ali!' He visited the University Hospital at Mona in Jamaica, where Professor John Golding, a renowned orthopaedic surgeon, confirmed that he needed surgery on his knee. However, the management refused to sanction an operation, sticking to the line that Wes was unfit. Perhaps more telling was their insistence that 'if you're a professional, and we're paying you, then you've got to play', and despite a succession of unremarkable performances in 1966-67, he retained his place in the West Indies side for the series against the 1967-68 English tourists.

14

A Team in Decline and Struggles with Injury

England's tour of the Caribbean in 1967-68 produced an evenly contested Test series. Each side came close to a win in the first two Tests: England were thwarted by an unbroken eighth wicket partnership of 63 between Sobers and Wes in Port of Spain, and in Kingston West Indies were two England wickets short of victory. As was often the case, Wes produced his best bowling at Sabina Park where he took four wickets for 63 in the first innings. The next Test in Bridgetown produced an uneventful, slow-scoring draw, with Wes again struggling on his home ground, although this time, he had a valid reason.

As part of the usual preliminaries before the Test match, a cocktail party was held in the Marine Hotel on the outskirts of Bridgetown. Wes attended with his wife Shurla, who was heavily pregnant with their second child. When they left the function, he drove her home and went to join the rest of the West Indies players at the team hotel. At 1am, he received a call from Shurla, asking him to take her to Bay View Hospital, where he stayed all night as his daughter Kerry was born on 28 February 1968. However, there were complications with the birth: the umbilical cord wrapped around the baby's neck, and for a while the situation was critical. Thankfully the danger passed, and Wes left the next morning to go to Kensington Oval for the Test.

Reporting for duty so shortly after the horrific life and death situation involving his daughter, he was relieved when Sobers won the toss and chose to bat first. Nevertheless, when Wes took the new ball in England's innings, he was still physically and emotionally exhausted. Under the circumstances, his figures of two for 98 from 32 overs were respectable and certainly no worse than usual at Kensington!

Comparisons between eras are inevitable. Whether or not change is for the better will always be a matter for debate, with opinion split typically along generational lines; however, irrespective of the charm of the 'good old days', progress has been an undisputed force for good in terms of player welfare. It seems inconceivable that such a relatively short time ago, top international sportsmen were expected to adopt a 'stiff upper lip' and to perform at times of trauma in their private lives.

The most significant action of the series took place in the Fourth Test, again in Port of Spain. For Wes the drama began on the eve of the match, as he was dropped for the first time in his Test career, ending his sequence of 44 consecutive Tests – a West Indies record – stretching back almost ten years to 1958. In the first three matches his injured knee had continued to prevent him from bowling at anything approaching full pace, and he had been relatively ineffective, taking seven wickets for 256 runs. News of his omission reached him from an unexpected source: his wife telephoned from Barbados and told him that she had just heard his 'cricketing obituary' on the BBC! Not being told face-to-face compounded his disappointment. When the selectors did eventually speak to him, they again failed to acknowledge that Wes was carrying an injury, simply repeating that he was not fit enough.

Wes accepted that his performances had been below his usual standard but, with the team lacking quality front-line bowlers, he struggled to understand the logic in dropping him. He assumed the role of spectator for the Fourth Test, with an inside view of events that sparked controversy and polarised opinion throughout the Caribbean.

After winning the toss and deciding to bat first on an excellent pitch, Sobers declared with the West Indies score on 526 for seven. England were bowled out for 404 and, when West Indies had reached 92 for two in their second innings, Sobers again declared, setting England 215 for victory in the 165 minutes remaining. After 162 of those minutes, it had become the most infamous declaration in history as England reached their target and won the match by seven wickets.

The fallout from the defeat was colossal, with Sobers facing a furious backlash from indignant West Indian cricket fans. His status – a cricketing genius who regularly carried the team single-handedly – was forgotten by the critics lining up to condemn him as a reckless risk-taker. Up to this point, he had been regarded as an excellent, astute captain, but the declaration in Port of Spain prompted a widespread clamour for his removal from the West Indies captaincy.

Sobers was unrepentant and remains so to this day. He admits that his dislike of negative cricket motivated him to try to force a victory but argues persuasively that his declaration was based on sound logic. Given a repeat of the circumstances, he would make the same decision. A common argument used by those berating Sobers was that, with Wes not in the team and Griffith injured and unable to bowl in the second innings, the West Indies attack lacked firepower. Wes refutes this totally and comes down firmly on the side of his captain:

> It was the fourth innings on a turning wicket in Trinidad. In the first innings, all the England wickets were taken by spinners; Charlie only bowled a handful of overs [three overs for no wickets] so they weren't going to miss him. We had the best off-spinner in the world [Lance Gibbs]; Willie Rodriguez was lethal on that wicket, his home wicket; Sobers could bowl left-arm orthodox or wrist-spin; Joey Carew had bowled 25 overs for 23 runs in the first innings; and Butcher had taken five wickets for 34 runs with his leg-breaks!

He also mounts a defence of Sobers on the issue of the required run rate. He points out that England had scored at less than 40 runs per hour throughout the series, and the declaration left them needing suddenly to double that scoring rate. Wes generously suggests that not enough credit was given to England for achieving their target: 'Rather than put all the blame on Garry Sobers, why not praise Cowdrey and Boycott for their excellent batting?'

The public's disappointment was understandable: defeat at home against England was a sign that the West Indies team was losing its grip on the number one status it had enjoyed for the previous three years. This was made all the more galling by the avoidable nature of the defeat, in a match West Indies had dominated and in which they lost only nine wickets. For Wes an unpalatable aspect of the episode was the behaviour of certain members of the team who turned against Sobers. Armed with the benefit of hindsight, players who had been united in supporting his declaration at the time later became vocal in second-guessing the decision:

> At that moment, I knew that West Indies cricket was struggling, because the love and the family spirit that was so much a part of our success was no longer there. There were cracks, divisions in the team like in the old days.

Wes's long-term assessment was to prove as prophetic as it was gloomy. More immediately, he made an unspectacular return to the side in Georgetown for the final Test. Disappointingly for West Indies, the result was another tense draw. Striving for redemption after events in Port of Spain, Sobers put in an astonishing performance, with scores of 152 and 95 not out and bowling analyses of 37-15-72-3, and 31-16-53-3. Despite his heroics, West Indies fell agonisingly short of squaring the series and retaining the Wisden Trophy, as England again clung on for the draw, this time with only one wicket in hand. For the first time since 1960-61 West Indies had lost a series and with it their place at the summit of world cricket.

For Wes, the 1967-68 series saw a continuation of the downward trend in his performance levels, with just nine wickets at an average of 39.22 (by far his highest in a series to date). The final Test in Guyana would be the last Wes played at home. His two wickets in the match were those of Boycott and Graveney, continuing his 'habit' of dismissing top-class batsmen. A personal highlight of the series was his match-saving performance with the bat on the final day of the First Test in Trinidad. Following on 205 runs behind, West Indies were on the brink of defeat at 180 for eight in their second innings when Wes joined Sobers at the crease with 90 minutes left in the match. Having lost their previous four wickets for just two runs, the situation looked desperate, but Sobers and Hall batted until the close of play, finishing on 33 and 27 respectively in an unbroken 63-run partnership.

A highlight of that season for Wes was his first one-to-one meeting with an all-time great West Indian: Learie Constantine invited Wes to join him for dinner at the team hotel in Georgetown before the last Test match. During their conversation Constantine suggested that Wes should add more variety to his bowling to compensate for his reduced pace. Wes was flattered that the great man should take such a keen interest in him, and he heeded the advice. Their meeting ended with Constantine confiding in Wes that it was not possible for anyone to feel more overjoyed than he was at the West Indies cricket team's rise to the top. He spoke with such passion that he was close to tears as he described what West Indies' success meant to him after the struggles he had been through. Wes was overcome with emotion as he listened.

A few days later, Wes suffered once more at the hands of the selectors. The squad for the 1968-69 tour to Australia and New Zealand was announced after the Fifth Test, and he was not among the 16 players originally picked. Again, his lack of fitness was given as the reason for his omission.

The decision to leave him out may have been logical had there been other fast-bowling options, but the shortage of good young fast bowlers was showing no sign of ending. With Charlie Griffith handicapped by a series of injuries, the pace attack of Griffith, King and Richard 'Prof' Edwards, an uncapped 28-year-old Barbadian, appeared thin for an arduous tour of Australia and New Zealand which included eight Test matches. This was obviously a view held by Sobers and Griffith, who told the board that if Wes did not go to Australia then neither would they. Furthermore, they stressed the need to investigate the problem with his knee. With six months before the start of the tour, there was time for Wes to have an operation and get back to full fitness. Faced with the prospect of Sobers' withdrawal, the selectors yielded, if only partially: Hall's name was added to the squad with the proviso that he must address his fitness issues by going on a five-mile run along the highway four mornings a week. Jeffrey Stollmeyer, a selector and member of the board, lived close to Wes just outside Port of Spain and was mandated to check that he stuck to the regime. To add insult to injury, Stollmeyer would position himself at a different point on the route each day to make sure that Wes was not shirking! Wes acceded to the board's conditions, partly due to his fondness of Australia. This would be his last tour there and he was determined to enjoy it.

To the surprise of no one – except presumably the West Indies selectors – pounding the roads of Trinidad for six months did not produce a miracle cure for Wes's injury, and he arrived in Australia for the 1968-69 tour in much the same physical condition as before. He understood the problem with his knee was likely to restrict him, and he went in the hope of rediscovering at least some of his old form. It was a forlorn hope: in the West Indians' early-season matches against state sides, his bowling was unexceptional, and he was not selected for either of the first two Tests, even though injury prevented Griffith from playing in the Second Test in Melbourne. In that match the West Indies attack laboured, and the team suffered an innings defeat so, with Griffith still unavailable, Wes was called up to play in the Third Test in Sydney. Three expensive wickets in another heavy defeat made it an unsatisfactory return to Test cricket for Wes; however, were it not for a bizarre incident, he would probably have retained his place in the side for the Fourth Test in Adelaide. Three days before the match, the West Indians played a one-day match against a South Australia Country XI in Loxton. Wes took four wickets for 24, including a hat-trick, but the gloss was taken off his day when he accidentally walked through a glass door at the team hotel, sustaining a cut to his forehead which ruled him out of the Test match.

Wes was recalled for the final Test, again in Sydney, and again the bowlers toiled with little success against the dominant Australian batting line-up. He took five wickets at a cost of more than 200 runs as West Indies lost the match by the huge margin of 382 runs to complete a 3-1 series defeat. The batsmen – again led by Sobers – performed adequately but, apart from Gibbs and Sobers, the bowling attack was ineffectual. Hall and Griffith finished as joint third leading wicket-takers with just eight each; as a testament to the team's struggles, Wes's Test bowling average of 40.62 was second behind Gibbs' 38.45.

With his knee troubles persisting, Wes concluded in hindsight that it had been a mistake to go on the tour. Up against formidable batsmen such as the Australian captain Bill Lawry and brilliant youngsters Ian Chappell and Doug Walters, he 'needed to be bowling at 95mph, not 82'.

On a brighter note Wes reached a significant landmark in the West Indians' first match of the tour against Western Australia in Perth. When he dismissed John Inverarity for the second of his three wickets in the hosts' first innings, he became only the fourth West Indian bowler – after S.G. (Sydney) Smith, Ramadhin and Sobers – to take 500 wickets in first-class cricket. By a remarkable coincidence Gibbs recorded the same feat six days later on the same ground when the tourists played a Western Australia Combined XI.

Every tour has its light-hearted moments, and Wes was constantly on the lookout for some fun. However, he was on the receiving end as the team prepared to make the journey by light plane from a country match back to Melbourne. The players' luggage, including their clothes, had gone ahead by road and, shortly before their departure, Wes became aware that his trousers had 'gone missing' from his room. Wes told Sobers: 'Skipper, the guys have got my pants ... with or without my pants, I'm on that plane!'

With their departure time approaching, Wes conceded that it was a good practical joke, but it had run its course ... now he wanted to be re-united with his trousers. As the atmosphere grew tense, one of his teammates suddenly appeared clutching a crumpled pair of trousers, having climbed the hotel's flagpole to recover them. Wes boarded the plane, thankfully fully dressed!

West Indies moved on to New Zealand for the second leg of the tour with morale at a low ebb after the chastening defeat in Australia. The cracks that began to appear the previous year against England became more evident after the opening match against South Island in Dunedin. Acting captain Kanhai left the team and returned to the Caribbean just two days before the First Test in Auckland. The reaction of the captain Sobers was characteristically matter-of-fact. He felt that if a player did not want to be there, it was better if he left, a view held by the rest of the team.

Wes was selected for the Auckland Test, and in New Zealand's first innings, he took his 192nd and final Test wicket when he had Glenn Turner caught at slip by Sobers:

> It turned out to be my last wicket, and I am pleased at least that it was the good opening batsman I got out! In Sydney a couple of weeks before, Ian Chappell was the last Australian I dismissed. Graveney, Chappell, Turner: I was still getting great batsmen out, even though I was no longer bowling at 95mph.

In the second innings, Wes was bowling well and had conceded just eight runs in his first eight overs. As he bowled the third ball of his ninth over, disaster struck. His left foot turned over in the deep rut made by the bowlers' feet repeatedly landing in the same spot. He fell heavily, and the next thing he knew he was lying flat on his back with a searing pain at the base of his spine. The other players gathered around him. Sobers grabbed him by the hand to help him to his feet, but Wes was unable to move. On 1 March 1969 his Test career was over. He was stretchered from the field and taken to hospital, an unbecoming way for such a wholehearted champion to make his final exit from Test cricket:

> I was 31 years old, and I'd had a good career. Everyone's body is going to break at some point, no matter what sport they are playing. When I first bowled a ball in competitive cricket, I was

nearly 18; imagine if I had been bowling fast from the age of nine or ten.

The team moved on to Wellington for the Second Test, leaving Wes behind in his hospital bed in Auckland with his torso covered in plaster of paris. During the Wellington Test the West Indies squad was announced for the forthcoming tour of England, due to begin just a month after the last match in New Zealand. Wes had expected to be omitted from the squad, but he was surprised that the selectors decided to drop the other three fast bowlers. Griffith was not at his best, King had failed to make an impression on the tour, and Edwards was trying to stake his claim in New Zealand after a disappointing time in Australia. Nevertheless, to discard them all seemed reckless given the lack of replacements:

> With my knee and back injury, I had no problem with missing the tour – or even not playing Test cricket again. But it was unfair on Griffith, Lester King and Prof Edwards, who bowled very well in New Zealand [in the three Test matches, Edwards was the leading wicket-taker with 15 wickets at an average of 23.46]. I was injured; fair enough, but they said Hall and Griffith were finished. I think that Charlie still had some years left in him.

In the two weeks after Wes sustained the injury in Auckland, his recovery progressed remarkably well. Incredibly he was even approaching match-fitness when team manager Berkeley Gaskin, Sobers, Hall and Gibbs met to pick the team for the Third Test in Christchurch. It was agreed that Hall and Griffith would make their final Test appearance, a gesture appreciated by Wes, who was looking forward to the opportunity of bowing out of Test cricket on a positive note.

On the morning of the match, when he, Sobers, and Gibbs went to look at the wicket, the captain welcomed Wes back into the team. Gibbs then surprised the others by expressing a preference for Holford over Wes, on the basis that the wicket appeared dry and would favour the spinners. Sobers disagreed strongly; he made the point that they knew the wicket was dry when they picked the team the previous evening. He instructed Wes to vote on the matter, effectively giving him the casting vote on his own selection. Although it would be his last Test match, Wes refused to vote for himself. He would play only if there was unanimity: 'I would never have voted for myself. I did not think it was the right thing to do.'

His Test career may not have ended on his preferred terms, but at least the final decision was his and fittingly, for a man of such high principles, it was guided by his sense of right and wrong.

At the conclusion of a Test career spanning more than a decade, Wes had played 48 matches, and was the leading West Indian wicket-taker with 192 wickets at an average of 26.38. He took five wickets in an innings nine times – and ten wickets in a match once – with best bowling figures of seven for 69 against England at Sabina Park in 1960. Almost certainly, his outstanding record would have been even better had the injury he sustained in India in 1966 been sensitively managed. The statistics are telling: up to that point, his first 38 Tests brought him 166 wickets at an average of 24.57, and a strike rate of 4.36 wickets per Test; handicapped by the knee injury in his final ten Tests, he took just 26 wickets at 37.92 and a strike rate of 2.6. In those ten Tests Wes was bowling as well as his knee allowed. Given the selectors' insistence on his lack of fitness, it is ironic that his fitness and athleticism were the very reasons he was able to play despite his injury.

To complete his Test career statistics: Wes scored 818 runs at an average of 15.73, including two half-centuries, and took eleven catches.

During the 1968-69 tour, the team spirit which had been such a feature of the glory years gradually dissolved. An indication of the disharmony within West Indies' ranks is provided by the extraordinary case of Seymour Nurse. Prior to the tour, Nurse had played in 21 Test matches, and had a very respectable batting average of 42.55. He performed unremarkably in the first four Tests against Australia before embarking on a spectacular run of form: beginning with the second innings of the Fifth Test in Sydney and continuing in New Zealand, he recorded scores of 137, 95, 168, 21,16 and 258. Although he was 35 years old, Nurse was physically fit and, unlike Wes, was expected to continue playing for West Indies. Instead, he called time on his international career immediately after his innings of 258:

> After that tour, Seymour went home, and he stopped playing Test cricket, although he continued to play first-class cricket for Barbados for another three years. He said he stopped because the remarkable camaraderie that we had experienced over the years was missing and had been replaced by insularity that he did not

wish to be a part of. I did not shed a tear when I knew that I had come to the end of my Test career, but he retired in the form of his life.

Until his death in May 2019, 'Casso' was a member of Wes's circle of close friends. Nurse was accorded an Official Funeral in Barbados, with the service held at Kensington Oval in the presence of cricketing greats past and present. Many of the island's dignitaries, including the Governor-General[1], the Prime Minister and cabinet ministers were also in attendance. Wes had the honour of delivering the sermon, during which he declared that 'in the 1960s, only Sir Garry[2] and Kanhai were rated above Seymour in my book.'

After concluding his Test career in New Zealand, Wes played a handful of matches for Trinidad and Tobago in 1969-70, the final year of his contract with WITCO working on the Wes Hall League. He finished the season with 15 wickets at an average of 22.53 and played a significant part in helping Trinidad and Tobago to their first Shell Shield championship. As in Test cricket a year earlier, in March 1970 his competitive first-class career ended in agony. Running up to bowl against Jamaica at Queen's Park Oval in the last Shell Shield match of the season, he felt a searing pain at the back of his foot as he stretched into his delivery stride. His Achilles tendon had completely snapped, and that evening in Trinidad he underwent a seven-hour operation. The surgeon was Dr Buster Robinson and, to this day Wes remains grateful for his superb work:

> I have not had a problem with it in 50 years, and a doctor even told me in 2018 what a pretty job Dr Robinson had done. She took a picture of the back of my foot to show the young doctors how to do it!

Back in Barbados after his stint in Trinidad, Wes had just one remaining wish as a professional cricketer: to conclude his career at Kensington

---

[1] From 1966 when Barbados gained independence, to it becoming a republic in 2021, The Governor-General of Barbados was appointed on the advice of the Barbadian Prime Minister by the British monarch to be her/his representative. It was considered the most important position in the Barbados Government.

[2] Sobers was knighted by Her Majesty Queen Elizabeth II in a ceremony held at Garrison Savannah in Barbados in February 1975.

Oval. He has always regretted not performing better on his home ground; a Test record of nine wickets in four matches at an average of 48.22 ranks amongst his worst at any venue. The closest he can come to an explanation is that perhaps his love of Barbados led him to try too hard. Happily, irrespective of past struggles at Kensington, he was granted the ceremonial farewell that his illustrious career deserved. On 30 March 1971, in the second innings of the match between Barbados and the Indian tourists, he bowled his last ball in first-class cricket. His match analysis was two for 61, and he retired satisfied that his farewell had been in Barbados.

15

Cricketing Memories and Reflections

The consistency of Wes's performances throughout his career is reflected in his first-class statistics: in 170 matches he took a total of 546 wickets, at an average of 26.14, compared with his Test average of 26.38. He took five wickets in an innings on 19 occasions, and twice took ten wickets in a match. His best bowling performance was seven for 51 for the West Indians against Glamorgan at Swansea in 1963. Wes scored a total of 2,674 runs, averaging 15.10, with one century and six half-centuries; and he took 58 catches.

Equally interesting to Wes are the quirky facts lurking beyond the record books, and he gives a couple of examples. Of the 55 grounds where he played first-class cricket, he failed to take a wicket at only one: 'Is that some kind of record?!' The ground in question is Stanley Park in Blackpool, venue for the West Indians' match against Lancashire in 1957. He is also pleased to count a stumping among his 546 victims: the occasion was a match at Hastings in 1963 between the West Indians and A.E.R. Gilligan's XI, when Essex batsman Geoff Smith was stumped by David Allan off some 'festival bowling' from Wes!

His postscript to his career looks beyond the statistics:

> They are numbers on a page for everyone to see. I look at it from the point of view that playing for my country was such a significant thing for me. I have often said that a great disservice done to our age is the disconnect between effort and reward. Our reward was not commensurate with our effort, but I would have played for nothing; I was very happy! People may be interested in your stats, but they *care* about how you made them feel, that is what they remember. People have said they have seen me taking off from the sightscreen at Sabina Park and Bourda, and they felt the excitement of it.

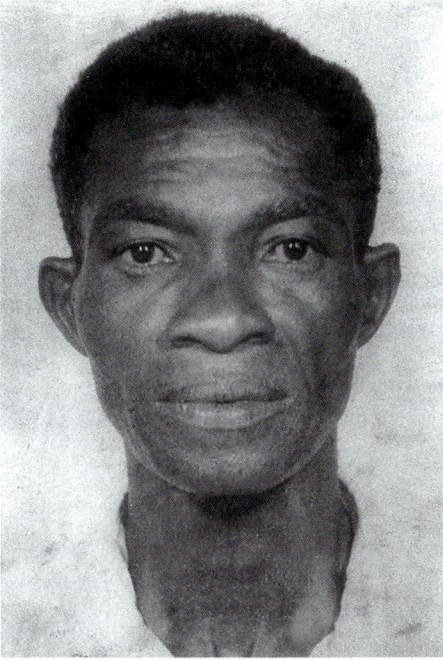

Wes's father Fred and mother Ione

Inspiring the children on a return to St Giles' School: 'Work hard, study for your exams and aim high – and as St Gilesians you can do it!'

England 1957: *(top)* Wes with Roy Gilchrist, docking at Southampton
(bottom) The Three Ws, Wes's heroes, at a cocktail party at the West Indian Club, London, the day after arrival. Sonny Ramadhin is standing between Weekes and Walcott.

left: Wedding day, 1964, with best man Frank Worrell
right: With Shurla and their first two children Sean and Kerry

12 September 2022: *(left to right)* Remi, Kerry, Wes and Sean

The tie at Brisbane

(top) Meckiff is run out off the seventh ball of the final over
(bottom) Amid the celebrations Wes walks wearily down the pitch

The draw at Lord's 1963

(top) Worrell runs out Shackleton as Wes celebrates with arms aloft

(bottom) The players run for the pavilion, with Wes *(second left)* in hot pursuit of Sobers

Wes in his delivery stride, the photograph
that inspired his statue at Kensington Oval
right: Four frames showing the stages of his action

Two prize scalps

left: Peter May bowled, his off stump shattered, Kingston 1960

below: Tom Graveney caught by keeper David Allan for 96, Lord's 1966

A popular figure in Queensland, at a deaf, dumb and blind children's picnic, but not so popular during the Brisbane Tied Test as he puts Norman O'Neill on his backside

Charlie Griffith *(left)* and Wes with Learie Constantine

England 1966: Wes with manager Jeffrey Stollmeyer and captain Garry Sobers

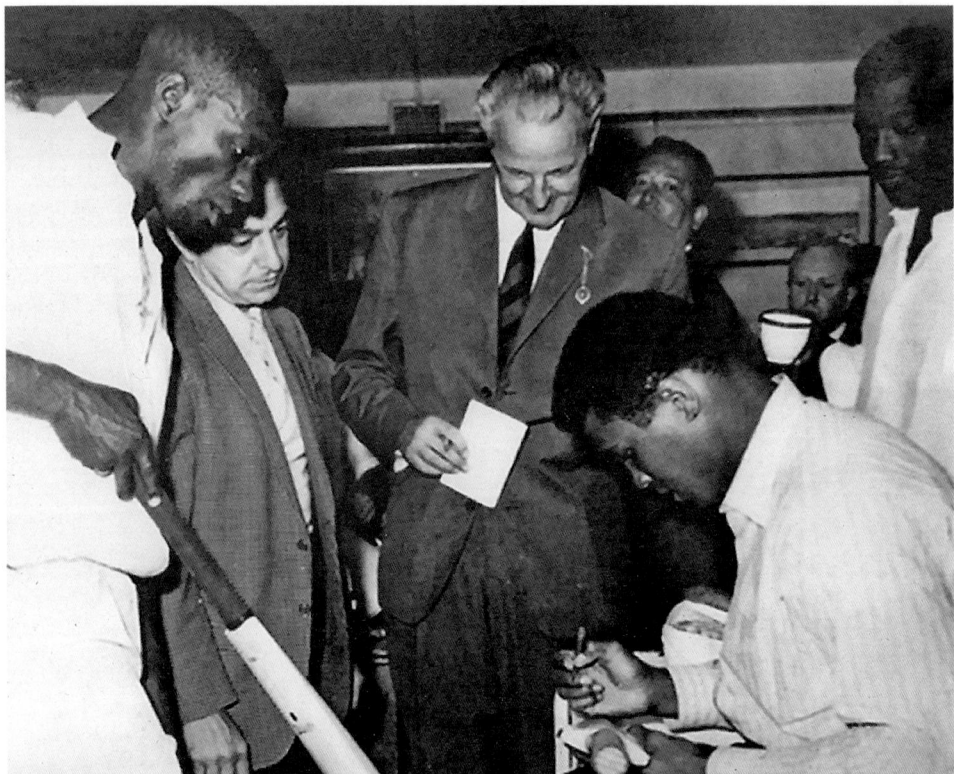

With two leading figures in the Civil Rights struggle

(top) Wes waits his turn as Muhammad Ali signs bats in the Lord's dressing room

(right) with Harry Belafonte

Wes, as Minister of Tourism, with Mick Jagger and Eddie Grant

Meeting Nelson Mandela in Johannesburg in 1993

Public recognition

left: Wes with his statue outside the Kensington Oval in Bridgetown

below: With friends and family at Government House after receiving his knighthood: *(left to right)* Wes's former permanent secretary Lionel Weekes, children Sean, Kerry and Remi, Wes, Rawle Brancker, Charlie Griffith

I did not take off from the sightscreen at Lord's, it was a bigger ground, but people have that memory of Wes ... that was how I made them feel, and that's a wonderful thing. But in another 15 or 20 years, no one will even remember Hall and Griffith ... it is not unusual now for bowlers to capture 400 wickets in Test cricket – some, of course, have taken many more – and future generations will judge all of us on the wickets we took. There aren't television recordings of all the games from those days, so when Hall and Griffith are dead and gone, and no one is around to talk about how they felt when watching them, how else are they going to be judged if not through the stats?

After 15 enjoyable years as a first-class cricketer, Wes retired from the game with countless happy memories, few regrets and the prospect of stimulating new challenges ahead. The end of a career is a natural time for reflection; at that point in his life Wes felt blessed that doing something he loved had given him such wonderful moments and the opportunity to meet so many interesting people. When Wes is asked to sum up his life as a cricketer, the response is not a verbal highlights reel of outstanding performances. Consistent with his belief that a cricketer's most important legacy is how he made people feel, Wes gauges his own accomplishments in terms of how they made *him* feel. In recounting memorable moments, his Test match career-best seven for 69 does not receive a mention, whereas he waxes lyrical about the beauty and mystery of a game that can produce moments such as when he shattered May's stump in the second innings of the same match. He overlooks his hat-trick against Pakistan in Lahore in 1959 – the first ever by a West Indian bowler in Test cricket – but describes at length the 'beautiful' feeling he experienced during the chaotic last over in the tied Test.

Photographs from his playing days are all Wes needs to jog his memory and relive the feelings he experienced. He was never a collector of souvenirs:

I have a few bits and pieces; the odd stump maybe. Peter May's stump that I broke is somewhere upstairs, I think. Nowadays players run off the field at the end of a game with their arms full of stumps and things. We never did that. Frank Worrell told us that when we get a wicket – even if we have bowled the best ball in the world – just stand there and shake hands with our teammates. He said if we go around hugging each other like footballers it gives the impression that we were not expecting a wicket! We never celebrated like that.

When he looks back and analyses his cricket career, Wes recalls that the fun he derived from playing was provided mainly by team camaraderie ... and batting! Bowling on the other hand was his serious business:

> My batting was my entertainment. When I was bowling, I did not see any entertainment in that. I never set myself up to be a fast bowler, it was just something that God allowed. How else could a 17-year-old boy who had never bowled a ball be playing for his country less than two years later? Bowling was my job, and it was my duty to take it seriously. When I was at the top of my run, it was no joke. When you see me with a ball in my hand, do not doubt me, you are standing between me and the Caribbean people. People knew that. I have *never* been sledged on a cricket field. The thing about sledging is that like every bully you pick on people who you think are weaker than you. So who is going to pick on Gilchrist? Or Griffith? Or Hall? They are just serving up punishment for themselves.

He frequently returns to the theme that in order to be successful a cricketer must be a good thinker:

> People feel that fast bowling is just a question of running up and delivering, but that is not so. You have to learn to bowl line and length, and then so many variations: a slower ball, a yorker and when to put that ball in the four and six-metre zones. Once you have mastered all those skills, you need to be able to set up batsmen. If a particular batsman does not like facing you, the easiest thing for him to do is to just drop his wrists and get a single to get away from you. My job is not to let him get a single; I am going to bowl six balls at him, because there is nothing better than bowling six balls at a batsman if he is vulnerable.

Mastering the mechanics of bowling is just the first part of the process, after which success at the highest level becomes a mental issue. Once Wes had a technique that he could trust, out-thinking opponents and applying pressure on them became paramount. At all times during his career Wes devised in advance the tactics he would employ against a particular batsman:

You have to do your homework and plan a strategy. All distinguished players are great thinkers, and I had to study and analyse the opposing players, to try and be one step ahead. Do people think that batsmen like Dexter, Cowdrey, May, Graveney, Davidson, Simpson and Harvey just get themselves out?

Wes was never sledged, nor was sledging ever part of his armoury. Good-natured banter yes but without any of the malice that has so often tainted the game. Even when bowling, he found time to intersperse business with moments of levity. Roy Virgin, the former Somerset and Northamptonshire batsman, describes an incident in the West Indians' tour match against Somerset at Taunton in 1966. Virgin was doing his best to negotiate a particularly hostile spell from Wes. He played forward to a delivery that nipped back off the seam and struck him an excruciating blow to the inner thigh. Determined not to show his pain, he did not flinch or wince; instead, he held his position on the front-foot and stared at Wes who had advanced to within a few feet of him in his follow-through. The two men stood face-to-face, before Wes broke into a grin: 'You can rub it, man. I know it hurts!'

Virgin expressed his affection for Wes as a person and his admiration for him as a player. He faced many great bowlers in his career, none quicker than Hall: 'He was extremely fast and one of the great outswinging fast bowlers. He was right up there with Fred Trueman, Dennis Lillee and later Richard Hadlee.'

Wes is grateful to have played cricket at a time when 'having a laugh' was very much part of the game, and when he talks about batting he becomes less intense and assumes his customary light-hearted demeanour. Despite several noteworthy innings, his fondest memories are of times when his batting added more to the mirth in the changing room than to the total on the scoreboard. In the modern era such an attitude would be considered unprofessional; in the 1960s, teams often contained three or four 'genuine' tail-enders of whom very little was expected. Wes became a victim of that mindset and took great delight in announcing to his teammates that 'I bat when it is necessary. I also bat fully cognisant of the fact that with Griffith and Gibbs behind me, there is always the very strong potential for a hat-trick!' Although at the time he viewed batting as an enjoyable release from the pressures of bowling, nowadays he reflects with some regret that he was a capable batsman who undoubtedly could have had more success. Bearing in mind his prowess as a schoolboy batsman, it disappoints him that the statistics – and his performances with the bat – fail to do justice to his ability. As he demonstrated in scoring his century at Fenner's in 1963, and six first-class half-centuries – two of them in Test matches – he was capable of producing valuable contributions when he fully applied himself.

Because the 'proclivity for comedic inspiration', first noticed and eloquently described by Worrell, came to the fore when Wes batted, spectators enjoyed the entertainment of a Hall innings. However, his antics were sometimes considered excessive by opponents. In the tied Test, for example, during the crucial 88-run ninth-wicket partnership between Alexander and Hall, Australian players felt that his horseplay went beyond acceptable limits. The two batsmen scampered many audacious singles, with Wes regularly threatening to run and goading the fielders to try to run him out. The opposition was probably frustrated at their inability to get him out and irritated because they felt that the joke was at their expense. Whatever their reasons, Wes felt no need to justify himself. He was playing the game his way and enjoying himself.

Batting with his captain seemed to inspire Wes to adopt a more serious approach, yet he remained on the lookout for a joke. In the Fourth Test of the 1961-62 series against India in Port of Spain, Wes went in last with the score on 346 for nine. Worrell wanted more runs and instructed Wes to 'hold on' and bat sensibly. Wes did as he was told and began to build an innings. With his score in the 20s, he played 'three serious cover drives'. Worrell came down the wicket to Wes with a smile on his face: 'Winfield, are you trying to make me look bad?'

'No, Sir, I am just trying to make you aware that there are Four Ws: Worrell, Weekes, Walcott and Wes!'

Worrell declared on 444 for nine, with Wes having made 50 in their unbroken 98-run last-wicket partnership. Back in the pavilion he announced to everyone that number eleven, W.W. Hall, had outscored the great F.M.M. Worrell, one of the finest batsmen in the world! Accusations that he was 'talking nonsense', were met with a withering reply. Wes haughtily pointed out that it was not a complex mathematical issue: if he scored 50 in a partnership of 98 with the skipper, 'who outscored whom?' The dressing room fell silent.

Five years later, in the Second Test against India in Calcutta, Wes joined Sobers in the middle with West Indies' first-innings score on 290 for seven. West Indies had won the First Test in Bombay but were troubled by the Indian leg-spinner Bhagwat Chandrasekhar, who took 11 wickets in the match. 'Chandra' was a very skilful bowler who bowled at a quicker pace than most spinners, making it extremely difficult to read his deliveries. A day had been lost due to the crowd riots, and Sobers was batting aggressively to try to make up for lost time. His assessment was that they needed 100 more runs; Wes's assessment was that the chances of that happening were slim: 'A hundred more runs, and Chandra's bowling? You've got to be joking! I cannot pick him, and I do not think anybody can except you.'

As usual, Sobers had an answer. When Wes was on strike, he would watch Chandra and indicate whether or not he was about to bowl a googly. If Sobers moved his bat, Wes could expect a googly and was safe to play the ball through the leg side. If his captain did nothing, Wes would either defend the ensuing leg-break or leave it to pass by the off-stump. The system worked to perfection. Wes batted beautifully, and at lunch he was feeling rather pleased with himself when Seymour Nurse sat down next to him with a puzzled look on his face.

'Blues, you've hit Chandra three times over mid-wicket ... are you pickin' him?'

The opportunity to make some mischief was too good to resist: 'Well, boy, you fellas didn't go to Combermere, you didn't learn how to play properly. I learned to pick at school. So, to answer your question: yes, of course I'm pickin' Chandra.'

Wes accepts that he should have stopped at that point; unfortunately he was unable to help himself:

'I have something to tell you, but please don't tell anybody.'

Nurse assured Wes that his lips were sealed.

'Sobers ain't pickin' Chandra. The skipper's strugglin', and I'm helpin' him.'

Sobers was out shortly after lunch as he continued to force the pace, leaving Wes to fend for himself against Chandra. The outcome was inevitable: 'The googly pitched on off-stump and nearly cut me in half! All I could do was jerk my bat towards it, and it came off the inside edge and I was caught at short-leg.' Sobers greeted him outside the pavilion:

'Well, Wes. I can't pick him, and it looks like you can't pick either ... you can't even pick rice. Now go along inside!'

Back in the pavilion, Wes informed his teammates: 'If you want the world to know your business, you can telephone, telegraph, telex ... or tell Seymour Nurse!' This time the dressing room erupted with laughter.

For the record, West Indies made 390 and won the match by an innings.

Wes also had had some fun with Sobers in Trinidad after their match-saving partnership in the First Test against England in 1967-68. Following on 205 runs behind, West Indies were untroubled at 164-2 until a collapse reduced them to 180-8 with Wes the next batsman. His innings began in jocular fashion: he strode to the wicket to replace Charlie Griffith, who had been bowled for nought by the Warwickshire seam bowler David Brown. All three stumps were flattened and, as they passed each other, Charlie's mood was not improved when Wes asked him for directions to the middle: 'Where do I have to go and stand exactly? I don't see any stumps out there!' Wes played and missed the first few balls he faced from Brown, prompting Sobers to instruct him to go back to schoolboy basics with bat and pad together in order to keep the England bowlers at bay. Both batsmen played with uncharacteristic caution, and when it became clear they had saved the match Sobers gave Wes *carte blanche* to indulge himself and play a few shots. Wes declined. He was determined to see the job through to the end and walk back with his skipper undefeated. The match ended with their partnership unbroken on 63 and, as they headed towards the pavilion, Wes made the tongue-in-cheek suggestion to his captain that the decent thing to do would be to allow him to walk off first. Sobers looked disdainfully at him and strode towards the pavilion, but a few feet from the rope he pulled up: 'Blues, you go ahead.' He probably regretted his gesture shortly afterwards when Wes told reporters that he had been worried because 'the batsman at the other end looked a little vulnerable!'

Reminiscing about batting with Sobers leads onto the subject of great players, beginning with those who Wes played with and against. Garry Sobers tops both lists:

> Sobers made 8,032 Test runs and took 235 wickets and 109 catches. But more than that, people remember how he made them feel! When you see him walk out with that gait, with his collar up, oh boy, that's what you remember.

In addition to Sobers' unparalleled all-round skills, Wes identifies qualities such as his physical courage and an intuitive feel for cricket: 'Everything came together to make him the greatest cricketer that ever lived.' Wes saw at first-hand many of Sobers' remarkable exploits, most of which are well-documented. He picks out a couple of lesser-known examples which help define Sobers as a special cricketer.

In 1963, with the series in England tied at 1-1, West Indies faced the prospect of playing the Fourth Test in Leeds without Sobers. Since the previous Test at Edgbaston he had been treated for a large and extremely painful whitlow on a finger. Sobers had it lanced in the hope that he would be able to play, but he arrived at Headingley on the morning of the match with his arm in a sling. An hour later, when Worrell announced an unchanged team from the previous Test, the players were as overjoyed as they were amazed. The side contained many highly talented individuals, but the knowledge that their talisman was in the team gave an enormous boost to morale. Sobers' teammates then watched in disbelief as he defied his pain and made scores of 102 and 52. In the second innings he bowled 32 overs and took three wickets for 90. West Indies won the match by 221 runs.

In January 1963 Brisbane was the setting for an astonishing example of Sobers' genius. He and Wes were playing for their respective state sides in a Sheffield Shield match between Queensland and South Australia. Early on the first morning, Sobers came in to bat with South Australia struggling on 17 for two and in need of a substantial innings from their West Indian star. Wes had the misfortune to drop him first ball, prompting Sobers to tease his friend that he would bat until the same time the following morning!

Wes was the fastest – and the number one – bowler in the world. He was bowling very well that day and, having already captured a wicket, his confidence was high as he began his next over to Sobers. He bowled a fast, rising ball in the six-meter zone, and Sobers went onto his back foot and savagely smacked it over the mid-wicket boundary for six: 'No other batsman had ever done that to me; even great hookers like Milburn always hit it backward of square.'

It was of little consolation that Sobers failed to live up to his prediction of batting until the next day; when he was dismissed shortly before the close of play, he had scored 196 and South Australia had progressed to 338 for six.

That evening over dinner, Wes was still smarting when he asked Sobers how he was able to react so quickly and hit him over the mid-wicket. Even now, the answer leaves Wes in awe:

> His explanation taught me a sobering lesson. He said that if my hand was forward of vertical at the point of release, he knew it would be a short ball, and he would be ready on his back foot to hit me out of the ground. Conversely, if my hand was more vertical, the ball would be released earlier and pitched up, and he would be ready to go on his front foot.

Sobers applied the same logic when fielding at short-leg to spin bowlers. If Gibbs released the ball a fraction later, he knew that it would not be flighted but pushed through faster and shorter, and he would move squarer to give himself the chance of a catch. The ability to identify the subtlest variations in a bowler's action with his naked eye, and the speed of thought and body to react, provided further confirmation that Sobers was operating on a different level. Wes rates him not only as the greatest all-rounder he has ever seen but also the best batsman, especially against fast bowling. It is telling that such a bright and knowledgeable man as Wes still seeks Sobers' opinion and advice on cricket matters:

> I don't believe there is anybody in the world who understands cricket like Sobers. That's a big statement to make about a man, but I believe he has the greatest cricket brain ever. Sobers was a genius. There is no more to be said.

Wes encountered numerous fine players over the course of his career, but he makes special mention of Tom Graveney, whom he held in the highest esteem as a cricketer and a man:

> I reckon Graveney was the best English batsman I played against, a great man as well as a great player. He had all the shots. He was a true gentleman, but when he hit you through the off-side, it hurt! Such perfect timing.

The most prolific English batsman against Wes was Ken Barrington, but he was happy to bowl at him:

> Barrington was the hardest to get out, but he was never going to destroy me. He was relatively easy to contain, unlike Graveney,

Cowdrey or Dexter. If those boys batted a whole day, you were in trouble; they scored runs quickly, especially Dexter. That England batting line-up of the 1960s was about the best I faced. Cowdrey, Barrington, Graveney, May and Dexter: You don't find five men like that in many batting orders; and then Parks, D'Oliveira and Titmus – give me a break!

Wes enjoyed the challenge of playing against such high-quality batsmen and was constantly striving to improve his game to compete with the best. He regrets that he did not see Neil Harvey in his prime but, of the other Australian batsmen, he had a very high regard for Norman O'Neill, Bobby Simpson, Doug Walters and Ian Chappell.

Richie Benaud ranks as one of his most formidable opponents, 'a brilliant captain and a very intelligent cricketer. Bowling or batting, he was always dangerous, you could never relax when he was around.' A teammate of Benaud, Alan Davidson, is considered by Wes to be the best all-rounder that he played against in Test cricket, 'a magnificent fast bowler, a very good batsman and as an all-rounder second only to Garry Sobers.' Like many of his opponents, Davidson – and his wife Betty – became good friends of Wes.

In more recent times, the two batsmen who stand out for Wes are Viv Richards and Brian Lara. Richards possessed colossal talent and a presence the like of which Wes has not seen before or since in a cricketer. Driven by intense pride in his African ancestry, and with supreme confidence, his brilliant batsmanship was just a part of what made him such a special cricketer. When applying his benchmark of 'the way he made you feel', Wes describes the thrill and anticipation felt by all of us who were privileged to witness Richards striding out to bat. Disdainfully chewing gum and with a sense of purpose, Richards intimidated opposition bowlers and fielders before he had even taken guard. The only batsman he rates as highly based on pure batting ability alone is Brian Lara:

It is difficult to compare batsmen of different eras. Sobers did not play with Richards or Lara – those are the three best batsmen I have played with or managed. Sobers is easily the best batsman I have seen against fast bowling. Lara is the best I have seen against slow bowling. Richards is the most devastating to all-comers.

If Gilchrist was the fastest bowler Wes saw, Frank 'Typhoon' Tyson was close behind. Playing for E.W. Swanton's XI in Wes's first-class debut in 1956, Tyson bowled 'so fast that he bowled Clyde Walcott before Clyde had time to move his bat.' In the second innings Walcott completely changed his batting technique to combat Tyson's extreme pace. He dispensed with his customary high backlift, keeping his bat down by his pads to cover his wicket. Normally an attacking batsman, he showed uncharacteristic restraint, relying on deflections to score runs. He made 130. It was not Walcott's most fluent innings, but his carefully thought-out solution greatly impressed Wes – as of course did Tyson's speed.

A bowler who consistently caused Wes discomfort was the England pace bowler John Snow. Wes liked to adopt a carefree batting style; sometimes restraint would have been a sensible policy:

> I loved flicking the ball on middle or leg stump to backward square, and John Snow was probably too fast for me to be flicking! He was a very good bowler, very accurate and he would bowl at the wicket until I missed one.'

In 1999 Wes conducted the service at the funeral of the great Barbados and West Indian cricketer Malcolm Marshall. Short of stature, and with a chest-on action, Marshall was the antithesis of Wes Hall the bowler. He challenged conventional thinking with his ability to bowl big outswingers despite his action. He skilfully used the full width of the crease either to draw batsmen into playing a shot to the ball that left them, or to angle the ball in at the stumps. Marshall was by no means the fastest bowler, but in Wes's view he was the smartest. In his sermon Wes stated that he considered Marshall to be the best fast bowler the world had ever seen: 'When I said those words, you could hear a pin drop; nobody had said that before. Since then I have heard many cricketers say that Marshall is the greatest fast bowler of all time.' Wes was equally impressed with Marshall's dignity as he approached the end of his life. Suffering from terminal colon cancer, Wes led Malcolm to Christ four weeks before he died at the age of 41 on 4 November 1999: 'I have never seen anyone die like that. He was so serene.'

16

A Tribute to the Three Ws

From Headley to Sobers Wes admired many of the greats, but from boyhood until his playing days his biggest heroes were the Three Ws. Wes has written this tribute to them.

Frank Worrell, Everton Weekes and Clyde Walcott: it was miraculous that these three great men were born within a radius of one mile in Bridgetown and in an 18-month period between 1924 and 1926. They became the most accomplished batting trio ever in world cricket and gained international acclaim in 1950 as part of the West Indies team that created history by winning a Test match at Lord's and a series in England. Along with Ramadhin, Valentine and Rae, they were immortalised in calypsos in the Caribbean for their part in the moment when we West Indians finally believed that we had arrived. Beating England in England was one of the greatest achievements in our cricket. But you can't look at cricket alone. It was part of the movement for change that was taking place in the Caribbean and in Barbados in particular. An Everton Weekes quote explains the symbolic importance of the tour: 'It was the end of the Empire as far as we were concerned.' When the Ws returned home in October 1950 after that historic tour, they could not vote in Barbados because they did not own land. Here they were, icons who were feted with motorcades and receptions in their honour in England, but when they got home they weren't allowed the vote. The introduction of the Adult Suffrage Bill the following year put an end to that, and all adult citizens got the vote. That meant a lot to me. I saw cricket as a big part of the process. The victory in England was a watershed; on the back of the Three Ws and Ramadhin and Valentine, it led to an awareness of the role black people had to play, and we could no longer be ignored.

When I was selected for the 1957 tour of England, I had only played one first-class match, and I looked in one direction for guidance and that was the Three Ws. As a youngster the things that impressed me most about them were their amazing ability, temperament, caring attitude, humility and how they handled pressure. And that was the amazing thing, all of them had all those qualities. As a young man on my first tour, I had no idea how to handle pressure, and there was a lot of pressure on us in 1957, especially on the Three Ws. They were injured – particulerly Weekes and Walcott – but they handled it. They would never chicken out when the going got tough. They played in pain. Even with their troubles, the way they made a neophyte like me feel comfortable in their awesome presence was so inspiring. It meant so much and said so much about them. They never pulled rank on me, and by putting me at my ease they made it enjoyable too. I was so impressed by them that I decided to use the time I had on my hands on that tour – especially during the Test matches – to do some research to learn all about them.

Frank Worrell and Clyde Walcott both began their first-class careers playing for Barbados in the same match against Trinidad in Port of Spain in January 1942. They were aged 17 and 16 respectively (Walcott made his debut on his 16th birthday); Walcott opened, and Worrell batted at number eleven since he was selected as a left-arm spin bowler. Worrell got six wickets and scored 29 in the first innings and never batted at number eleven again. They both quickly established themselves as class players, and over the next few years they made some huge scores and were involved in massive partnerships[1]. Both players were products of the secondary school system: Worrell went to Combermere, and Walcott – who was from a well-known family of civil servants – went to Harrison College. Those two schools along with The Lodge School played in

---

[1] In February 1944, against Trinidad in Bridgetown, Worrell (308*) was involved in an unbroken fourth-wicket partnership of 502 with John Goddard (218*); and in February 1946, also against Trinidad in Port of Spain, Walcott (314*) and Worrell (255*) shared an unbroken fourth-wicket partnership of 574. At the time this was the highest partnership in the history of first-class cricket. In that innings Weekes was dismissed for 0!

the first division of the BCA, and Walcott would have been playing against men in senior cricket from the age of twelve; Worrell from 13. Because they were playing in the BCA every Saturday, they were spotted early and selected to play for Barbados at a young age. Weekes did not go to high school, and so did not play organised cricket at school. So much talent must have gone by the wayside. Weekes left school when he was 14 and played BCL cricket from then until he joined the Barbados Regiment of the British Army aged 18. He then played in the BCA competition for the Garrison Sports Club and made his first-class debut on 24 February 1945 against Trinidad. He was two days short of his 21st birthday, several years after the other two; obviously if he had gone to Combermere or Harrison he would have played for Barbados when he was 16, so he lost four years. When he eventually did play, he batted out of position as an opener – without success – but as soon as he was moved to his proper position of number four he showed his true form.

The Second World War delayed the Ws' Test debuts until the 1947-48 home series against England. The series was very significant for us: we won against England for only the second time, and also George Headley became the first black man to captain West Indies. He pulled a muscle in the First Test, and Stollmeyer was made captain, but he got injured too, so Gomez was captain in the Second Test. Goddard was made captain for the Third Test, and after West Indies won they kept him for the last Test in Jamaica, and he remained captain until 1953. Worrell scored a lot of runs, but Weekes and Walcott had moderate series, and Weekes was dropped for the last Test to make way for Headley to return. Walcott kept wicket so well that he was retained. He was a big man and wasn't too keen on keeping wicket, but he was a master at reading Ramadhin. That was his real strength as a wicketkeeper; batsmen couldn't read Ramadhin, so it gave us a big advantage. Headley was injured again before the Fifth Test, and Weekes was recalled. After a delayed flight to Jamaica he replaced the popular Jamaican J.K. Holt in the field, and the crowd was hostile towards him for taking the place of their local man. When we batted, he made a brilliant 141, and he was the darling of the Jamaican crowd.

That was the first of his five consecutive Test centuries, four more on the tour of India the next year, and it would have been six, but he was wrongly given run out when he was on 90. His record still stands.

After his success against England in 1947-48, Worrell fell out with the board over players' pay, and he did not go to India in 1948-49. Instead, he toured India the next two years with a Commonwealth team and had tremendous success, scoring 1,129 runs in ten matches at an average of 80.64. On the second tour he was captain of the side and showed that he was a born leader. He was a man of principle, the first man to really challenge the board.

Over the next few years the Ws dominated West Indian cricket and were the greatest middle-order triumvirate the world has ever seen. As they became senior players, they endured the ignominy of junior men being appointed to captain them. Both Walcott and Worrell were vice-captains; Walcott on the 1957 tour of England captained by John Goddard and Worrell in the 1959-60 series against England when Gerry Alexander was captain. Finally Worrell was rightly given the job in 1960. Worrell was just so dignified in everything he did. He always spoke to you in a calm way. His wisdom resonated with me and stayed with me through my career, things he used to say that were so true and that helped me achieve perspective. One of the most valuable lessons he taught me was that players needed to have the right attitude to perform at their best and that, if you're playing every day against top international cricketers, not every day will bring joy. Obvious really, but how many people have that mindset? It helped me see things in a more logical way and play with the right attitude. He used to say, 'The best, with a bad attitude, is no longer the best,' and, 'It's not how good you are, but how you play under pressure.' Again, how true. How many times do you see talented players without the right mindset lose to a strong-willed opponent with less talent? The biggest compliment he ever paid me was in his foreword to *Pace Like Fire*, when he said 'Wes Hall ... can take his "licks" like a man.' To me he is saying I showed character and had learned the perspective he believed we should strive for. I had cricket in its proper place, as he always did. Coming from him, that meant so much.

The Three Ws paved the way for the great players that followed them: players like Sir Garry, Kanhai, Sir Viv and many others. They contributed immensely to our cricketing heritage, a heritage that is a source of hope and pride for all West Indian people. That heritage is our point of reference, the touchstone of our identity. Here are three great men, who for 15 years demonstrated the value of true merit, and once their merit was fully recognised, the democracy that we now cherish was finally assured. The wisdom of these men and the way they conducted themselves proved to everyone that black West Indians were ready to take on roles of responsibility and that excellence could no longer be ignored. Since Worrell, all of the successive captains from Sobers to the present day have been selected on merit, and this because of the principles established by the Three Ws. Learie Constantine said he hoped he would live to see the day when people no longer got into a team or became captain by means of landed value or ethnicity. In 1960 Worrell was the first one who was captain on pure merit, and Constantine lived until 1971.

The Three Ws could have lived anywhere in the world when they retired, but they chose to come back home to make further contributions. That is a big point: they chose to make a difference in the Caribbean. Sir Frank and Lady Worrell lived in Jamaica, where he was a very popular warden of Irvine Hall at The University of the West Indies. He mentored countless students and, with his calm manner, he was a really good man to have to help them with any problem. Many top professionals, including politicians, sat at Frank Worrell's feet as students and listened to his philosophy on life. He later did the same thing at the St Augustine campus in Trinidad, and he was revered there as well. Worrell died in 1967, a year after Barbados gained independence. He was 42. If he had lived, he would have been Governor-General or whatever the authorities wanted him to be. He had been in the Senate in Jamaica; he achieved so much in those 42 years.

Sir Clyde and Lady Walcott settled in Guyana, where he gave yeoman service coaching on the sugar estates. The wonderful thing about his coaching in Berbice was the talent that emerged: Solomon, Kanhai, Butcher, Madray. Once he got the district producing cricketers, it led to others like Kallicharran. Walcott also captained Guyana and later served as an administrator, and so he was very instrumental in the rise of the Guyanese team. He returned to Barbados as Industrial Relations Manager at Barbados Shipping and Trading, a big job. He served on the board of the BCA and was elected president of the WICBC and subsequently president of the ICC, the highest office in cricket. He is the only West Indian to hold the post: a very capable and successful man. I was very privileged when Lady Walcott and her family asked me to deliver the eulogy at his funeral. That was a big thing for me.

Sir Everton lived in Barbados. After his last Test in 1958 he became the first cricketing coach of Barbados. It was a government appointment, they didn't even know what title to give him, they just asked: 'Will you come and improve our cricket?'! He continued playing for Barbados and in 1959 he captained the side. Like Walcott he served on the BCA and WICBC. He worked as a hotel management executive and served on the Police Service Commission for over 20 years. He served on the Public Service Commission into his early nineties, until his health began to fail. He was a very clever man, and he played bridge at international level. Weekes was so bright, I believe that if he had gone to secondary school he could have been a professor. He had an engaging personality and delivered the greatest one-liners in the world!

In the foreword to the 2007 book, *Mastering the Craft: Ten Years of Weekes 1948-1958* by Everton Weekes and Hilary Beckles, Owen Arthur[2] wrote: 'Through his excellence on the cricket field, Sir Everton helped in a fundamental way to change Barbados for the better, forever, by proving that true excellence cannot be constrained by social barriers.'

Everton Weekes died on 30 July 2020 and is buried next to the other two Ws in a plot beside the cricket ground at The University of the West Indies' Cave Hill campus near Bridgetown. The cricket stadium there has been named The Three Ws Oval in their honour, the brainchild of Professor Sir Hilary Beckles, Vice-Chancellor of The University of the West Indies.

[2] The Right Honourable Owen Arthur (1949-2020) was the prime minister of Barbados from 1994 to 2008. He was the country's longest-serving prime minister.

On a personal note I owe a great deal to Sir Everton. I would probably never have played for Barbados or West Indies had I not been strongly recommended by him, and I am eternally grateful to him for that. Sir Everton Weekes was a great and valued friend to me. Sir Frank Worrell charted my career path and was a mentor *par excellence* to me. Sir Clyde Walcott was a cricketing prodigy who developed into a multi-dimensional, multi-talented professional who excelled as a player, selector, manager, referee and President of the WICB and ICC. There is empirical evidence that the Three Ws' myriad contributions to West Indian and world cricket have left a legacy that will never be equalled, far less surpassed.

I am eternally grateful to have played with these three West Indian cricketing giants.

Part Two

Life After Cricket

17

A Career Crossroads

After the 1968-69 tour of Australia and New Zealand, Wes returned to Trinidad for the last year of his contract with WITCO. Injury had brought an end to his international career, and he would play just a few more first-class matches. He was starting to think about life after cricket and had tentatively considered various options, including turning his hand to cricket commentary. Given his command of language and knowledge of cricket, it is highly likely he would have been a success; however, as a husband and father of two young children, he decided it was time to settle down with the family in Barbados. Entertaining as Wes Hall the commentator undoubtedly would have been, losing his contributions elsewhere over the next 35 years would have been a heavy price to pay. Numerous calls to serve were to follow, beginning in the last few months of 1970.

The call from Father Pantin – SERVOL
On completion of his work with the Wes Hall League in 1970, Wes was called to embark on a life-changing task. He speaks with passion about SERVOL and considers it his defining experience, lifting him above cricket and making him aware of what he wanted to do with his life.

In a moment of self-examination, Father 'Gerry' Pantin, a Catholic priest, questioned his role as a teacher at St Mary's College, an illustrious middle-class school in Port of Spain, when just a few blocks away in Laventille Hill children faced extreme deprivation. The neighbourhood was home to some of Trinidad's poorest people, many of whom lived in awful conditions and, after years of neglect, social unrest erupted in the form of violent protests in 1970. Thousands of people – mostly youths – took to the streets in riots which became known as the 'Black Power' demonstrations.

Father Pantin saw the riots as a cry for help, and he decided to respond. He was unsure what form his action would take, but it was clear to him that his first step should be to enlist the services of Wes Hall. Father

Pantin had seen from Wes's coaching work on the island that he was a man of compassion and humanity who achieved results, improving lives along the way. The priest gained permission from Hugh Henderson at WITCO to speak to Wes about an exciting new community project. Once this was granted, Father Pantin's brother Clive organised the meeting. (Clive Pantin was the headmaster of Fatima College in Port of Spain, one of the leading schools in Trinidad. As a volunteer who helped with the administration of the Wes Hall League, he knew Wes well.) Having unknowingly convinced Father Pantin of his special qualities, Wes was taken aback when he received the call to accompany the priest to Laventille.

He was unsure what to expect, or that he was the right person for the job, but despite his uncertainties, something told him he should do it. Father Pantin assured Wes that he was very popular with the people there and, as they set out to walk up the hill, he insisted on Wes leading the way and speaking first.

It was not uncommon for people to come into such neighbourhoods accompanied by reporters and cameras so that they could publicise the charitable donations they were giving, and so visitors were treated with suspicion. The approach adopted by Father Pantin was very different: he wanted simply to ask how they could help. He believed that making assumptions about what people wanted was patronising. He would listen to them to find out what *they* wanted and, instead of handing out unconditional charity, ask them to make a contribution: 'We went there to listen to them and show them respect. Neither of those things had happened before.'

A short way up the hill they introduced themselves to a group of men. Wes assured them that he and Father Pantin had no ulterior motive, and he asked how they could help. One of them said they would like a football. At this point Father Pantin entered the conversation. He promised the men that if they gave him half of the cost of a football, they would bring one the next day. When the spokesman replied that he had no money, Father Pantin pointed out that they had enough to buy beer and cigarettes. He told them to club together and that he and Wes would see them on their way back down the hill. A couple of hours later, the men were waiting, ready to hand over the money; the next day, Father Pantin and Wes brought the football. This was the first of many philanthropic deeds, each one delivered with the message that 'the more you can help yourself, the more we can help you.'

As word spread of the two men who spent every day walking through the community, curious locals came out of their homes to see this unusual pair. Wes and Father Pantin were joined by a local resident, Carl Weekes and, by engaging in 'rap sessions' with various street-corner groups, they gradually overcame any hostility. On one occasion, after Father Pantin had explained their work to some bystanders, a member of his audience – clearly a man of means – was so impressed that he offered a house free of charge for them to use as an office. They gratefully accepted and established their headquarters in the house, and on 8 September 1970 SERVOL – Service Volunteered for All – was officially born.

Wes took the view that the vast majority of those in need were decent people who happened to be the victims of circumstance and that SERVOL's job was to try to give them the chance in life they deserved. He identified enormous potential in Laventille. It already had one of the world's leading steel bands – sponsored by WITCO – and the area was famed for speciality jewellery made from shells: 'Those people in Laventille Hill were very talented, and many of them very quickly began to display leadership qualities.'

The SERVOL house became a hive of activity as more and more people came out to help and to be helped, including a group of female volunteers from the Catholic Church. As Fathe Pantin and Wes gained the confidence of the community, the results were spectacular. An especially popular initiative called 'On the Street where you Live' took the form of regular street parties held in various locations for the residents of three or four of the neighbouring streets. The area took on a more hopeful atmosphere, with young people going to classes and clubs and playing football and cricket. Talks were given by skilled people: sports coaches; tradesmen to encourage youngsters to take on apprenticeships, and office workers to teach typing skills. The job of convincing boys and girls to make the next step was more difficult; they were often reluctant to leave home to go and work in the city, because despite the problems – and the high likelihood of a prison sentence – this was the life they knew. However, over time, and with the help of some gentle persuasion, increasing numbers of them chose to make the move.

Father Pantin involved local merchants and businessmen, who undertook to provide sponsorship and donate items. The most notable was the generous pledge by the department store Kirpalani[1] to send a

---

[1] Kirpalani was founded in Suriname in 1936 and expanded into Caribbean locations, including Trinidad.

truckload of goods that could be sold to raise money. The private sector's contribution was most welcome, but the biggest source of funds was the SERVOL Poor Man's Dinner. The event was held at The Hilton Hotel, with guests paying 100 Trinidadian Dollars for a meal of soup and a crust of bread. Obviously it made an enormous profit. At the dinner, Father Pantin and Wes circulated among the guests, telling them about their work and securing more donations in the process. Among the many eminent people at the inaugural Poor Man's Dinner was Dr Eric Williams[2], the Prime Minister of Trinidad and Tobago, whose constituency included Laventille. He congratulated the organisers and assured them of his continued support for the programme. The Poor Man's Dinner became an annual fundraising event and is a highlight in the island's social calendar.

SERVOL's mission statement succinctly outlines its aims:

> SERVOL is an organisation of weak, frail, ordinary, imperfect yet hope-filled and committed people seeking to help weak, frail, ordinary, imperfect, hope-drained people become agents of attitudinal and social change in a journey which leads to total human development. It does so through respectful intervention in the lives of others and seeks to empower individuals and communities to develop as role models for the nations.

The policy of allowing people to decide how they would be helped, and then insisting that they were active participants, gave them control of their destiny – and often self-respect – for the first time. Wes sums up SERVOL's ethos: 'We had to move people beyond poverty and into opportunity. It is born out of love for your fellow man.'

The success of SERVOL was not to everyone's liking. Black Power leaders were unhappy with the positive work that Fatherr Pantin and Wes were doing on their recruiting ground; in a letter to Pantin, one of them wrote that if Wes did not leave the island 'it would be pace like fire!' Of course, Wes interpreted this as a threat and one which was especially worrying for the father of two young children. Fortunately he was spared the dilemma of making a choice, as he was due to return to Barbados at the end of the

---

[2] Dr Eric Williams (1911-1981) became the first prime minister of Trinidad and Tobago when it gained independence in 1962. He served until his death in 1981.

year after his coaching stint with WITCO ended in August 1970. He left Trinidad with 'a heavy heart'.

During his four years in Trinidad Wes displayed his abilities as a gifted communicator and organiser. Motivated by his desire to help others, his accomplishments would have been a credit to anyone, let alone an active top professional sportsman. Father Pantin arranged a farewell party for Wes at The Hilton Hotel, with food cooked by the locals as a token of their appreciation. Wes felt flattered by the many tributes, especially Father Pantin's insistence on describing him as a 'co-founder of SERVOL', without whom it could not have succeeded. Wes reserves a special place in his affections for Father Pantin:

> An amazing man: a saint, but a saint with a sense of humour. So humble, yet so bright. He changed my life, and he changed so many lives. Not only the lives of the people in Laventille but also the lives of many of the privileged members of society, who were moved by Pantin to make a significant contribution to this cause. He would be worthy of a Nobel Prize.

From those beginnings in Trinidad, SERVOL went from strength-to-strength under the guidance of Father Pantin. After Wes left Trinidad, seven soldiers from the Trinidad and Tobago Defence Force were seconded to help with SERVOL's programme in Laventille, and they adopted the practice of asking the SERVOL question: 'How can we help you?' This approach is still used as the first step in the organisation's objective of helping communities to achieve self-development. SERVOL refused to undertake ambitious, large-scale projects requiring major funding from outside finance. On the basis that development of this nature is unsustainable, it preferred to set up viable micro-projects which were clearly defined and achievable. By empowering people in this way, it sought to act as a small catalyst for the social change needed in the Caribbean. SERVOL's models could then be implemented on a society-wide scale by larger organisations with access to greater resources and capital.

Between 1970 and 1976 SERVOL consolidated its activities in Trinidad by establishing community-based pre-schools; training courses in numerous trades; a bakery; consumer co-operatives; a youth farm; sporting and cultural projects; and adult literacy classes. This ambitious range of projects was expanded even further in the 1980s with the development of an early childhood intervention programme and an adolescent training programme for teenagers. SERVOL extended its model across the Caribbean by inviting trainers and field officers from the other territories to visit Trinidad for instruction so that they could set up projects in their own countries. These leaders returned home with the common goal of helping to bring about a caring, sharing society wherever they were operating.

SERVOL has continued to grow since Father Pantin's death in 2014. Hundreds of thousands of people have benefitted directly from the programme, and numerous centres throughout Trinidad and Tobago, and elsewhere in the Caribbean now operate under the SERVOL name.

SERVOL itself traces its origins to 'one day when a priest and a cricketer walked up Laventille Hill', a notion that seems as absurd to Wes now as it did then: 'I knew I could play cricket, but helping people in Laventille? It never crossed my mind!' He considers what he did there to be one of the most worthwhile things he has done in his life: 'It was so gratifying and brought me closer to reality, and at the time I knew without doubt that it was my best moment.' Even though he worked with Father Pantin for only six months before his WITCO contract ended, the experience affected him profoundly: 'That call to serve – or divine intervention, I don't know – was central in defining my journey. It told me that I should live a life of duty and service.'

The call from Dr Eric Williams

In September 1970, while Wes was busy in Trinidad with SERVOL, his great friend Garry Sobers accepted an invitation to take part in a double-wicket tournament in Rhodesia. Ian Smith, the country's Prime Minister, had resisted calls for majority rule, and consequently his regime was declared illegal by the international community in 1965. The controversy was fuelled when Sobers described Smith as 'a tremendous man to talk to'. In reality Sobers was guilty of nothing more than naivety. He had been assured that there was no racial discrimination involved in the selection of the teams and, despite his insistence that he would have declined the invitation had Rhodesia not made progress in promoting multi-racial sport, his attendance was seen by many observers as a tacit endorsement of Rhodesia's racist policies.

The episode caused uproar in the Caribbean, particularly from outside Sobers' native Barbados where his good character was well known. Trade unions and newspapers were ferocious in their criticism; the governments of Guyana and Jamaica – in the form of Forbes Burnham and Michael Manley, the respective prime ministers – threatened to ban Sobers unless he apologised. There were even rumours that India would cancel their tour of the West Indies scheduled for early 1971 if the matter remained unresolved.

Wes's involvement in the saga began when he arrived home late one evening and saw two police cars parked outside his house, with their lights flashing. Fearing for his family, he rushed inside in a state of panic. To his relief, a police officer explained that they were there because Dr Eric Williams, the Prime Minister of Trinidad wanted to see him immediately. Wes replied that he would go in the morning, but the officer was insistent. Wes was taken to the government building, where Dr Williams outlined his concerns over the escalating controversy surrounding Garry Sobers' trip to Rhodesia. Williams asked Wes for his reading of the situation and what he thought Sobers would want to do. Whilst Wes was mindful of the dangers of speaking on someone else's behalf, based on the Garry Sobers he knew, he felt confident in his answers. He assured Dr Williams that Sobers was a kind, genuine man who would never knowingly do anything to cause offence. The Prime Minister was further encouraged when Wes opined that Sobers would not have gone on the tour if he had suspected his actions would arouse such deep feelings among the West Indian people and that he would now be desperate to rectify matters.

Wes had confirmed to Dr Williams that he was the right person for the job. A strategy was agreed whereby Wes would fly to Barbados the next morning and embark on a day of intra-island diplomacy. Thus Wes became Dr Williams' emissary, effectively charged with resolving a sensitive international issue. Dr Williams would inform Mr Manley of developments and then, assuming Wes achieved the desired results, they would contact Mr Burnham, the most militant and outspoken of the prime ministers.

The following morning Wes caught the first flight from Trinidad to Barbados, where his arrival was expected: 'I just walked straight through at the airport, they gave me VIP status!' He headed from the airport to Sandy Lane where he knew he would find Sobers on the golf course. They arranged to meet later that afternoon to craft a statement after Wes had discussed the issue with the Prime Minister of Barbados, Errol Barrow – who knew Sobers well – and other relevant parties. Mr Barrow and Wes drafted an outline statement, and the Prime Minister was happy for Wes to work with Sobers on the final wording. First, Wes observed protocol by consulting other interested parties. He visited the Barbados Minister of Home Affairs, Philip Greaves[3], and Captain Peter Short, president of the BCA, so that by the time he arrived at Garry Sobers' house, the draft statement had been fully approved: 'There was no point in going to Garry first and getting a statement, and then finding out later that it wasn't right.'

Wes caught his return flight to Trinidad at 7pm. On arrival, he was greeted by a policeman, who told him that 'The Doc' wanted to see him. The officer escorted Wes through passport control to a waiting car and, after a debrief in his office, Dr Williams delivered a positive verdict. He spoke to Manley, Barrow and Burnham, who all agreed that the day's efforts had produced a neat, effective solution which avoided blame or recrimination.

Garry Sobers issued a statement in association with Mr Barrow, addressed to Noel Peirce, the president of the WICBC. The following is an extract:

> I therefore wish to convey to you and the members of the board, my sincere regrets for any embarrassment which my action may have caused, and to assure you of my unqualified dedication whenever I may be called on to represent my country, the West Indies, and my people.

The statement was accepted by the protesting governments, and a crisis had been averted.

It is an indication of how highly Wes was regarded that the Prime Minister of Trinidad and Tobago had selected him to perform this task. Wes was honoured to be entrusted with such a huge responsibility, but 'Boy! That was a lot of diplomacy in one day! Other people could have done it, but Dr Williams chose me because I was in Trinidad at the time, and I was close to Garry.' Wes's modesty clouds reality: in his work for WITCO with the Wes Hall League, he had demonstrated maturity and resourcefulness beyond his 33 years, and people had started to take notice. It is debatable whether any other cricketer before or since – with the possible exception of Worrell – would have been called upon in this way.

[3] P.M. Greaves (b.1931) is a former cabinet minister and deputy prime minister. He was knighted in 2009 and was acting Governor-General of Barbados from 2017 to 2018.

18

Businessman, Politician, Cricket Administrator

Wes had impressed many people with his work in Trinidad, and his services were in demand when he returned to Barbados.

Return to Cable & Wireless

At the culmination of his work developing youth cricket in Trinidad, Wes coached the West Indies Young Cricketers on their successful tour of England in July and August 1970. While in London he was asked to model shirts at a promotion event for Barbados Sea Island cotton[1]. A Cable & Wireless board member was present, and he asked Wes when he was going to work for the company again. Wes registered his interest, and shortly afterwards he received a call from Cable & Wireless' London office, offering him the position of Staff Welfare Officer with responsibility for the entire Caribbean, from the Bahamas in the north to Guyana in the south. After consulting his good friend Branford Taitt, a politician and Combermere school friend, Wes accepted the job, and in January 1971 he began work at the company's office in Sunjet House in Bridgetown.

Cable & Wireless enjoyed a reputation for prioritising the well-being of its workforce, and Wes fitted easily into that culture. With his interest in industrial relations, he looked forward to dealing with problems in the training school, staff grievances and sponsorship requests from the company's offices in the region. Working closely with the Human Resources Department headed by Pedro Welch, Wes insisted on dealing with issues promptly and – wherever possible – in person, which meant he was required to travel extensively. The work was demanding but rewarding.

Shortly before Wes re-joined the company, it moved its Caribbean headquarters from Dover in Christ Church to an ultra-modern, multi-storey development in Wildey in St Michael, built on rough ground

---

[1] Grown in Barbados, Sea Island cotton is a variety of extra-smooth cotton renowned for producing luxurious, high-quality fabrics.

in an abandoned cotton field. The company always prioritised good recreational facilities for workers' entertainment outside office hours, and the management team (which included Sonny Gilkes, Wes's captain on that fateful day in 1955) successfully negotiated with Head Office in London for finance to build a new sports club as part of the development. It included tennis courts, a football pitch and a cricket pavilion, as well as indoor facilities and a lavishly appointed clubhouse. All sporting activity at Boarded Hall ceased and relocated to Wildey. Wes had mixed feelings: he was impressed by the new set-up, but remained nostalgic for the intimacy of the old pavilion at Boarded Hall:

> It is important for players to realise that the better the facilities they have, the better they can become. However, like any sports club, it's about the people: *they* make it, not the building. Just because you have a better pavilion does not mean you are going to enjoy it more.

The call from the Governor-General to serve in the senate

In September 1971 an uneventful morning at Cable & Wireless was interrupted by a telephone call from the office of Sir Winston Scott[2], the Governor-General of Barbados, requesting a meeting with Wes that afternoon. Assuming that Sir Winston would want to discuss cricket, Wes accepted the invitation. Following the usual pleasantries, Sir Winston began talking about Wes's celebrated cricket career and, with the conversation progressing much as he had expected, Wes was totally off guard when Sir Winston got to the point. Having followed Wes's work in Trinidad with the Wes Hall Youth Cricket League and SERVOL, he considered him to be worthy of service to his country at a higher level. He therefore had the distinct pleasure of appointing him as one of the seven independent senators in parliament's upper house.

Modelled on the Westminster system, the Parliament of Barbados comprises two chambers. At that time the elected lower house – the House of Assembly – was made up of 24 constituency Members of Parliament (this increased to 27 in 1981 and 30 in 2003). The upper house, the Senate, comprised 21 appointed senators: twelve represented the government, two were from the opposition, and the remaining seven

---

[2] A.W Scott (1900-1976) was a fellow St Gilesian and a doctor. In 1967 he was knighted and became the first native Governor-General of Barbados.

were independent (non-political) senators chosen by the Governor-General to represent a cross-section of Barbadian society.

Wes was overcome. It would be a privilege to serve, but he questioned his suitability: he was only 34 years old and, apart from exercising his right to vote, he had never been involved in the political process. Nor had he ever given politics much thought. He worried that his relative youth and lack of experience would hinder him: 'I was not a lawyer; how would I navigate the jargon in the various debates?' Unlike a senator who was expected to vote along party lines, it would be his responsibility to choose right from wrong before each vote in the Senate. Despite his uncertainties he placed his trust in the values that his mother had taught him. He was confident that his judgement would be guided by his conscience and what he felt was right. Above all, he relished the opportunity to make a meaningful contribution by helping to improve people's lives. Wes thanked the Governor-General for his kind words and the confidence he had placed in him and humbly accepted the appointment.

Later that evening Wes called his great friend and erstwhile teammate, Rawle Brancker, to tell him the news. Brancker chuckled: 'Blues, boy, you beat me to it!' He was about to call Wes to say that *he* had accepted the Governor-General's invitation to become an independent senator! For both, it was a wonderful feeling of *déjà vu* and reassurance to know that, just as they were at Combermere, they would be seated together for the next five years in the chamber of the upper house.

Combining his duties at Cable & Wireless and in parliament was made easier by the fact that the Senate sits for just 20 to 25 days a year. Nonetheless Wes was kept extremely busy, especially as he had acquired yet another role – in cricket administration. From 1970 to 1972 he was a member of the BCA board, and he also managed the West Indies team for the Test match against India in Barbados in April 1971. (At the time the board kept costs down by appointing a manager from the island where the Test was played; hence Wes held the position for one match only.)

Wes still found time in his hectic schedule to play cricket. After his final first-class match for Barbados against the Indians, he returned to captain the Cable & Wireless team in the BCA intermediate division. He had come full circle, back to where his adult cricketing career began so spectacularly; only now the fresh-faced rookie had become the decorated international star. One of his early matches produced a notable encounter.

Cable & Wireless faced Foundation School – a good side, considered slightly less strong than the main three high schools – and a young fast bowler, Joel 'Big Bird' Garner.

Cable & Wireless batted second and, with Garner inexplicably absent from Foundation's attack, Wes scored 148 to help his side establish a first-innings lead. Wes told Garner he should bowl in the second innings and soon regretted the advice: 'They set us 70 to win, and Bird bowled us out for 45!' In the manner of Wanderers' Billy Knowles 15 years earlier, Wes went straight to the management and urged them to employ 'this 18-year-old boy who would one day play for West Indies.' Shortly afterwards, Garner was enrolled at the Cable & Wireless training school in Dover, and the two of them were soon playing alongside each other in the company team. Wes once again donned pads and gloves and took his place behind the wicket to keep to Big Bird. The side was very successful, reaching the final of the knock-out cup competition in consecutive years, although they lost on both occasions to elite division opposition in the form of Empire and Police respectively. Interestingly Hall and Garner are the only players to progress to Barbados and West Indies straight from the BCA intermediate division.

Working for Banks Breweries and Managing West Indies
In December 1974 Ian Clark, the Managing Director of Banks Breweries Ltd, invited Wes to address the workforce at the company's Christmas lunch. Banks was one of the leading companies on the island and a member of the conglomerate, Barbados Shipping and Trading Company Limited (BS&T, also known as the 'Big Six'). Wes agreed and delivered a thought-provoking speech in which he emphasised the point that talent alone does not win championships in sport – or guarantee success in other walks of life – and must be augmented by a work ethic and discipline. His speech was extremely well received, and he enjoyed meeting the workers afterwards.

It had not occurred to Wes that there may have been an ulterior motive behind Banks' interest in him, and he was surprised to receive a follow-up invitation to lunch with Mr Clark. Mr D.J. Leacock, Chairman of Banks Breweries, was also present, and he got straight to the point: the management hierarchy at Banks had for some time been monitoring Wes's progress and had taken particular note of his performance as an independent in the Senate. With his employment background, Wes possessed all the credentials for the new post of Personnel and Public Relations Manager, and Mr Leacock offered him the job at their first meeting.

Wes had enjoyed four happy and successful years at Cable & Wireless and had no particular desire to leave the company. However, he had been very impressed by both men and by everything he had seen at Banks, especially the company's far-sighted commitment to initiatives which would benefit the community, including donations to schools' sporting and social programmes. Wes was interested in developing this aspect of the company's activities, and he also looked forward to the opportunity of utilising his skills in industrial relations when negotiating with the Barbados Workers' Union (BWU). He accepted Mr Leacock's offer and handed in his resignation to Cable & Wireless, who made it clear that they had no intention of standing in his way. He left with the company's blessings and was grateful to part company on such good terms. He even carried on playing for – and captaining – the Cable & Wireless cricket team.

Wes's personal life suffered a setback around this time. He had gone from being an international sportsman to a company executive, both very demanding and immersive careers requiring him to spend a great deal of time away from home. With his additional cricket and parliamentary responsibilities, the pressure told on his marriage, and he and Shurla divorced in 1976. Their third child Remi had been born in October 1974, and he and Kerry remained with their mother at the family home in Christ Church, while Sean lived with Wes.

At Banks the amalgamation of the personnel and PR functions into a single role gave Wes a far-reaching brief ranging from staff welfare to negotiations with unions. Mr Clark saw this as part of a new, professional approach to employee relations. The company was well-managed throughout, and Wes felt it was important that his newly created function fitted into the structure. He took responsibility for establishing an expansive base of knowledge and expertise – an 'institutional memory' – so that his department could begin contributing as quickly as possible to the smooth running of the company.

As the person in charge of negotiations with the BWU, Wes needed to be familiar with the workers and their roles in the company. In order to understand the business and learn the jargon, he took it upon himself to spend his first three months working the night shift in the brew-house, getting to know people and observing every detail of the brewing process. He encountered a skilled, highly motivated workforce, who appreciated his honesty. Christopher Walters, a brewhouse and cellar supervisor and union delegate, recalls 'a person true to himself and true to his friends. His attitude was the same toward management and the workers – often to the chagrin of some of the management!'

Wes can proudly boast that during his nine years at Banks there was never a strike nor any other form of industrial action. This was partly due to the enlightened approach of management which existed before he arrived: for example, workers were encouraged to offer their opinions and were rewarded when their suggestions were put into practice. As someone whose first instinct was always to ensure that the workers were treated fairly, Wes applauded such engagement with the workforce. At the same time he remained mindful of his responsibility to his employer and trod the line skilfully:

> I wasn't going to give a ten per cent wage increase for a two per cent argument. It was like cricket, you play it fair but tough; sometimes very tough, and I was looking for someone who would understand the company's ability to pay, and then we would be able to work together to look for ways to bridge the negotiable gap.

That person presented himself in the form of the BWU representative LeVere Richards: 'He was a strong man and a tough negotiator, but he was also very fair and rational.' Over the nine years Wes spent with Banks, he and Richards developed an outstanding working relationship. Every two years the two men headed negotiations and never failed to reach an amicable settlement, although neither allowed their mutual respect to interfere with their professional obligation to the people they represented. Banks was always satisfied with the agreements brokered by Wes, and the union appreciated his integrity. The process was helped by the open-door policy Wes adopted for the workers; they knew that he was fair at all times and were happy to work with him. He applied a simple philosophy wherever there was a need to manage people with differences: 'You have to be courteous and put yourself forward in a such a manner that people can deal with you. You have to go in with an open mind.' He received formal recognition of this when he was made an associate member of the BWU, and Wes and LeVere Richards remained good friends up until Richards' death in 2022.

With the welfare of workers his priority, Wes regularly counselled employees on money-management and encouraged them to invest part of their annual bonus in Banks shares. Those who took his advice realised healthy returns when the company was sold in 2015.

During the inaugural World Cup – played in England in 1975 – Wes suggested that production should be halted to allow workers to listen to the radio commentary; they could then make up the time by working late. Mr Clark gladly agreed, and 'the men were happy, it did a lot for morale', especially when West Indies, captained by Clive Lloyd, went on to lift the trophy. Wes also helped boost morale by forming a band to represent Banks at the annual Crop Over festival[3]. The two months of festivities reaches a climax with a lavish carnival parade on the first Monday in August – Kadooment Day – and the bandleader is responsible for organising a costumed band to take part. With his extrovert personality Wes was an ideal bandleader and, as well as winning a few prizes, they had great fun parading through the streets!

Banks was actively involved in numerous sports and, like Cable & Wireless, the company was deeply committed to cricket. Virtually every employee played cricket, and the company team was strong. A culture of cricket ran through the organisation and Wes, of course, was perfectly in accord with that ethos. As in many other areas, Mr Clark was the driving force behind the policy of recruiting cricketers:

> Mr Clark was a Scottish master brewer and a most amazing character and one of my heroes. He joined Banks in the company's infancy in 1961 as head brewer and invented several successful drinks. He was a man-manager and he loved sports, particularly cricket. He was well-known for employing cricketers: on Monday mornings he would tell me he had read

[3] The Crop Over Festival is a harvest festival, traditionally celebrating the end of the sugar cane harvest. It dates back to the 1780s when Barbados was the world's leading producer of sugar.

about a couple of players who performed very well in the BCA over the weekend and ask when I was going to interview them. And I would reply that the interviews were already set up! Clark would chuckle and continue to his office.

Such was Mr Clark's determination to raise Banks' profile that he employed numerous other famous Barbadian sportsmen, including cricket stars Vanburn Holder, Gordon Greenidge and Malcolm Marshall and the bodybuilder Darcy Beckles[4].

Wes thoroughly enjoyed working at Banks, and the company looked after him very well. A four-bedroom house within walking distance of the brewery was included in his employment package, and in 1979 he was granted six months study leave on an advanced course in Industrial Relations and Human Resource Management at the Industrial Society in London. This typified Mr Clark's – and Banks' – vision: 'It was a terrific job, working with genuinely good people.'

Wes was offered the position of tour manager for the 1983-84 West Indies tour of India, and Mr Clark was happy to grant him the time off. He took the view that having an employee in such a prestigious position could only reflect well on the company. This stance was supported by Mr Bert Banfield, who had taken over as chairman following Mr Leacock's retirement. In fact, this had long been company policy: like Wes, Clyde Walcott was employed as a personnel manager within the Big Six group of companies and had managed West Indies at World Cups and on tours.

Wes was thrilled at the prospect of being involved with Clive Lloyd's exciting world-champion Test team, but he needed to be satisfied that his absence would not cause too much difficulty for Banks. He was able to delegate much of the responsibility for public relations to his secretary Eunice but, before he left at the end of September, he made sure that he had reached agreement with the union in the wage negotiations: 'I would never have gone and left someone else to finish the negotiations, that would have been immoral.' Mr Clark then took responsibility for industrial relations, and Wes's decision to manage the team was an easy one. Sadly – in more ways than Wes realised at the time – Mr Clark retired in 1983 and returned to the UK.

[4] Bodybuilder Darcy Beckles won many regional and international competitions including the Mr World title.

The tour was a success. West Indies won the Test series 3-0 to consolidate their position as the number one team in the world. The managerial experience gained in his post-cricket career served Wes well in his new role. He took to the job quickly, helped by the fact that the team was settled and successful under the long-time captain Lloyd.

Andy Roberts missed the first four of the six Tests with injury. He had been the first of his generation of great West Indian fast bowlers, and it was clear that his distinguished career was nearing its end. However, he was still worthy of his place in the team, and his recovery in time for the Fifth Test in Calcutta raised the question of who should make way for him, with the other bowlers performing well as West Indies established a 2-0 lead in the series. The question was answered when one of them, pace bowler Wayne Daniel, revealed that he was suffering from a niggling injury. Roberts was brought in as his replacement and took four wickets in the match to help West Indies to an innings victory. He also excelled with the bat: his 68 was his highest score in Test cricket, and his ninth-wicket partnership of 161 with Lloyd still stands as a West Indies record. Wes had added cause to feel pleased for Roberts, who had arrived in India with 197 Test wickets to his name. Mindful of the insensitive treatment he had received at a similar point in his Test career, he did not want Roberts also to fall agonisingly short of 200 wickets: 'I felt good that Andy got his 200 Test wickets, as I knew what it would mean to him.'

In 1984 the WICB again asked Wes to manage the team, this time on the 1984-85 tour to Australia. He felt that the series was particularly important in the light of Clive Lloyd's announcement that he would retire from Test cricket after the Fifth Test in Sydney. As the captain of West Indies for ten years, Lloyd had masterminded the strategy of employing four fast bowlers to deliver a relentless pace onslaught. With an equally aggressive, high-quality batting line-up at his disposal, his West Indies team dominated world cricket. Obviously replacing him would be difficult. As a firm believer in the importance of succession planning within an organisation, Wes was keen to manage the team and to oversee the transition. The tour of Australia would allow him to assess the candidates and make an informed recommendation to the board:

> We needed to do things in a professional way by appointing the best man to captain the team, not like in the old days when we

chose him because we liked him, or because of the colour of his skin, or because he was the best player. Those things don't make a good captain.

As a matter of routine Wes sent his application for four months' unpaid leave to chief engineer Mr Les Debeger, who had replaced Ian Clark as Banks Breweries' general manager. With wage negotiations successfully concluded and not due to re-commence until 1986, Wes fully expected the board to grant permission as usual. However, his confidence was misplaced: under the new regime, managerial approval was no longer a formality, and the request was denied: 'It was obvious that I did not have the support of Mr Debeger.' Furthermore, Wes was told that if he went on the tour, his employment would be terminated. He contested the decision, pointing out to the chairman Mr Banfield the kudos to be gained by helping West Indian cricket. He cited numerous precedents: Clyde Walcott had been granted leave to manage West Indies on several occasions, including on the 1980 tour of England when Cammie Smith, another Big Six manager was his assistant. To add insult to injury, Smith's application to accompany the 1984-85 tour as assistant manager was approved! Wes drew attention to the inconsistency in company policy and asked for an explanation. None was forthcoming. He went even further and made sure that cover would be in place during his absence by enlisting the help of his friend Collis Blackman, a leading industrial relations expert, who pledged in writing to step in and deal with any problems that may arise – free of charge.

Banks' management still stood its ground. Totally exasperated, Wes confirmed that he was going to Australia and not even the threat of dismissal would change his decision. When Banks' treatment of Wes became widely known, it drew the ire of the cricket fraternity and public, with Sir Garry Sobers, Charlie Griffith and Rawle Brancker especially critical. His friend David Simmons[5], an eminent lawyer and chairman of the National Sports Council, wrote to Banks on Wes's behalf in an attempt to resolve the *impasse*. Faced with the company's continuing intransigence, a meeting was arranged between Banfield, Debeger, Wes and Simmons. Thanks to Simmons' efforts, Wes received assurances of

[5] D.A.C. Simmons (b. 1940) became Chief Justice of Barbados in 2002. He was knighted in 2001.

a satisfactory pay-out from Banks and wrote to the chairman accepting the terms of his departure. His final act was to thank the staff for their invaluable support during his 'nine wonderful years' at Banks.

Wes had made a great personal sacrifice to serve West Indies cricket, but he had no regrets. It was a privilege for him to manage a team still regarded by many as the greatest ever seen. West Indies' dominant form continued in Australia and, despite strained on-field relations with their hosts, they had remained popular with the Australian crowds, helped by the presence of the man described by Wisden as 'the affable Wesley Hall'.

Wes looks back with satisfaction on the part he played in the choice of Viv Richards as Lloyd's replacement as captain. Richards' position as vice-captain made him Lloyd's heir apparent. He had the support of selectors and players, and the tour confirmed Wes's belief that he was the right man to lead the world champions to further glory. Wes therefore recommended Richards unreservedly: 'The appointment of Richards may well have happened anyway, but I was glad if I influenced the decision.' Richards' captaincy would prove to be an unqualified success: between 1985 and 1991 West Indies did not lose any of his 13 series in charge. At Richards' request, Wes managed the first of those, the four-match home series against New Zealand in 1985 which West Indies won 2-0.

Before leaving for Australia, Wes had arranged to rent a house in Grazettes Gardens and, while he was away, his son Sean moved there from the Banks company house where they had lived for the previous decade. Arriving at the new house on his return from Australia was tangible confirmation to Wes that his Banks days were over. He was not the only person to feel sad: he had many friends at Banks, and it seemed nobody wanted him to leave or agreed with the decisions that led to his departure.

19

Member of Parliament and Government Minister

Wes's five-year term in the Senate ended following the 1976 general election. Governor-General Sir Winston Scott died in August of that year, and his acting replacement Sir William Douglas did not offer Wes a seat in the new parliament. Wes had never been particularly interested in joining a party and, as an independent senator, he had appreciated having the freedom to vote on each issue according to its merits. He entered debates with an open mind, listened to the speakers from both sides and based his decisions on the facts as they were presented. He therefore judged issues solely on his perception of what was right and voted accordingly: 'One day the people over there would hate me; the next day the other side would hate me, but they soon got used to it!'

The call from Errol Barrow to run for election
Wes's political career was reignited in 1981 by a call from Errol Barrow, the leader of the opposition DLP. The party had been ousted from power by the Barbados Labour Party (BLP) in 1976, and Barrow wanted Wes to join the DLP and stand as a candidate for a seat in the Assembly in the forthcoming election. Several factors discouraged Wes from accepting the offer: he had no strong affiliation to the DLP; and the general election was only six weeks away. Another obstacle existed in the shape of the incumbent member of parliament in the St Michael west-central constituency which Wes would contest. Vic Johnson was a government minister and an experienced, wily politician, 'a very good man and a formidable foe'.

After much thought Wes overcame the first objection, concluding that the DLP's ethos chimed closely with his belief that people from the proletariat had a positive role to play in the country's future. He had become aware of 'professional politicians', who were divorced from the ordinary people they were elected to represent, and he vowed that he would do things differently. However, the practical issues remained: in addition to the strength of the opponent, getting around the constituency and canvassing 7,000 people in six weeks was unfeasible. Wes turned down Barrow's request, but after discussing the matter with his old school friend Branford Taitt, himself an MP, he was persuaded to change his mind. He sought and received the approval of his employer, Banks, and stood for election. Taitt was an extremely skilled campaigner, and he promised to show Wes the ropes, free of charge. Although the odds were stacked heavily against him, Wes lost to Johnson by just 52 votes as the DLP again found itself in opposition. Having entered elective politics, Wes had declared his party allegiance and so could not be considered by the Governor-General for selection as one of the seven independent senators. With twelve of the remaining 14 seats in the Senate going to the BLP government, just two nominations remained for the DLP leader Errol Barrow. Encouraged by the energetic campaigning which had brought Wes so close to victory in a seemingly unwinnable contest, Barrow invited him to take up one of the seats. The other appointee was Evelyn Greaves[1], 'a marvellous politician, a strategist of the highest order'.

Together, the two of them performed magnificently in the Senate. They frustrated the government to such an extent that the Prime Minister Tom Adams changed the Senate's timings so that prime-time radio coverage no longer coincided with opposition speeches! Wes derived no particular pleasure from the filibustering tactics that he and Greaves employed – 'it was slightly underhand, yes' – but justified them on the grounds that just two seats in a 21-seat house was an unfair representation for his party.

This second term in the Senate did a great deal for Wes's political education. As an independent senator he had enjoyed being able to indulge his principles; now, the obligation to defend his party's stance taught him the pragmatism he would need to negotiate the cut-and-thrust of party politics.

> Some people were very disappointed in me because I gave up my independence, but really, when you are trying to get two sides together, the chances are you won't, all you can do is give your view. Barrow spoke to me a lot and I learned so much from him. He was a colossus.

His exit from Banks in late 1984 left Wes without a job for the first time since leaving school in 1955, and with no regular income he was forced to

[1] E.E. Greaves (1940-2018) served multiple terms as an MP and cabinet minister and was High Commissioner of Barbados to Canada from 2008.

use his savings to pay the rent and to buy a replacement for his company car. In the absence of any other employment, and with over a year to go before the 1986 general election, he decided he would contest the St Michael West Central seat for a second time. Unlike in 1981, when he had just six weeks to prepare, he would have the time to give himself the best chance of being elected to parliament. He spent the year canvassing his constituency, a very densely populated area, delivering the message that he would always be there to fight for his electorate.

Branford Taitt again devoted hours of his time to helping Wes, despite having to defend his own seat in the neighbouring constituency of St Michael South West. He offered plenty of vote-winning advice, including the need to keep records of his constituents and to prepare by researching the families in the street he was about to canvass. Above all, Taitt stressed that an MP must always be available to his constituents and that, as their representative, he should put their needs before his own. In a slightly Machiavellian aside, he made the point to Wes that this would pay dividends only if he was noticed. For instance, attending the funeral of a constituent and sitting at the back is pointless: 'Make sure everybody sees you!' Coming from such an honourable man, this amused Wes and left him in no doubt that he was in good hands: 'So much of what I learned about politics and the way it worked came from Branford Taitt; from encouraging me to go into politics to going on the campaign trail, he was there with me.'

The differences between the two main political parties in Barbados were far less marked than in most western democracies. The DLP was founded in 1955 when Errol Barrow led a number of BLP members in a breakaway to form a more people-orientated alternative; hence the ideologies of both parties are rooted in common socialist principles. Electoral success was therefore often determined by the popularity of the candidate, and Wes set out with a vision and zeal which endeared him to voters. Having established a reputation as a free spirit who acted on his conscience, Wes was able to convince people that they could rely on him to act with integrity. His message was simple and irresistible, and he enjoyed being of service.

With ample time to make sure that everyone was aware of his philosophy and policies, Wes trudged the streets for days on end, knocking on every door in St Michael West Central. He outlined his priorities: job creation; investing in decent housing; increased security so that all citizens could feel safe; and the provision of recreational facilities. Wes was rewarded with spectacular success, defeating Johnson by over 1,000 votes in the 1986 general election, a result that he would repeat (with a slightly reduced majority) in 1991: 'I knew that having won once, I would do the job right and win again.' Thus began eight years as an elected MP.

The call from Errol Barrow to serve as a minister

Wes's success in 1986 was replicated by DLP candidates across the island as the party regained power with a landslide victory, winning 24 of the 27 seats. Again Errol Barrow – this time as prime minister – had bold plans for Wes. He asked him to be a minister in the new DLP government. Given Wes's background in industrial relations and cricket it made sense when Barrow put him in charge of both the Ministry of Labour and the Ministry of Sport. The work would be demanding, but Wes was happy to be involved in areas so close to his heart. He was less prepared when the Prime Minister went a step further and made him Minister of Community Development – known colloquially as 'social cement' – with responsibility for youth development and old age welfare. Like Worrell and Pantin before him, Barrow identified special qualities in Wes, whose maxim 'What is life, if not a life of service?' was about to be tested to the full. He considers himself fortunate to have had as his parliamentary secretary Ms Maizie Baker-Welch (now Dame Maizie), who brought a wealth of experience in the areas of women's development and youth and senior citizens' affairs.

Barrow's admiration for Wes was reciprocated. The 'Father of Independence' had man-management skills to rival Frank Worrell: 'He was a born leader. He made decisions when they needed to be made, and more than 70 per cent of the time he was right.'

One of Wes's more satisfying accomplishments during his first year as a minister was to introduce an official Labour Day in Barbados. Hitherto, the first Monday in May was workers' day, but BWU representatives put the case to Wes that 1 May should be officially declared a public holiday. The idea appealed to him both as a religious man and as a proud member of the proletariat. Noting God's example in putting Adam in the Garden of Eden to work the land and allowing Joseph – a carpenter – to be the earthly father of Jesus, Wes gladly agreed to the union's request, as it was an important reminder of the dignity of labour.

The first year as an elected MP and cabinet minister was a good one for Wes. He felt honoured that people had put their trust in him and considered him worthy of representing them. St Michael West Central was a constituency of contrasts with some serious social issues, home to affluent residents living in large houses and those for whom life was a struggle. It was vital to Wes that he should be accessible, and he moved into a house in his constituency with his son Sean and daughter Kerry.

On 1 June 1987, three days after the DLP had celebrated its first year in office, Barbadian politics – and indeed Barbados – was rocked by the news that Errol Barrow had collapsed and died at *Kampala*, his beach house close to Paradise Beach Club in St Michael. Wes was in Switzerland at a labour conference when Deputy Prime Minister Erskine Sandiford[2] was sworn in as Barbados' fourth prime minister later the same day. He implemented a cabinet reshuffle, and among the new appointments Wes was given the job of Minister of Tourism and Sport. It was an inspired move on the part of Sandiford, amalgamating the two ministries with a view to developing 'sports tourism', whereby sport would be used as a vehicle to encourage tourism, the island's leading export. Among other things it was hoped that by scheduling sporting events outside the most popular months, the scheme would reduce the seasonal fluctuations in tourist activity and lead to increased overall revenue.

Wes was very happy with his new role, which presented him with a great opportunity 'to do something special for the people of Barbados'. Unfortunately, not everyone on the island shared his enthusiasm for his appointment. As the engine of growth in the island's economy, tourism was of paramount importance to Barbados, and some prominent individuals openly questioned the wisdom in handing over responsibility to 'a cricketer'. Wes was dismayed by the insults. Most of what he had accomplished since his playing days had been informed by lessons he learned from cricket, and many cricketers before him had achieved great success in other fields. With his humble beginnings, he could only imagine that his detractors were motivated by classism. Whatever the reason, the negative comments were proved to be hopelessly wide of the mark by Wes's performance over his seven years in charge of the ministry.

[2] L.E. Sandiford (b. 1937), a career politician, became the fourth prime minister of Barbados in 1987 and was knighted in 2002.

With the two ministries combined, Wes would need to orchestrate strategy relating to both sport and tourism. Success would be dependent on sectorial linkages: an increase in visitor numbers would have to be matched by infrastructure developments and a greater food supply, whether home-produced or imported. Manufacturing, health, agriculture and transport were all essential to the continued expansion in tourism and should therefore grow at the same pace. This would allow the economy to develop in a balanced, sustainable way which would also improve the living standards of the local population.

Wes soon discovered that the sporting infrastructure was woefully lacking, and he made it a priority to allocate funds to the development of facilities throughout the island, continuing a programme of building new cricket pavilions and upgrading existing ones in every parish. The showpiece was the gymnasium and multi-sports complex at Wildey on the outskirts of Bridgetown. With the agreement of its Chinese financial backers, the gymnasium was originally planned as a 2,500-seater venue. Delisle Bradshaw, who held several ministerial portfolios in the previous BLP administration, had been instrumental in promoting the concept of the gym, and Wes credits him with doing a good job in early negotiations with the Chinese. However, Wes focused on the longer-term future of the centre, and was more ambitious in his plans. In his opinion, Barbados needed a sports facility with a capacity of 5,000 seats; also, he favoured the idea of two 50-metre swimming pools instead of one. He asked a visiting Chinese delegation to increase the level of funding and eventually received the go-ahead more than a year later: 'People got nervous during that time, but I turned the sod and I opened it in 1992.'

Among the many sports catered for at the complex – named the Sir Garfield Sobers Gymnasium – was tennis. Wes had never played the game in his life and, much to his discomfort, it fell to him to deliver the ceremonial first serve at the opening of the new court. As he dutifully tossed the ball up, he joked to the audience, 'This is how Arthur Ashe does it'. Nobody was more surprised than Wes when he served an ace! Mr Peter Symonds, president of the Barbados Lawn Tennis Association, asked him to repeat the feat, but Wes declined: 'I retired with a 100 per cent record!'

The opening ceremony in November 1992 was a colourful affair. Wes booked the gospel singer Paula Hinds to perform at the event, and he was delighted when Gregory Armstrong, the former Barbados and Glamorgan fast bowler, used his contacts to secure the services of the inimitable Harlem Globetrotters, who captivated the audience with their dazzling basketball skills.

Wildey provides floodlit football and hockey facilities with artificial turf pitches, and it caters for numerous other sports, including cricket, volleyball and basketball. Upkeep of the gymnasium has been a priority for successive governments, and the site has developed into a multi-use venue capable of hosting concerts, exhibitions and conferences. It is also the headquarters of the Barbados Olympic Association. Wes derives much satisfaction from what he accomplished at Wildey: 'It's a thing of beauty, and I am very proud of it. Every time I pass there, it makes me feel good!'

South Africa's exile from international cricket lasted from March 1970, after the Test against Australia in Port Elizabeth, until the process of dismantling the apartheid regime was under way in 1991. Their reintroduction into world cricket came in a series of three ODI matches in India in October and November, and they were due to participate in the World Cup in Australia in February and March 1992. Nelson Mandela, a fervent cricket fan, was very keen that his country's return to Test cricket should be against West Indies in the Caribbean. Wes was equally enthusiastic, and as Minister of Tourism and Sport he was in a position to help make it happen.

The world cricket community may have been satisfied that the time was right for South Africa's readmittance, but the visit of a South African team to the Caribbean was a very delicate issue, and Wes wanted to be sure that sufficient progress had been made. Sir Garry Sobers and the president of the Barbados National Olympic Committee, Austin Sealy[3], visited South Africa and provided positive feedback, and a short tour of the Caribbean was arranged for April 1992. A single Test match in Barbados would follow three one-day internationals, one in Kingston and the other two in Port of Spain. West Indies won all three of the one-day matches, and the teams travelled to Barbados for the climax of the tour. Wes was

---

[3] A.L. Sealy (b. 1939) served as a distinguished sports administrator from 1970. He was Barbados' ambassador to the United Kingdom and Israel in the 1990s and continues to practise as a business consultant. He was knighted in 2015.

called into action before the mini-tour had even begun: the South African contingent did not have the required entry visas, and so he went to the airport to personally sign in each member of the party.

On 18 April 1992 South Africa's first Test match for 22 years took place at Kensington Oval. West Indies triumphed by 52 runs in a match dominated by South Africa until they their last eight wickets for just 25 runs, with Curtly Ambrose and Courtney Walsh taking all ten wickets between them.

Wes is proud to have played an active role in facilitating this historic occasion. Naturally he abhorred apartheid, and being involved in organising one of the events marking the end of the regime meant a great deal to him. He salutes the will and commitment of Dr Ali Bacher[4] and all those who were involved[5].

Without question Wes's greatest achievements in government were in the field of tourism, confounding the critics who questioned his suitability as custodian of the islands 'crown jewels'.

Every year one of the biggest challenges a minister faces is meeting the Minister of Finance to defend the allocation of funds for his or her ministry. In his first year Wes and his team at the Ministry of Tourism and Sport successfully argued their case and negotiated an increase in funding, enabling them to travel extensively to promote the Barbados tourist industry at overseas conferences and exhibitions. Wes played a major role on these marketing trips, where he eschewed the ministerial limousine and instead travelled with the marketing and sales staff on the 'team bus'. The results were spectacular and, although statistics do not tell the whole story, record visitor numbers are a good indication of his success: in 1989, two years into Wes's tenure, Barbados recorded over 460,000 long-stay arrivals, an all-time high and an increase of 90,000 on the year before he became minister. The breakdown of the figures reflected the work he had done. His first act as minister – after consulting his permanent secretary and senior members of the Barbados tourist board – had been to re-open the Barbados tourism office in Germany: within

---

[4] Dr Aron 'Ali' Bacher (b. 1942) is a former South African Test captain. He was the first director of the United Cricket Board of South Africa when it was formed in 1991.

[5] Bacher worked tirelessly to re-integrate South African cricket. In 1991 he and Steve Tshwete, the head of the sports desk of the African National Congress, combined to lobby successfully for the readmission of South Africa into the ICC.

four years the German market trebled to almost 66,000. His promotional drive in the UK targeted new areas such as Wales and Yorkshire, and this led to Britain contributing the greatest numerical increase in visitors, up from 47,000 in 1986 to 118,000 in 1989. Cruise ship visitors increased by almost 90 per cent to 430,000 over his seven years as minister, and in addition to quantity he addressed the issue of quality (in terms of visitor spending) by encouraging them to visit attractions and events on the island. Wes ensured that complaints from visitors were taken seriously but also took the opportunity at the annual Tourism Week to remind hotel and ancillary workers of the difference between service and servitude.

The Gulf War of 1991 and world economic recession had a disastrous effect on an already struggling Barbados economy, not least its tourist industry. With a drastically reduced budget, Wes faced a different type of challenge, yet he succeeded in motivating his staff in Barbados and marketing teams abroad to such an extent that by the time he left office in 1993, numbers had recovered to close to their peak levels. Contrary to the opinions of his detractors, his fame as a popular sportsman was an asset.

In the early 1990s there was a growing clamour to provide casinos in Barbados, with many people believing that gambling would attract more visitors to the island. However, the idea was at odds with Wes's Christian beliefs, and he resisted in the face of mounting pressure in parliament. When challenged to come up with alternatives, he struggled to find an argument which did not make him appear self-righteous until – in a moment of inspiration – he announced that he wanted to promote 'wholesome tourism', a phrase which is still in use to describe faith-based tourism. Nobody was likely to criticise an initiative linking tourism with healthy pursuits, and the concept fitted his sports tourism brief. He had the idea of holding an annual festival celebrating the Christian faith, timed to coincide with one of the major public holidays in the USA so as to attract large numbers of Americans. Assisted by an organising committee, Wes took charge of coordinating the event. He wrote to all the denominations in Barbados asking for their support, and the committee invited several overseas gospel singers and preachers to perform at the inaugural 'Gospelfest', to be held at the Wildey gymnasium in May 1993. Among them was the famous American gospel singer and television star, Dr Bobby Jones, whose participation was a major coup and gave the event instant credibility. Wes happily obliged when Jones asked if room could be found in the schedule for a young Texan singer called Kirk Franklin. Franklin captivated the audience and went on to top the charts shortly afterwards. As a gesture of his gratitude, he waived his usual fee when he appeared at the second Gospelfest. He has since become a leading name in gospel music.

Gospelfest has been staged every year since 1993, when approximately 2,000 overseas visitors attended. Responsibility for organising the event was passed on to a committee chaired by Adrian Agard, under whose guidance it has grown in stature to become a highlight of the island's social and cultural calendar. Gospelfest now occupies a week in May running up to the US Memorial Day holiday and features gospel talent in the fields of drama, dance and comedy as well as music. The festival attracts large crowds to shows across multiple venues, with attendances in excess of 10,000 not uncommon for some of the concerts. The official Gospelfest website proudly proclaims the scale of the event, with artists and visitors drawn from all over the world; it also recognises that 'the festival was the brainchild of the then Minister of Tourism, Wes Hall.'

Since the mid-1980s a scheduled Concorde service from London to Barbados had been a significant factor in the development of the island's tourism industry. Barbadians were proud of Bridgetown's status as one of only four regular destinations in the western hemisphere, along with London, Paris and New York. When British Airways was rumoured to be considering withdrawing the service in the early 1990s, Calvin Hope, Barbados' Assistant Sales Manager for Tourism in London, arranged a meeting there between Wes and the company chairman, Lord King. During the early-morning meeting Wes employed his diplomatic skills to successfully plead the case for Barbados, and Concorde continued to fly to the island until the plane was withdrawn completely in 2003. As an acknowledgement of the part played by Barbados in Concorde's story, one of the aircraft resides next to the airport as the centrepiece of the Barbados Concorde Experience.

Of his numerous trips, one to London in 1992 is especially memorable. It featured a cricket match in which a combined Commons and Lords team took on a West Indian side made up of politicians and former cricketers, captained of course by Wes! In a distinctly uneven contest,

Sobers celebrated reaching his half-century by hitting three consecutive sixes off the bowling of MP Bill Cash, prompting a rueful comment from Cash in his after-dinner speech that evening: 'Sir Garry, I'd just like to say that to bowl at you is the highlight of my cricket career. I also want you to know that my name is Cash, not Nash[6]!' On that visit to London, Wes had the honour of addressing the House of Commons. By then, having spent many years in the Barbados Parliament, he was a seasoned public speaker, but nothing he had experienced previously compared to the excitement he felt that day when he spoke in Westminster.

Wes was an extremely capable and successful government minister, who worked unrelentingly to serve his people and his country. Ministers did not enjoy the luxury of a holiday, yet he brought the same enthusiasm and energy to the office every day. He struck a balance between leading from the front and delegating responsibility to his trusted staff. His kindness and approachability inspired their loyalty, and they still talk of him fondly. Wes made friends too numerous to mention but particularly wishes to acknowledge his secretary, Mrs Cecile Cummins, 'for her outstanding patience and dedication to duty', and two permanent secretaries, Lionel Weekes and Edward Layne, 'for the work they did for me and Barbados – they were the best in the business!'

---

[6] Batting for Nottinghamshire against Glamorgan in 1968, Sobers made cricket history when he hit all six deliveries of a Malcolm Nash over for six.

20

The Greatest Call to Serve

The fifth of his mother's pivotal life-lessons came more than 30 years after the previous one, when her reassuring words had inspired him following the disappointments of the 1957 England tour. In 1988, as Minister of Tourism and Sport, Wes led a drive to incentivise Barbadian expatriates in Britain to promote Barbados as a tourist destination. Participants would visit areas outside London which previously had not been targeted, and rewards would be offered based on results. During an event to publicise the initiative, a young lady asked Wes a couple of routine questions, followed by a comment that could hardly have been more incendiary: 'You seem to be very good with these middle-class people, returning nationals ... I just wonder how you would be with poor people.' To challenge him in this way guaranteed a hostile response. He reminded her in no uncertain terms that he was from the proletariat and that he was the only government minister who had lived in government housing.

Wes was unaware that the occasion – including his angry outburst – was being televised, and so he was surprised the next day when his mother confronted him over his behaviour. After commenting that the man she saw on TV was not the boy she raised, she delivered her simple verdict: 'What you really need is to have Jesus in your life.'

Wes protested that he had been provoked by an insensitive remark, but his mother refused to accept that as an excuse. He quietly left her house and, although they lived only a few hundred yards apart, they did not see each other for three weeks, when his mother eventually broke the ice by bringing him a meal. In the meantime Wes had thought about her words a great deal. He began to doubt that he was as good a person as he had previously thought. Maybe he upset people. Maybe he was ignoring the advice she gave him after his first day at Combermere when she urged him to be 'better, not bitter'. Whichever was the case, she had laid the foundations for the most meaningful event in his life.

The call to serve God

Shortly after that unsettling incident, Wes led a delegation on a 'sports tourism fusion' trip to Miami, Florida. Always ready for a good time, he arranged a party to boost the rapport between the Barbadian contingent and their hosts. With the help of his good friend Colin Mayers, Barbados' Consul-General in Miami, Wes organised the food and drink, a sound system and music. The event was to be held in the Barbadians' hotel, The Marriott Miami Downtown, on the Sunday evening. It promised to be a busy day: at the invitation of Marjorie Nelly, one of the American netball officials, the entire group was to attend the morning service at her church, The New Way Assembly. The preacher's sermon was based on Chapter 3 of the Book of Philippians: 'Everything I have gained is a loss when compared to the surpassing greatness of knowing Christ my Saviour. I want to know Christ and the power of His resurrection.'

Wes found the message profoundly moving. Tears filled his eyes as his mother's voice repeated: 'You need Jesus in your life.'

> Boy, it hit me so hard! It propelled me to the altar to give my life to God. That is the day I was saved, and the realisation dawned that through God's grace, He had done for me what I could not do for myself. I asked God to forgive my sins and promised that I would serve Him in spirit and in truth as long as I live. It is the most amazing thing to happen to me – truly something supernatural, as the feeling of untold happiness and
> peace rested on my heart and filled me up.

Wes decided not to attend the party: 'I asked my permanent secretary and the consul-general to supervise the event. The rest of the visit to Miami became a blur.'

The bishops at the church, Billy and Catherine Baskin, invited Wes to their home for lunch and spent the rest of the day counselling him and helping him to understand the gravity of what he had experienced at the altar. They issued him with an open invitation to stay with them whenever he was in Miami.

The immediacy of the change was overwhelming, and the usually gregarious Wes returned to Barbados a regenerated, pensive man. He joined an evangelical Pentecostal church, The Abundant Life Assembly, situated in Bank Hall, St Michael, a few hundred yards north of Empire

Cricket Club. He became a regular in the congregation and would sit at the back of the church so as not to draw attention to himself or cause a distraction.

The pastor and founder of the church, Reverend William Cuke, spent many hours talking to Wes. Equally supportive was Bishop Dr Lionel Clarke, a Combermerian school friend who also served as permanent secretary to Wes in the government: 'He was my boss in church, and I was his boss in government!' Bishop Clarke had for many years been the pastor at Bethel Evangelical Church in Grazettes, where his mother and grandmother had worshipped since their move to the area in 1958.

Committing himself to God entailed major changes for Wes: the role of minister of tourism and sport required him to attend countless meetings and social gatherings. Furthermore, he enjoyed this aspect of the work and, by his own admission, 'the essence of my existence was life in the fast lane'.

> Jesus had a divine nature and a human nature, but he did not sin. I have only a human nature. I knew, therefore, that I could not let my humanness get in the way of my godliness. This imperative of change was the test that I had to overcome. And I did.

When he was a young man, cricket had provided him with a welcome opportunity to escape the strict church regimen imposed by his mother and grandmother:

> I see now that God was always there for me, every day of my life. God did not move; I moved! I let go of the scarlet thread, but I picked it up again and found my way back to Him. Though I did not know it, God saw all my imperfections, and He understood my needs. Since I gave my life to God in 1988, I have tried my best to be Christ-like and to walk the 'Christian walk', I have constantly striven to lead a better life.

Many of Wes's friends were sceptical about his new-found faith and doubted his ability to fully commit to God. Some gave him weeks; some months, but more than 30 years later he has never wavered, and his real friends have a more genuine love and deeper regard for Wes.

Having responded to the life-changing call from God, Wes began preparing to be a representative of Christ while working as a government minister. He travelled regularly to the USA to see the Baskins, and one evening over dinner Bishop Billy dropped a bombshell by asking him to deliver the sermon in church the following morning. Wes protested that it was too soon, but Billy told him that he had been instructed by God. Desperate for a reprieve, he turned to Catherine, but she nodded in agreement with her husband: 'That's right, Wes: you should do it.' The next morning, he delivered the sermon, the first of many on his visits to Miami. The Baskins were also happy to support Wes by accepting his invitation to attend the first Gospelfest along with a contingent from their church.

After his experiences in Miami, Wes preached at various churches in Barbados, and on each occasion his mother was in attendance. She derived enormous joy from knowing that her son had let Jesus into his life and that he was not afraid or ashamed to boldly preach the gospel wherever and whenever he was asked to do so ... such as at Bethel Evangelical Church on 25 December 1993! He was becoming more confident in the pulpit; nevertheless, when Bishop Clarke asked him to deliver his first Christmas morning sermon, he was slightly apprehensive. This was his mother's church, and the occasion guaranteed a packed congregation. Wes asked Bishop Clarke why he had chosen the Christmas sermon. The bishop replied: 'Your mother told me you are ready.'

When Wes saw his mother that Christmas morning, she was resplendent in a turquoise dress and a tan hat. He recalls that 'she was radiant, she was beaming and so happy'. He paused the sermon to draw the congregation's attention to her appearance and drew on a biblical analogy:

> Old Simeon, who, having taken the infant Jesus in his arms, gave thanks to God, saying 'Lord, now lettest Thou Thy servant depart in peace, according to Thy word, for mine eyes have seen Thy salvation, which Thou hast prepared before the face of all people.

Eleven days later, on 5 January 1994, Ione died suddenly of a heart attack. Obviously Wes was devastated and also troubled by the apparent prescience of his words on Christmas Day. Over time reason allowed him to dispel these thoughts, and he was satisfied that his mother had departed this earth in peace.

The bishops were impressed by Wes's sermons and began facilitating his path towards ordination. Finally, in 1998, following completion of his theological studies, he was ready to be ordained. The ceremony was to be held at New Way Assembly ten years after that fateful Sunday there. Bishops Billy and Catherine Baskin would proclaim him a Minister of the Gospel. Reverend Cuke chose Reverend Basil Yarde to travel to Miami as the representative of Abundant Life Assembly.

Wes was happy that Reverend Yarde, 'an amazing singer', was to take part in the ordination programme, witnessed by Colin Mayers and other friends and church members. A regular service was first held in the packed church, and then Reverend Yarde provided the link between the service and the ordination, singing the chosen song, *I Pledge Allegiance to the Lamb*, written by the American singer/songwriter Ray Boltz.

Wes describes the atmosphere, and the unforgettable experience of the anointing:

> His powerful, spirit-filled rendition rang through the hushed congregation and touched every person present, as the Holy Spirit moved throughout the room. It was as if God Himself was orchestrating the perfect precursor of what was to follow. The prayers from the two bishops, Billy and Catherine Baskin, further heightened the charged atmosphere; everyone was praising God, and the presence of the Lord filled the room – the *sine qua non* of worship. I did not have a beard like Aaron, but the moment the oil was poured on my head and flowed over the side of my face and all the way down into my shoes, it was an out-of-body experience. More dream-like than when I walked to the altar and gave my life to God ten years before – this was not just 'giving', it was total surrender; total commitment to a life of service to God. I have felt the presence of the crowd on cricket fields all over the world, calling out my name and trying to get close to touch me. I have felt the presence of the crowd during political campaigns cheering me on; but there was no comparison to feeling the presence of the Lord in that congregation.

During the ceremony, the prophecy was spoken over Wes that he would travel all over the world to preach. This took him by surprise: 'I am no Billy Graham; I must admit I was a little disappointed, because I had hopes of settling into service at Abundant Life Assembly.' However, he soon started receiving calls and letters inviting him to travel and preach throughout the Caribbean, the UK, USA and Australia. He was now officially a servant of the Lord.

Before embarking on his travels, Wes was invited by Dr Lionel Clarke to preach at the Easter Sunday morning service at Bethel Evangelical Church. Fittingly the first sermon since his ordination was to be held in his constituency, at the church attended by his mother, grandmother and aunt.

Wes had known Reverend Cuke long before joining Abundant Life Assembly in 1988: 'He was a humble man and a useful leg-spin bowler who had played for Wanderers Cricket Club.' When invited to speak in his praise at a Pastor Appreciation Service, Wes spoke of his gratitude for the guidance and kindness the pastor had extended to him over the years. Reverend Cuke's thank-you letter to Wes included an amusing message: 'When a great leg-spinner combines with a great fast bowler, we will never be beaten!'

Shortly after his ordination in 1998, Wes accompanied Reverend Dr Lucille Baird on her regular prison ministry visits to Glendairy Prison. He tried to encourage inmates to develop a vision for their future, to write it down so that it becomes more real, and to come up with strategies to help them achieve it. As an extension of the ministry, he offered counselling to inmates, and he also included Desmond Haynes to help with the cricket coaching sessions. Wes shared with the prisoners the lessons that had helped him through difficult times in his life. Successes were gratifying, such as when an impeccably dressed man came over to him at a service station, smiled and said: 'Nobody can make me inferior without my permission.' He was quoting the words that Wes had first heard from his mother and which he had passed on to the prisoners. The man had followed Wes's advice and, after leaving prison, he had worked hard and established his own successful tour business.

In 2000 Wes was invited to preach at St Martin-in-the-Fields church in Trafalgar Square in London, at a service to commemorate the 100th anniversary of the first West Indies tour of England. He shared the duties with the Bishop of Liverpool, Lord David Sheppard, the former England Test cricketer. The two had met on the cricket field just once, in MCC's tour match against Queensland in November 1962, and Sheppard had enjoyed the better fortunes on that occasion. He opened the batting against Wes and scored 94 as MCC posted a huge total. Nevertheless, Sheppard's sermon reflected the feelings of the many batsmen who had experienced Wes bearing down on them from 22 yards:

> I just wish to tell you that I am so pleased to see Wes here today. As I see him in his cassock and his surplice and his collar, I want to say he looks like an angel. But don't be fooled: with a cricket ball in his hand, he's a devil!

Wes was continually in demand to preach in Barbados and overseas. This was partly due to his celebrity status, of course, but increasingly he built a reputation as a compelling speaker whose sermons were sincere, inspirational and amusing. In the last 30 years he has read the eulogy at every funeral on his father's side of the family and those of numerous prominent figures from the cricket world including Malcolm Marshall, Roy Gilchrist, Sir Clyde Walcott and more recently Tony Cozier, Seymour Nurse and his best friend Rawle Brancker.

The day before Cozier died, he asked Wes to conduct the service at his funeral. Wes promised to deliver the sermon but regretted that he would be unable to perform the sentencing due to his own ill-health at the time. Cozier's response was emphatic: 'No, I want you to do everything. You can do it; I know you can.' He was right. Wes's heartfelt salute to his friend concluded with a stirring farewell:

> So Tono, as you repose in your mahogany silence, let the records show that we love you and will never forget you. Oh, warrior of words, you have written your name on history's page. So, go to the plan that God has for you. A plan holier than any prophet can describe. A plan greater than the best minds can conceive and richer than human language can explore. May you rest in peace and rise in glory.

Reverend Dr Ivan Broomes, the senior pastor at Abundant Life Assembly, appointed Wes an associate minister at the church in 2003, a position he held until retirement in 2012. Since then, in his continuing efforts to serve God, he has discovered a welcome benefit of old age:

> When you're getting old, your physical attributes wane. Your mental faculties wane: I can remember all the words of *She*

Stoops to Conquer, which I learned over 70 years ago, but I can't remember if I fed my dogs this morning. But when it comes to your spirituality, as you grow older, you develop spiritual muscles, and you are a lot stronger ... If you are a Christian, you are able to deal with things that otherwise would lick you. You gain spiritual strength.

21

Meeting Nelson Mandela and Farewell to Politics

A highlight of Wes's time as tourism minister came in February 1993. South Africa was hosting a triangular series of ODIs featuring Pakistan and West Indies, and Wes was a member of the West Indian delegation for the team's match against Pakistan at Wanderers Stadium in Johannesburg. The occasion was charged with emotion, and the stadium erupted when Nelson Mandela was introduced. Mandela's entourage then made its way towards the crowded VIP area where he was to meet some of the dignitaries, including Wes and Al Gilkes[1], the man who brought this story to light.

Wes was hoping to get the chance to deliver a letter to Mandela from the Governor-General of Barbados, Dame Nita Barrow[2], who had campaigned against apartheid for many years and visited him in prison. He need not have worried. As Mandela started to make his way through the crowd, he looked up and his eyes fixed on Wes. He smiled and cried out, 'Is that the great Wes Hall?!' before rushing to embrace a bemused Minister of Tourism and Sport. Wes handed over the letter and opened the conversation by expressing his sympathy that Mandela's incarceration would have prevented him from indulging his love of watching cricket and following many of the great West Indian players. Mandela's reply was unexpected. He explained that he may not have been able to see his 'comrades' during his 27 years in prison, but he had read about their exploits. As he reeled off a succession of great names from Headley – via Hall, of course – to Richards, it was clear that the West Indies cricket team was a source of immense pride to him.

He was pleased that Wes had been taken by Ali Bacher to see some of the promising young cricketers in Soweto, and he paid tribute to

---

[1] Al Gilkes is the head of a public relations and communications company and contributes a regular column in *The Nation* newspaper.

[2] R.N. Barrow (1919-1995) was appointed the first female Governor-General of Barbados in 1990. She was the elder sister of former prime minister Errol Barrow.

the excellent work of Conrad Hunte, whose role as South African cricket's National Development Coach involved youth coaching in the townships.

Mandela noted that Wes was minister of sports and tourism in Barbados; he was extremely interested in the fusion of the two and the concept of sports tourism which Wes had done so much to promote. Their conversation far overran the allotted five minutes but, before his staff finally managed to move him on, he requested Wes's business card, hugged him and promised he would be in touch: 'Sport can change the world. Sport has more power than politics, for sport can build bridges between nations that politics cannot.' His enthusiasm was inspirational. As a minister whose brief included sport, these words from a world leader-in-waiting[3] filled Wes with optimism.

The encounter with Mandela left a lasting impression on Wes:

> Like Muhammad Ali, this great man didn't talk to me as if he was the star and I was the doorman, he talked to me as a person. He was down to earth and dignified. Meeting him was one of the highlights of my life. I knew that I was in the presence of greatness.

Wes's political career ended in controversial circumstances. He resigned from the cabinet in February 1994, citing 'a fundamental difference' with the Prime Minister, Erskine Sandiford. After the retirement in 1993 of Mrs Patricia Nehaul, Director of the Barbados Tourist Board, the board changed its name to the Barbados Tourism Authority, a statutory board, and Section 9 of the Act establishing the authority stated that 'the Authority shall, with the approval of the minister, appoint the CEO and the Deputy CEO.'

The following is Wes's account of events:

> I have no desire whatever to cause any distress to Prime Minister Sandiford or his family by regurgitating events which gave none of us any pleasure, so I shall not dilate upon the circumstances that led to a motion of no confidence. Briefly, what happened was this:
>
> The directors of the Barbados Tourism Authority, for which I was responsible, made a recommendation to fill two

[3] Mandela became the first democratically elected and the first non-white president of South Africa in May 1994.

vacancies, those of CEO and Deputy CEO. I approved the Board of Directors' recommendation of Mr Tony Arthur – the Director of Marketing – to act as CEO until they found a suitable replacement. Prime Minister Sandiford gave the 'green light' to advertise the vacancies and ten persons were interviewed. Among the four who were shortlisted, Tony Arthur was number three. In the meantime, a senior civil servant, Mrs Avril Gollop, was seconded to the authority, and she wrote to me saying that she was 'advised to inform me that a Miss Sylvia Lynch would be acting as Deputy CEO of the new Barbados Tourism Authority.'

The board then hired the Barbados Institute of Management and Productivity (BIMAP) to carry out an executive search for suitable replacements of CEO and Deputy CEO, with my approval. Following the executive search, Mr Hudson Husbands and Sylvia Lynch were selected. Again I supported the board's decision and submitted the two names to cabinet for approval. A few weeks later, I left for South Africa to meet with Nelson Mandela, and during my absence Prime Minister Sandiford acted as Minister of Tourism. I returned to find that he had fired the entire Board of Directors and was in the process of selecting a new one. The Prime Minister's action was very embarrassing for me. I thought it was an injustice to the members of the board who had shared the accomplishments of the previous seven years.

Prime Minister Sandiford refused to agree to the recommendation that Hudson Husbands be appointed CEO but approved the appointment of Sylvia Lynch as Deputy CEO. He then shuffled me out of the Ministry of Tourism and into one with disparate and disconnected subjects such as transport and public works, labour and industrial relations, community development, welfare, family and youth affairs and sports.

Evelyn Greaves succeeded me as Minister of Tourism, but there was still no tourism CEO. The board of directors sought applicants and, after a rigorous process, made a recommendation for Cecil Miller (now deceased) to be approved as CEO by Evelyn. However, Prime Minister Sandiford did not allow him to bring the usual cabinet paper seeking cabinet's collective approval for the appointment. Instead, the Prime Minister moved Evelyn Greaves from the Ministry of Tourism and appointed himself as the minister.

The Prime Minister and Minister of Tourism created a new board of directors and, in a jiffy, his nominees – Tony Arthur as CEO and Sylvia Lynch as Deputy CEO – were appointed to the two most senior posts at the Barbados Tourism Authority. And Prime Minister Sandiford played one more card. Contrary to the usual and hallowed practice of bringing matters such as these to cabinet for discussion and approval, he merely sent his nominees for 'noting' by cabinet, thereby effectively denying any discussion of the matter. I submitted my resignation from cabinet two days later.

This whole matter created much disquiet within the Democratic Labour Party. It attracted national attention and created fodder for the opposition Barbados Labour Party. Religious leaders from eight denominations, as well as the former ministers, met with the Prime Minister to try to heal the rift, but with no success.

June 7 1994 was perhaps the most controversial and painful day in my political career. On that day the House of Assembly was convened to debate the no-confidence motion brought by the leader of the opposition, Owen Arthur (now deceased), against Prime Minister Erskine Sandiford.

Evelyn and I both thought that Prime Minister Sandiford's actions were an affront to our ministerial status and, as a matter of principle, we felt compelled, along with Harold Blackman (now deceased) and Keith Simmons, to vote with the opposition against our then political leader on the motion. Leroy Trotman[4] (now Sir Roy) also voted with us.

Historically, that no-confidence motion was an epic political event in the history not only of Barbados but also of the Commonwealth Caribbean. I am content to explain that, on a matter of the highest political principle, I felt obliged to vote in

[4] C.L. Trotman (b. 1944), a teacher and leading trade unionist, became General Secretary of the BWU in 1992. An MP since 1986, he resigned from the DLP over the government's economic policy in 1993 and sat as an independent. He was knighted in 2002.

support of the motion that would ultimately cause the downfall of the government in which I was a minister. The principle concerned the appropriateness of a prime minister to seek to have persons of his own choice appointed to positions of seniority in a statutory board without according due respect to the substantive minister responsible for the statutory board and the directors of that board. It was a case of prime ministerial overreach.

What troubled me most was that I had to leave; but the support from my branch executive bolstered my confidence when they forwarded a resolution on behalf of the constituency to the annual conference that year pledging their loyalty to me.

I have made reparation for the mistakes I have made in my life, and I just could not vote as some would have wished, and my response was calm and resolute.

My position was that I love my prime minister, but I don't love him more than I love the party.

I love the party, but I don't love it more than I love my country.

I love my country, but I don't love it more than I love God.

Anything that I consider to be wrong, I will speak against it. I bear the Prime Minister no hatred; to do so would be – as Jesus said – an act of committing murder in my heart (1 John 3:15).

History is the study of past events, particularly in human affairs, and this event caused me no pleasure. Prior to reaching this point in our history, the Democratic Labour Party had lost a large number of supporters when Dr Sir Richard Haynes[5] (now deceased) left the party with three other parliamentarians. I pleaded with Prime Minister Sandiford to heal the party with no success.

After losing the vote of no confidence, the Prime Minister announced a general election to be held on Tuesday 6 September. Of the DLP members who voted for the motion, only Harold Blackman – standing as a National Democratic Party candidate – contested the election, and the party won just eight of the twenty-eight seats.

---

[5] Dr R.C. Haynes (1936-2013) held the position of Chief of Medical Staff at Queen Elizabeth's Hospital in Barbados. He was Barbados' Minister of Finance 1986-87, before resigning from the DLP following a dispute with Prime Minister Erskine Sandiford. He was knighted in 2003.

His political career at an end, Wes was left to contemplate the prospect of unemployment. Not only did Wes face an uncertain future, but he was also saddened by the hurtful comments made by people who were unhappy with his role in the political turmoil. He received a timely boost in the form of a visit from Rawle Brancker, his trusted friend since their first day at Combermere when they were eleven years old: 'He had been as solid as a rock and there for me every step of the way.' That evening Brancker's support was as unwavering as ever and largely unspoken except for a few gratefully received words: 'Blues, I know you, and I know that whatever happens I can shut my eyes and back you.'

Wes is grateful for his time in politics. It had given him the opportunity to serve and, after 18 years as a parliamentarian, he was able to say that he had not once voted against his conscience. When he joined the DLP and sat for the first time as an opposition senator in 1981, Wes had become aware of the need for political manoeuvring to defend his party's position. Once his relationship with God became known, opponents were swift to accuse him of piety, and at times he faced outright hostility, but he refused to succumb to blind allegiance, or animosity towards the opposition:

> Barbados is a tiny island, only 166 square miles in size, and I was at school with these guys; we go to the same church, play the same game, go to the same parent-teacher meetings, and we celebrate together at Crop Over time! But we are on different sides: does that make them my enemy? Certainly not. Our friendship will never wane.

Ability to see beyond political differences influenced Wes's conduct in the political arena and helped him to relate to those who disagreed with him. He vowed to work for his constituents, including those who would never vote for him. Wes recounts an occasion during his (ultimately unsuccessful) first campaign in 1981 when his conciliatory approach to political opponents paid dividends. While canvassing door-to-door, his campaign helpers advised him that it was pointless stopping at a particular house, as the old man who lived there with his five children was a confirmed opposition supporter who would never be swayed. Wes ignored the warning and went on his own to speak to the homeowner, who politely expressed admiration for Wes the cricketer and distaste for his politics. However, he was impressed that Wes had taken the trouble to talk to him, and he allowed him inside to speak to the children, all of whom were of voting age. Wes's message obviously resonated with them: 'All five voted for me.'

Wes's morale was at a low ebb following events in parliament, but his faith was restored by an upturn in fortunes which came when he most needed it: 'That's the way God operates!'

Working for Butch Stewart at Sandals
A few days after leaving government, Wes was contacted by a lady on behalf of Gordon 'Butch' Stewart[6], the Jamaican founder and owner of the luxury Sandals hotel chain, requesting a meeting with Wes. The meeting took place in Barbados two days later. Stewart was aware of the most recent political developments in Barbados, and he got straight to the point, asking Wes what he planned to do for work. Somewhat unenthusiastically, Wes replied that he had nothing specific in mind and that maybe he would not work anymore. Stewart's response was emphatic. He expressed his admiration for Wes and confidence that he was the right person to come and work with him. The offer of a job was a relief for Wes, especially coming from a man for whom he had a long-standing respect. After mulling over the offer for a few days, Wes accepted, and they quickly agreed terms.

Wes held the title Director of Corporate Relations, with responsibility for spearheading Sandals' involvement in community relations and corporate sports sponsorship and for developing its international profile. He would be based in Barbados as the chief liaison between Sandals and the governments of the Caribbean islands where the company had a presence.

His remit also included facilitating the ambitious plans for developing the Barbados operation: earlier in 1994 Butch Stewart had bought the Cunard Paradise Beach Hotel on the island's south-west coast, with a view to rebuilding and completely refitting it to the high standards of the Sandals brand. It was an immense project, and Wes was tasked with

---

[6] Gordon 'Butch' Stewart (1941-2021) founded the luxury hotel Sandals Resorts in 1981. He was Chairman of Sandals Resorts, Beaches Resorts and many other companies in the Caribbean, USA and Great Britain.

organising the groundwork for everything from legal matters to security arrangements. He was supported by just three members of staff: Judith Cobham, his secretary, accountant Shirley Garnes and Ewart Jackson, who oversaw the team of security guards. He was involved with planners, architects and engineers, but progress was slow: finally in 2001, after seven frustrating years of delays, setbacks and litigations beyond the control of Butch Stewart and Wes, Sandals reluctantly decided to call a halt to the venture. Knowing how much Mr Stewart wanted to establish Sandals in Barbados, Wes felt a sense of relief on behalf of his boss. He set about the final task of winding down the operation at Paradise Beach, convinced that one day Sandals Barbados would become a reality.

Eventually, after a further twelve years, Wes's optimism was justified when Butch Stewart successfully negotiated an agreement with the Barbados Government to establish two properties on the south coast of the island. At the opening of the first, Mr Stewart hosted a dinner for Wes and his daughter Kerry; Paradise Beach was finally 'water under the bridge'.

On leaving Sandals, Wes wrote to thank The Honourable[7] Gordon 'Butch' Stewart for the graciousness and generosity he had extended to him and his family. Sadly Butch Stewart died in Miami in January 2021, leaving Wes saddened by the loss of a loyal and trusted friend.

[7] Stewart was awarded the Order of Jamaica (OJ) in 1995. Considered the equivalent of the British knighthood, the order permits members to adopt the title: 'The Honourable'.

22

Managing West Indies in Turbulent Times

Shortly after Wes had started working at Sandals, the WICBC asked him to manage the team on the tour to England in 1995. This time Wes did not need to worry about whether he would be granted leave by his employer. Butch Stewart embraced the opportunity to lend support to West Indian cricket, and Sandals also became the first West Indian entity to sponsor the cricket team on a tour of England. David Roper, Director of Industry Relations at Sandals Resorts International, took on an enormous workload in masterminding the marketing blitz. He organised promotional and publicity initiatives on a scale that had never before been undertaken by a touring West Indies side. During their four months in England, the players took part in golf days and gave up their free time to appear at special events where they could engage with the public and promote the Caribbean tourist industry and in particular Sandals. The new concept was fully embraced by the players and left a lasting, positive memory in the minds of English fans.

West Indian cricket was at a watershed: against Australia at Sabina Park in early May, they lost the Fourth and final Test, and with it the series 2-1. This was their first series defeat since March 1980 in New Zealand, and the run of 29 unbeaten series is a record which still stands. Unfortunately that defeat was sufficient for the ICC to relieve West Indies of the number one position in the world Test rankings and to replace them with Australia (whose victory over West Indies took their unbeaten run to six series). The ending of their proud unbeaten record provoked a furious reaction in the West Indies; the press turned on the players, and the West Indian public demanded answers, all of which heaped additional pressure on the tourists. With the first match in England taking place just ten days after the Sabina Park Test against Australia had ended, there was minimal opportunity for the players to regroup after their disappointment.

Having attended the Jamaica Test, Wes noted that the West Indies team of 1995 was a far cry from the world-beaters he had been privileged to manage a decade previously. Most disturbing to him was the cultural shift which had taken place in the dressing room. The sides led by Lloyd and Richards were packed with strong, determined characters who conducted themselves professionally. They had the view that those drying the socks and bringing the drinks onto the field were just as important a part of the team as the players. By contrast, the 1995 squad was characterised by questionable attitudes and indiscipline which was reflected in performances on the field. The only survivors of the previous era were Walsh and Richardson: 'They were the epitome of that team's discipline and work ethic; they were manageable'.

In 1995 West Indies toured England without an assistant manager. Wes took on extra administrative duties, such as organising tour logistics and managing the accounts, a task made easier thanks to Allan Smith, a Barbadian chartered accountant, who set up an accounting system at no cost to the WICB. Wes established a chain of command comprising himself, coach Andy Roberts, captain Richie Richardson and vice-captain Courtney Walsh. He emphasised the importance of accountability at each stage, beginning with the players, but warned that if they failed to take responsibility the system would break down. Unfortunately this proved to be the case on more than one occasion. Together with Andy Roberts, he would spend much of the next four months preoccupied with off-field issues.

The tone was set early in the tour. West Indies' star batsman Brian Lara requested permission to leave England to attend to some personal business at home in Trinidad and to return in time for the First Test at Headingley in early June. Wes consulted Roberts and, after gaining the board's approval, they agreed to the somewhat unusual request, stipulating that Lara must be back for the match against Northamptonshire which preceded the Test. Lara arrived back on time and helped West Indies to a winning start in the Test series, but not for the last time on the tour there was a feeling among other players that he was receiving preferential treatment.

The first disciplinary incident involved the Antiguan pace bowler Winston Benjamin. He played in the three early-season ODIs, but a knee injury limited his appearances in the first-class matches and he missed the first two Tests, at Headingley and Lord's respectively. Between those Tests the tourists played Durham, where he was referred to the nearby Washington Hospital; Wes paid the doctor's fees, yet despite requests the report on Benjamin was not forthcoming. A few days later at Lord's, Wes was surprised that Benjamin bowled a long spell in the nets and then declared himself unfit when asked to bowl to the captain. Matters came to a head in the tourists' next match, at Oxford against Combined Universities. Again Benjamin told the coach he was unfit to play, yet the next morning he joined his teammates kicking a football on the outfield. Wes asked for an explanation; the bowler failed to provide one, and at a meeting of the management team it was decided to make a recommendation to the board that Benjamin should be dismissed from the tour. The board agreed, and Wes informed him that he was to be sent home. Arrangements were made for Benjamin to travel from Oxford to London for his flight home to Antigua.

The following morning Wes called a team meeting to explain the decision. He asked if anyone would like to comment on the matter. Nobody spoke.

As it transpired, Benjamin was suffering from an illness, something Wes did not discover until after the tour when he received a doctor's bill relating to Benjamin's treatment in Durham. In his 2015 book, *Time to Talk*, Sir Curtly Ambrose states that Benjamin was 'extremely ill' and expresses the opinion that he was treated unfairly. At the time the only condition Wes was aware of was the knee injury. Bearing in mind how his own injury had been handled in the latter part of his career, Wes always tried to empathise with players. Had he known about the illness at the time, he would have managed the situation differently but, given the information made available to him, he had taken the appropriate action:

> I enjoyed a very good relationship with Benjamin. In the absence of an assistant manager, he had helped me with the players' meal allowances on the tour. I find it sad and disappointing that Benjamin – or Ambrose for that matter – had not felt able to talk to me about his illness. Both were on good terms with me.

The major flashpoint came a month later at Old Trafford following the Fourth Test match. After winning the Third Test at Edgbaston inside three days, West Indies arrived in Manchester with a 2-1 lead in the series. Their form had been patchy: good performances were interspersed with some spectacular, embarrassing defeats, most notably by an innings against Sussex at Hove and against the Minor Counties in a one-day match at Reading.

At Old Trafford, despite scores of 87 and 145 from Lara, West Indies lost the match by six wickets, having set England a second-innings victory target of just 94 runs. England's run chase was less comfortable than it may appear. West Indies even scented an unlikely victory after tea on the fourth day when the hosts were 48 for four (effectively five, with Robin Smith on his way to hospital with a fractured cheekbone after being hit by an Ian Bishop bouncer). In an attempt to push for the victory, Richardson ignored the fact that Ambrose was struggling with an injury and brought his top bowler back into the attack in place of Kenny Benjamin, who had taken two wickets and was bowling very well. The move backfired doubly: Ambrose failed to make further inroads into the English batting, and he was unfit to play in the Fifth Test at Trent Bridge.

The Old Trafford Test illustrated the fine margins in cricket. West Indies believed they could have won the match and extended their series lead to 3-1, instead of which the teams were tied at two Tests each. This remained the final score after the last two matches were drawn. Criticism of Richardson's tactics was made with the benefit of hindsight. Well as Benjamin was bowling, the captain's decision to turn to Ambrose, the world's leading bowler, was understandable: 'Captains and coaches the world over make gut decisions, and when they don't work out, it just has to be accepted.'

Wes was concerned by the inept and undisciplined performances he witnessed against Sussex and the Minor Counties, and now defeat at Old Trafford brought the Test series all square. He had also noticed a gradual worsening of the off-field conduct of certain team members and called a meeting to address the issues. Players were given the opportunity to express their views, but most were quiet and reserved. Many of them were seeking to establish a place in the Test side and, as such, they were reluctant to make their voices heard. Wes wanted to foster an atmosphere in which everyone felt entitled to express their opinion; otherwise, 'the younger players never say a word, and you don't learn a lot when that happens'.

The first to speak at the meeting was Ian Bishop, and he was typically forthright. He encouraged the youngsters to do the little things right, such as practising properly in the nets; this was the kind of constructive input Wes had been hoping for. Bishop then went on to bemoan indiscipline within the squad. He criticised Curtly Ambrose and Kenny Benjamin for being over-vocal and distracting others and opined that Winston Benjamin's expulsion was overdue. The next person to speak was Lara.

He was critical of Richardson's decisions and blamed him for allowing standards to slip, views he claimed were shared with most of the squad (although nobody supported him at the meeting). Wes invited Richardson to reply, and the captain's response was measured and pointed. He said he would step down if the players were unhappy with his captaincy, but he was not prepared to bow to egotistical people with agendas and ambitions.

At that point, Lara rose and announced: 'I retire', before leaving the room.

Ambrose then responded maturely and without rancour to Bishop's criticism. He had been unaware that he was considered a disruptive influence, and he stated his intention to retire from Test cricket at the end of the series. He emphasised that he was committed to the remainder of the tour, which at least lifted the mood for the remainder of the meeting.

Later that evening Wes invited Lara to his room to talk through the situation. Several times during their conversation Lara stated that 'cricket is ruining my life'. Wes was unable to persuade him to change his mind, and the next morning the team set off for the county fixture in Somerset without their star player. The following day WICBC President Peter Short called to say that Lara had requested a meeting with the West Indies management and that he would be bringing Lara to Taunton. At the meeting Lara repeated that cricket was ruining his life and cited a couple of perceived injustices. After swiftly dealing with these minor grievances, Wes pointed out that far from ruining lives cricket is the ever-present force that brings West Indian people together and serves as the heartbeat of Caribbean life. He went further by suggesting that there are great sportsmen who are insecure despite their brilliance; it is their insecurity which ruins their lives – as it would do whatever their career – and he resolved to provide support for Lara. Short commented that cricket had been the making of Lara, and he should recognise his responsibilities. Lara took note and asked to be allowed to re-join the tour.

Lara took his place in the side for the next match against Gloucestershire at Bristol. There were no more incidents involving him on the tour, and he was able to put the controversy behind him. In the final two drawn Tests he batted brilliantly, scoring 152 at Trent Bridge and 179 at The Oval. Lara's magnificent batting – 765 runs at an average of 85.00 – illuminated a series which produced some scintillating cricket, played in front of packed stands. The next highest run scorers were England's Graham Thorpe and Mike Atherton with 506 and 488 respectively. When asked to nominate England's man of the series. Wes chose the captain Atherton, 'the difference to the result of the series. He led from the front and took the fire of the West Indies pace bowlers unflinchingly.' Wes identified the 24-year-old Barbadian opening batsman Sherwin Campbell, with 454 Test match runs at an average of 45.40, as the most promising of West Indies' youngsters.

Wes was also greatly impressed by the performance of the team's four fast bowlers. Curtly Ambrose, Courtney Walsh, Ian Bishop and Kenny Benjamin all made significant contributions and between them took 97 of the 102 England wickets to fall to bowlers in the series. Prior to the Third Test at Edgbaston Wes compared the pitch to Jacob's coat of many colours, but he refused to criticise, believing it was the home side's prerogative to prepare a pitch of their choosing. He did, however, feel that England miscalculated: 'They would never have dreamt of having a wicket like that in the '70s and '80s, but in '95 we still had the best four fast bowlers in the world.'

In addition to being the world's best fast bowler, Ambrose was a motivational presence in the dressing room, as he showed when his impromptu speech after the defeat by Sussex reinvigorated the team when it was at its lowest ebb. Clearly he still had plenty to offer, and the combined persuasive powers of Wes, Roberts and Walsh encouraged Ambrose to reconsider his decision to retire. Happily for West Indies, he played on for the next five years.

The drawn Test series meant that West Indies retained the Wisden Trophy, but Wes was left to reflect that he had presided over a tour which had seen Winston Benjamin sent home for disciplinary reasons and four other players fined by the WICBC for misconduct. Ironically – given the length of the charge sheet – Wes was the antithesis of the confrontational, authoritarian manager. His empathetic, 'player-focused' style almost certainly kept the number of incidents to a minimum, especially considering the febrile atmosphere among the party. Wes prided himself on looking after his players. His first loyalty was to them, and if anyone needed support he would provide it:

> I tried to be a man-manager; that was always my reputation as a
> manager. Whatever the problem is, just let me know and I'll go

in to bat for my players and deal with the consequences. I learned that from Frank Worrell. You could go to his room any time and confide in him, and I hoped my players felt the same about me. Take the business with Winston Benjamin: I don't understand why he didn't reveal his sickness to me so that I could help him.

The infamous visit to Taunton featured an example of his approach to player welfare. Jimmy Adams was hit in the face by a bouncer from Somerset's Dutch fast bowler Andre van Troost. Adams suffered severe facial injuries requiring an operation, and even though it was obvious he would play no more cricket that summer Wes kept him in England for a further month to ensure that he received continuous treatment from top surgeons.

After such a joyless tour Wes could have been forgiven for turning his back on team management, but he felt duty-bound to honour his contract and try to find answers to the problems that were undermining West Indian cricket. His end-of-tour report to the board was a candid appraisal of the reasons for the friction within the party: he spoke of conflicts, disrespect, and bad attitudes among the players. Years later, Wes's plan – based on an enlightened approach to player well-being and the need to set cricket's structure on a more professional footing – resembles a prophecy. Among his recommendations, he called for:

- an end to indiscipline and a return to the game's traditional values.
- the introduction of professionals to offer psychological counselling, a role which he saw (and still sees) as being as important to player welfare as a coach, trainer, or physiotherapist.
- the development of an academy – 'a finishing school for young cricketers' – which would not only hone skills but also recognise the importance of the mind in cricket and raise the level of intellectual preparation and discipline required for the modern game.
- investment in a human relations development plan, featuring regular training workshops and guest lectures, with ex-players and administrators invited to participate. This would help players to improve mentally, spiritually, socially and economically.
- measures to ensure the preservation of West Indies' cricketing heritage and the establishment of public archives, where research can be conducted using multiple resources: books, articles, photographs and footage of old film.

- governments to become involved in a tangible way, such as by contributing to a 'cricketers' fund' that would allow players to have retainer contracts.
- the WICBC to receive all the benefits commensurate with its status as being one of the important institutions in the West Indies.
- a region-wide coaching programme, in order that everyone involved with West Indian cricket would be working towards the same goal.

His report paved the way for several initiatives in West Indian cricket, most notably paid managers, retainer contracts for players, a commitment to marketing the game and establishing an academy. One of his arguments in favour of a cricket academy resulted from the indiscipline he witnessed on the 1995 tour; he concluded that if young players are steeped in the history of West Indian cricket and can develop a sense of how they fit into it, they will be more likely to behave appropriately. Ironically the 1995 squad, which had proved so difficult to manage, produced more coaches and administrators than any West Indies team before or since: 'It is therefore obvious that these guys had a renewal of the mind and realised the necessity for discipline, a good work ethic, and commitment to the task.'

Impressed by his progressive thinking and commitment, the board asked Wes to continue as manager for the 1996 World Cup in India, Pakistan and Sri Lanka. Once again he was happy to serve; and once again he was to endure a rollercoaster ride of emotions and fluctuating fortunes.

West Indian cricket can rarely be accused of being dull, and the 1996 World Cup was a case in point. The journey to India got things off to an eventful start: the team was due to fly from Barbados to New Delhi via London and Mumbai, an arduous trip even if everything went according to plan. However, shortly after the plane left Grantley Adams International Airport, it had to return to Barbados when one of the engines caught fire. Concerned that they would miss connecting flights and the World Cup opening ceremony, Wes contacted the British Airways manager, Elvin Sealy, who hastily arranged for the team to fly to London early the next morning on Concorde. Upon touching down in London, the captain's announcement caused much mirth: 'Guys, I did say we would arrive in two hours and 40 minutes, and I wish to offer an apology ... we took two hours and 41!'

Described in *Wisden* as 'surly and unattractive', the team stuttered in the early stages of the competition with just one win – against Zimbabwe – in the first three matches. One of their two 'defeats' was the fixture against Sri Lanka, which West Indies forfeited (as did Australia) after refusing to play in Columbo due to security concerns. Matters reached a nadir in the penultimate group match against Kenya in Pune: West Indies were dismissed for 93 following a lamentable batting display in which no batsman managed to score 20 runs, with only Chanderpaul and Harper reaching double figures. The 73-run defeat was described by Wes in his report to the board as 'perhaps the most astonishing result in the history of world cricket ... [it] shocked and humiliated the West Indian team'. It left them needing to beat a strong Australia side in the final group game to be certain of avoiding the ignominy of failing to qualify for the quarter-finals.

Undoubtedly the absence of Carl Hooper, who had withdrawn from the squad shortly before the tournament, was a huge blow, but the problems clearly ran far deeper. With players unwilling to discuss matters voluntarily, Wes called a team meeting to discuss the debacle against Kenya, insisting that they should come up with some answers. The players were unanimous in accepting that the match was a team disaster and that everyone should share responsibility. When some were critical of the captain Richie Richardson, Wes asked Richardson what he had to say. In an impassioned response the skipper expressed his love for his teammates and reassured them that as long as he was captain he would do everything in his power to help them. He concluded with a rallying call for them to put an end to the bickering and to pull together. There followed a constructive discussion on the strategies they would use against Australia.

Inspired by a superb innings of 93 not out by Richardson, a rejuvenated West Indies beat Australia in Jaipur by four wickets with seven balls to spare. However, news reached Wes from home that the next day's board meeting would include a discussion on relieving Richardson of the captaincy after the World Cup:

> I told Richie about the meeting and that the Trinidad representative had been saying that the team's performance was so bad they

needed to look at the captain, coach and manager. With a nine-hour time advantage, I suggested that Richie write his resignation to the board. He did and resigned his position to take effect at the end of the tour. Before the planned meeting I faxed it to Steve Camacho, CEO of the WICB, with a cover note asking him to pass it to the board.

While Wes was averting Richardson's probable embarrassment by encouraging him to 'jump before he was pushed', another problem was brewing. On 7 March, four days before the quarter-final against South Africa in Karachi, Brian Lara showed Wes a page from the previous day's *Trinidad Express* newspaper which had been faxed to him from Trinidad. It featured excerpts from an article in a Delhi-based magazine called *The Outlook*, detailing incendiary comments Lara had made to the Kenyan players in their dressing room after the match in Pune. His outburst caused controversy on two fronts. Under the headline: 'We have a bad team and a bad management', he criticised West Indian cricket, citing disharmony within the team and claiming that he and other players from Trinidad and Tobago were the victims of discrimination. Obviously a senior player breaking ranks so spectacularly was embarrassing for West Indian cricket, but at least 'in-house' squabbles had little impact further afield.

Unfortunately the same could not be said of the second part of Lara's tirade. He told the Kenyans that 'it wasn't that bad losing to you guys. You are black ... Now a team like South Africa is a different matter altogether. You know this white thing comes into the picture. We can't stand losing to them.'

Wes took an extremely dim view of the deceitful journalist who smuggled a tape recorder into the private space of the dressing room, but Lara's behaviour was nonetheless inexcusable. It fell to Wes to try to diffuse the situation, and before the party left India for Pakistan he called Dr Ali Bacher, Managing Director of the South African Cricket Board, to arrange a meeting in Karachi. Wes and Bacher had always got on well. Their mutual respect had been a driving force behind South Africa's readmittance Test match in Barbados in 1992, and the good relationship between the two countries since then was a significant factor in the South Africans' tolerant response to the Lara affair. Upon arrival in Pakistan, West Indies' management team and Brian Lara met South

Africans Dr Bacher and Peter Pollock, convenor of selectors of the South African Cricket Board. Throughout the meeting the South African delegation was extremely cooperative and understanding, and the tone remained convivial. Lara apologised for the unnecessary trouble he had caused. He stated that he had been indulging in the usual dressing-room banter over a few drinks with the Kenyans and that his words had been taken out of context. He added that he had nothing against South Africa and was looking forward to playing them. The South Africans accepted Lara's apology, and the potentially explosive situation was diffused with a minimum of fuss. In his manager's report on the 1996 World Cup, Wes says: 'His statement appeared to have been well received by the press since no further mention was made of this matter.' The report omits to point out that, perhaps more than anyone else, Wes can be credited with bringing this unfortunate saga to a conclusion.

Thoughts could finally return to cricket and the quarter-final in Karachi. West Indies batted first, and a magnificent 94-ball 111 by Lara – inevitably – illuminated their innings of 264. Spin bowlers Harper and Adams then starred with the ball as West Indies completed a 19-run victory over the previously unbeaten tournament favourites, South Africa. Incredibly West Indies were in the semi-final.

The semi-final against Australia in Mohali was largely dominated by a confident West Indies team. Having restricted Australia to 207 runs, they batted sensibly, and needed 43 runs to win from nine overs, with eight wickets in hand. Victory seemed a formality until Chanderpaul's dismissal for 80 triggered an extraordinary collapse in which the last eight wickets fell for 37 runs. With Richardson left stranded on 49 not out, Australia were handed a five-run victory. President of the WICB Sir Clyde Walcott was reduced to tears, while Wes described it as 'the worst day I've had in cricket'.

Although the team was inconsistent in the tournament, there were several good performances, and for the first time since 1983 West Indies reached the semi-final of a World Cup. Wes focuses on the positives when he reflects on the campaign. Notwithstanding *Wisden's* unflattering verdict on the squad, he saw an improved culture from the 1995 tour of England, and his report to the board stated that 'the conduct of the West Indies team was exemplary'.

He admired the way Richardson conducted himself throughout such a difficult period, remaining dignified and focused on doing what was best for the team. Compared to his predecessors Clive Lloyd and Viv Richards, both of whom exuded enormous presence, Richardson was quiet and unassuming:

> I will allow the words of Khalil Gibran[1] to speak for me: 'Tenderness and kindness are not signs of weakness and despair, but manifestations of strength and resolution.' This is the Richie Richardson I know and celebrated when he was knighted Sir Richard Benjamin 'Richie' Richardson in February 2014.

Wes left the job when his contract expired at the end of the World Cup. He returned to his duties at Sandals but was soon to be involved in West Indies cricket again when he was appointed chairman of selectors in November 1996. In order to perform the new role properly, Wes attended as many of the inter-island matches as possible. This necessitated taking time off work and, with the number of matches increasing, he began to feel that he was prevailing on Butch Stewart's goodwill. He came to the conclusion that combining the two roles was not feasible, and he resigned from his selection post in 1998. Steve Camacho wrote to Wes expressing the board's gratitude, and the following extract from his letter is a glowing tribute to years of service to West Indian cricket:

> It certainly will be remiss if I do not reiterate our appreciation of the outstanding service rendered by you during your term of office. There can be no doubt that your leadership and commitment to West Indies cricket proved invaluable at a most difficult time.
>
> I have been closely associated with you for over 30 years first as a player, then in the employ of the WICB during your stints as both manager and chairman of selectors and can only say that our cricket has been only the better for your ability, integrity and experience.
>
> On behalf of the Board ... despite the valedictory tone of your [resignation] letter ... may I convey the hope that you will not be lost to our cricket.

That hope was to be realised three years later.

---

[1] Khalil Gibran (1883-1931) was a Lebanese-American writer, poet and artist, whose most famous book *The Prophet*, published in 1923, has been translated into over 100 languages and sold over 10 million copies.

23

WICB Presidency

In 2001, shortly before leaving Sandals, Wes received a call from his good friend Stephen Alleyne, a leading actuary and president of the BCA. Alleyne wanted to nominate Wes for the WICB presidency, which was vacant following the resignation of Pat Rousseau, the Jamaican lawyer who had occupied the role since 1996. With Clarvis Joseph resigning as vice-president, the board – and West Indian cricket – were in a state of turmoil: the steady decline in the team's performances and results had been accompanied by player unrest and policy disagreements within the board. It was clear that Rousseau's successor would need exceptional diplomatic skills.

Alleyne recognised the need for a strong replacement to be installed as quickly as possible. If Barbados could put forward a good candidate, he would then try to gain the support of the other five associations[1] which 'owned' West Indian cricket. Never one to shirk a challenge, Wes welcomed the prospect of helping to revive the cricketing fortunes of his beloved West Indies, and he confirmed his interest. Alleyne had already sounded out representatives of the Trinidad board – with favourable results – and within a few days, he confirmed that Wes would be elected unopposed.

Wes liked and respected Rousseau, and his first act as president was to visit him in Jamaica to learn more about the situation he was inheriting. Rousseau was a charismatic figure who had achieved a great deal during his tenure, including the introduction of some initiatives Wes had proposed in his manager's report on the 1995 tour of England. Wes had ambitious plans, and the meeting gave him an insight into the issues he would need to address alongside the pursuit of his own agenda.

Experience had taught Wes that change via committee tends to be a lengthy and often frustrating process, so he set himself a target of ten years

---

[1] The six territorial cricket associations are: Barbados Cricket Association; Guyana Cricket Board; Jamaica Cricket Association; Leeward Islands Cricket Association; Trinidad and Tobago Cricket Board; Windward Islands Cricket Board of Control.

to achieve his goals. Circumstances conspired to limit his tenure to just two years, yet few chapters in his life have been more eventful.

While in Jamaica Wes made an appointment to see Professor Rex Nettleford[2], Vice-Chancellor of The UWI, and his deputy, Professor Hilary Beckles. He wanted to discuss a matter that had concerned him for many years: namely the lack of synergy between sport and education. The concept of the student cricketer was the vision of Sir Frank Worrell, who argued that youngsters should not be forced to choose between a cricket career and university. Wes cited the example of three talented Barbadian cricketers – batsmen Colin Blades, Tony King and Lewis 'Guinea' Yearwood – who had gone to study at The UWI, Mona, in Jamaica. He was convinced that they, and many others, would have been Test cricketers if they had played at a high level while at university. Instead, commitment to further education curtailed their cricketing ambitions and, although King and Blades went on to play first-class cricket for Barbados, they made just 21 appearances between them.

Wes's message, that academic study and a career in cricket should not be mutually exclusive, met with widespread approval. He suggested the extension of cricketers' degree courses by a year or two, but since then The UWI's leadership has gone much further. Additional tutoring, mentoring schemes, flexible assessment and examinations and summer schools have been introduced along with college sports programmes and sports-based degrees, suggesting that his thinking was ahead of his time.

The first WICB meeting chaired by President Hall ran late – until 2am! All of those present were officials in some capacity, and he thought it right that he should hear their views. Among the invitees were representatives of women's cricket and, as Wes listened with interest to their comments, it occurred to him that there should be a place for women within the WICB. After discussing the matter with his daughter Kerry, the thought became a firm conviction. She pointed to evidence of the upward mobility of females in virtually every walk of life, from those occupying senior roles at the university, to engineers and pilots. During Wes's spell as president, for the first time, women were given positions of authority within the WICB. He appointed the former Trinidad and West Indies player Ann

---

[2] R.M. 'Rex' Nettleford (1943-2010) was a Jamaican scholar, social historian and choreographer who served as The UWI's vice-chancellor from 1998 until 2004.

Browne-John to the WICB's cricket advisory committee and Vaneisa Baksh to its World Cup board. Predictably he faced criticism from some quarters for breaking with tradition but was unapologetic:

> We pioneered women's cricket without realising that it would be successful. People wondered why I went with it, but I did it because cricket is a great game, and it is only fair that women and girls should have the opportunity to enjoy it like boys do.

It was only when Wes took up office that he became aware of the precarious financial state of West Indian cricket. The situation was so serious that the domestic season was in jeopardy, and his first task as president was to borrow $4 million in order that the WICB could continue to run its four-day cricket competition, the Busta Cup[3].

Rousseau sought to involve former West Indies cricketers by inviting them to a cricket convention in Jamaica, where they were encouraged to pass on their knowledge to current players. Wes applauded the initiative but wanted to take the idea further: 'I felt that we had as much talent as anywhere in the world, and I wanted youngsters to be coached by the greats.' Having played with 'a genius whose knowledge and instinct for the game were unparalleled', Wes was baffled why Sir Garfield Sobers – and other icons – were not used by the WICB as cricket gurus for young players. Unfortunately the financial constraints dictated that neither Rousseau nor Wes were able to press ahead with this plan. Instead, Wes invited a number of former players to serve on the cricket committee in a voluntary advisory capacity; all accepted and gave exemplary service. With the working brief 'Where do we go from here?', the committee's remit would extend to all matters pertaining to cricket. Committee members included Sir Everton Weekes, Sir Garfield Sobers, Sir Vivian Richards, Andy Roberts, Michael Holding, Gordon Greenidge, and Ann Browne-John. Obviously they had empathy with players, who in turn respected them. With such influential personnel on the committee, recommendations led to changes in policy, such as West Indian cricketers returning from playing in South Africa no longer being required to play a full season in the West Indies in order to re-qualify for the Test team.

[3] From 1998-99 until 2001-02 the Trinidad-based soft drinks company SMJ, manufacturer of the Busta brand, sponsored the Caribbean domestic 4-day competition.

A long-standing bone of contention for Wes had been the unwieldy structure of West Indian cricket. Pat Rousseau had taken the step of appointing professional coaches and managers, rather than somebody who could afford to take six months off from their job to go on an overseas tour. Successful candidates were chosen not only for their knowledge of cricket but also based on their wider skill sets. Wes wanted to extend this model to the board itself, which comprised two representatives from each of the six member associations in addition to the principals, such as the president, vice-president and CEO. As a result there were typically 18 people on the board, and consensus was often difficult. For many years Wes has advocated replacing this cumbersome set-up with a skills-based board, made up of a maximum of nine individuals irrespective of their island of origin. They would then be responsible for selecting suitably qualified experts to sit on various cricket sub-committees. Unfortunately, as when he was Minister of Tourism and Sport, his ambitious ideas were often vetoed by more cautious colleagues, and frustratingly the board is still organised along the same lines. He views this inertia as a symptom of an age-old problem in the region: 'We need to stop playing politics, stop currying favour with people and start to do what's best for West Indian cricket.'

Between 1995 and 2001 the Test team slipped from top of the world rankings to eighth place, above only Zimbabwe and Bangladesh. Wes welcomed the introduction of new countries into the Test arena, but with the qualification that established nations must not be stripped of their full Test status to accommodate them. Unlikely as this was for West Indies, it was vital that they did everything possible to stay ahead of the newly admitted teams. One of Wes's proposals was that the WICB should introduce a coordinated coaching structure throughout the Caribbean. In preparation for the tour of Bangladesh in late 2002, he instructed the coaches in each territory to work on improving the batsmen's techniques against spin.

In 2003 the West Indies Players Association (WIPA), the players' union, was incorporated. WIPA negotiated on behalf of the Test players with the board's acting CEO Roger Brathwaite, and if no agreement could be reached the matter would be referred to the board president. Wes was satisfied with the arrangement; he was an experienced and skilled negotiator, and player welfare had always been a major consideration for him. At a dinner for members of WIPA and the WICB, Wes told his audience how pleased he was that the framework was now in place for players to negotiate formally with the board. He fostered an excellent relationship with the players and their WIPA representatives, but such were the tensions within West Indian cricket that even this was not enough to prevent two player strikes.

The first strike took place prior to the 2003 World Cup, which was to be held in South Africa, Zimbabwe and Kenya. The board had negotiated a $175,000 sponsorship deal with Indian steel company ISPAT, $40,000 of which was to be spent on a training camp for the squad. They had hired the American motivational speaker Bob Wieland[4], and in addition Sir Everton Weekes and Andy Roberts would address the squad.

Wes told the players that the remaining $135,000 would be shared between them, but they demanded the full $175,000. The training camp went ahead as planned, and on the day of the press visit the team went on strike, causing maximum embarrassment for the board. Wes did not question the players' right to strike, but he was nonetheless disappointed:

> They waited until the press came, and they went on strike. It was unreasonable, but it was their prerogative to strike. The timing was very embarrassing for both the sponsors and the board. To this day I am still friends with all of them; just because they went on strike doesn't change that.

The players felt that the board was authoritarian and regarded them as mere recipients, leading to an implicit lack of trust. Wes urged them to enter discussions in a spirit of good faith based on his usual tenets: understand the ability to pay, accept a *quid pro quo* and work towards bridging the negotiable gap. Sadly his appeals fell on deaf ears; a few weeks later, on the eve of the semi-finals of the four-day Carib Beer competition[5], the players chose to strike again. This time they wanted pay increases for Test and first-class cricketers and backdated compensation for loss of earnings resulting from injury. A settlement was reached whereby players' match fees were raised, and a total of $110,000 was paid to eight cricketers who had suffered injury.

[4] Vietnam War veteran Bob Wieland lost both legs in a landmine accident in 1969. He recovered to become a power lifter, marathon participant and motivational speaker. Between 1982 and 1986 he walked on his hands from coast-to-coast across the USA.

[5] From 2003 until 2008 Carib Breweries, a Trinidadian beer company, sponsored the 4-day competition.

In 2000 the England and Wales Cricket Board had led the way in awarding central contracts to twelve of its senior players. Wes pledged to make retainer contracts a cornerstone of his presidency, and the issue was made all the more pressing by the players' disputes:

> We needed to move to another level, where there must be a spirit of conviviality in negotiations. Retainer contracts, a Collective Bargaining Agreement (CBA) and Memorandum of Understanding (MOU) would go a long way towards preventing a recurrence of such action.

Wes enlisted the help of his friend and political ally Evelyn Greaves, an expert in industrial relations, and commissioned Jamaican Michael Hall[6], the WICB's chief cricket operations officer, to draft the retainer contract as well as a CBA and MOU. He advised WIPA President Dinanath Ramnarine – an extremely able negotiator whom Wes liked and respected – to hire an industrial relations professional to conduct the negotiations on their behalf. Under the new structure human resources professionals would be advising both management and players and, instead of negotiating on behalf of 15 players in the Test squad, WIPA would represent all cricketers in the Caribbean. The contracts were implemented a few years later, and the following extract from the official WIPA website recognises the part played by Wes in formalising player/board relations within a legal framework:

> Former West Indies player and former WICB President Rev. Wesley Hall set relations between players and the WICB on an industrial relations platform, and the association has sought to ensure that this continues to be enshrined in a Memorandum of Understanding and Collective Bargaining Agreement.

The conduct of players had been worsening in recent years, with several leaving or being sent home from overseas tours. Wes sympathised with young men thrust into an alien environment, but he believed that, if they were to achieve their potential, discipline was essential. Drawing on the case of his friend Roy Gilchrist, Wes arranged for players to have access to professional psychologists and was pleased to be able to deliver on the

[6] Michael Hall held the position of WICB's Chief Cricket Operations Officer between 2001 and 2003. He was CEO of WIPA before becoming Director of Operations for the Caribbean Premier League in 2013.

promise he made in his sermon at Gilchrist's funeral, that never again would anybody be sent home and not receive counselling.

Wes had noted that communication and transparency were not among the WICB's stronger points, and he resolved to improve media relations and increase its public voice. Around the time he became president, the board was working with a Barbadian PR firm, Saunders-Franklyn & Associates, and it was to everyone's good fortune that the company hired a young, enthusiastic sports reporter as its media relations specialist. Adriel 'Woody' Richard was a family friend whom Wes had known for years, and his knowledge of the game, its personalities and the cricket media were invaluable to Wes's plans. Woody conducted an overhaul of the board's internal communication systems, but his major impact was in raising the media profile of the WICB. He expanded the mailing list from just a handful of counterparts to thousands and relayed West Indian cricket news to every major newspaper, radio station and television network. By populating cricket websites, he enabled people around the world to access direct messages from the WICB instead of having to wait for second-hand information. Newspapers around the Caribbean began to carry weekly WICB columns, frequently written by Woody.

During Wes's presidency around 200 media releases were sent out, a vast improvement on previous output. Although there was much more that Wes wanted to accomplish in this area, on reflection he is happy to have laid the foundations which would help the WICB to improve its transparency and to become more interactive with the media and the public.

In Wes's second year as president, West Indian cricket returned to profitability for the first time in four years, recording all-time high revenues of $20 million, boosted by a $7.7 million share of the profits from the 2003 ICC World Cup in South Africa. Gate receipts from the subsequent home series of four Test matches and seven ODIs against Australia provided evidence that West Indian cricket was alive and well. In addition Carib Beer's sponsorship of the regional competitions augured well for the domestic game.

Wes backed up his belief that emerging nations should be encouraged, inviting Kenya to take part in the four-day competition in 2003-04. He feared that lack of exposure to first-class cricket would inhibit the development of their young cricketers and lead to a reversal of the progress Kenya had made. Sadly, despite their involvement in the Carib Cup, he was correct.

Pat Rousseau had lobbied at the ICC for West Indies to be granted the 2007 Cricket World Cup, and in 1998 his campaign reached a successful conclusion. Wes would be working with a talented team on the World Cup committee, and he focused on the opportunities rather than the obstacles. Sadly he was unable to see the task to its conclusion, as ill health was to force him to stand down from the presidency after two years.

West Indies defied the predictions of many naysayers by staging a generally well-run tournament. Unfortunately, it was marred by setbacks beyond the control of the hosts, and Wes looks back on the event with mixed feelings. He was particularly frustrated at the rules dictating supporters' behaviour in the grounds. Like many West Indians he had been aggrieved when the whistles and horns favoured by West Indies supporters were banned from cricket grounds in England. Now, under the terms of the agreement with the tournament's 'hospitality partners', spectators at the World Cup were forbidden from indulging in the West Indian tradition of taking picnic baskets and rum – as well as musical instruments and conch shells – into their own grounds. Of course, he understood the importance of attracting commercial sponsorship but was pleased that in last few days of the tournament the ICC relaxed its regulations, and the traditional Caribbean party atmosphere returned. This illustrated the point he had been making for years: that cricket's failure to respect and embrace different cultures was likely to lead to matches being played in a sterile environment devoid of local flavour and colour.

Happily the lessons of 2007 were heeded, and things were very different when the West Indies next hosted an international cricket competition, the ICC World 20/20 in 2010. David Morgan, who was ICC president between 2008 and 2010, even invited spectators to 'bring your musical instruments, your songs and cheers, your flags, banners and colourful costumes'. The tournament – won by England – was an unqualified success. Wes felt vindicated: 'At least they listened, and they learned that worldwide we need to appreciate people's culture and differences.'

One of Wes's great regrets was that he was unable to remain WICB president for ten years as intended. Towards the end of his first two years as president, while he was on official ICC business in Dubai, he began to develop severe abdominal pains, which became more acute by the day. Back in Barbados, he received a preliminary diagnosis of prostate enlargement. Understandably concerned that he was suffering from cancer, Wes sought the opinion of eminent Barbadian medical professionals, surgeon Professor Errol 'Mickey' Walrond[7], a trusted friend, and gastroenterologist Dr Ed Layne[8] in Atlanta, Georgia. Dr Ed conducted further tests and diagnosed diverticulitis – which could have been responsible for the infected prostate area – and a bulbous bladder. At almost 250 pounds, Wes was also grossly overweight. Dr Ed admitted him to Emory University Hospital in Atlanta, where he was treated for diverticulitis, and provided him with a detailed nutrition programme. With continued monitoring by Dr Ed, Wes's health gradually improved and within a couple of years, he had lost approximately 65 pounds.

Having been 'very sick, and frightened too', Wes is grateful for the friendships of the members of the Miami Dolphins, a swimming group who met at Miami Beach in Barbados early every morning. Swimming with them six days a week for almost ten years and taking part in their social activities contributed in no small way to his physical and mental recovery.

Fearing that his health problems were potentially very serious, Wes did not seek re-election in 2003. Sadly, the episode had brought a premature end to his presidency of the WICB: 'I am very happy to have served, but I wish I could have done more. If I knew I would serve one two-year term only, I would not have accepted the call; but God knows best.'

---

[7] After studying at Guy's Hospital in London, Professor E.R. 'Mickey' Walrond (b.1936) was a pioneering surgeon and one of the leading medical figures in the Caribbean, noted among other things for his work in combating the spread of AIDS. He received numerous honours including a knighthood in 2011.

[8] Dr E.A. Layne is an eminent gastroenterologist who left Barbados to study at Harvard Medical School. He has practised in the USA and is Honorary Barbados Consul for the state of Georgia.

24

A Final Tally

Wes's life of full-time employment came to an end at the age of 66; not that retirement in the conventional sense was ever likely to be an option for him. Since the day in Miami, Florida in 1988 when he was 'saved', Wes had considered it his privilege to be chosen to dedicate his life to God. He gladly accepted the lifestyle changes he had made over the previous 15 years, and he had constantly striven to achieve a level of devotion and purity of thought to match his deeds.

Relinquishing the WICB presidency allowed him to serve God in an 'official' way for the first time since his ordination five years earlier. As an associate minister at his church, Abundant Life Assembly in Bank Hall, he was responsible for supporting the minister. In addition his popularity and reputation for entertaining oratory ensured that he was continually in demand to perform christenings, weddings and funerals. On many occasions his trademark request that God 'loosen my tongue and unlock my jaws' resulted in him abandoning his planned speech in favour of an unscripted one.

Commitment to God may have become the dominant motivation in his life, but he still found time to take on numerous other roles and responsibilities, each one inspired by an eagerness to enhance the common good. These included: sitting on the boards of Combermere School and the Barbados National Sports Council; serving as a Justice of the Peace in Barbados; and membership of the Barbados World Cup Board in 2007.

Wes has received many honours and awards in recognition of his lifetime of achievement. Foremost among them is the knighthood announced in the Queen's Birthday Honours list in 2012; he was knighted on 22 October 2012 by the Governor-General Sir Elliott Belgrave in a ceremony at Government House in Bridgetown. Wes considers himself fortunate that he 'happened to be chosen' from a team that included many great players, a self-deprecating observation which overlooks the fact that he was knighted for 'services to sport *and the community*'. It is unlikely that any of his contemporaries – or for that matter cricketers from any other era – have contributed more to the latter category.

The UWI awarded him an honorary Doctorate of Law in 2005, allowing him to append the title 'Dr (LLD, Hons)' to his name, along with those of his numerous other honours. These include: the Barbados Gold Crown of Merit; the Hummingbird Gold Medal from Trinidad and Tobago; and induction into the ICC Hall of Fame. Honorary life memberships were bestowed on him by the BCA, the Barbados Turf Club, Marylebone Cricket Club and Melbourne Cricket Ground, to name but a few. The Hall and Griffith Stand at Kensington Oval commemorates one of Test cricket's great fast-bowling combinations.

Although Wes is proud and appreciative of the recognition he received, 'no number of accolades is comparable to the joy of being a Christian and becoming a priest.' He understands the fickle nature of fame, something he had witnessed as a young man, with the example of Roy Gilchrist:

> When Gilly was sent home, he was the greatest fast bowler in the world, but you never heard about him after that. No day is sacrosanct, and you have to understand that as famous as you are, it only takes one silly thing to ruin everything. On and off the field, you are as good as your last performance; it's a *cliché*, but it is true.

Along with the acclaim that has come his way, Wes has endured his share of difficulties. One of the more unwelcome legacies of a 15-year fast-bowling career was the physical toll it took on his body. The knee injury has left him with a permanent limp, but he has been troubled far more by chronic back pain. In 2015 a scan showed the extent of the problem: 'When you see my MRI ... boy, it's not pretty! It shows that the human body was not designed for express fast bowling!' His layman's assessment was backed up by the professional one of Mr John Gill, a leading consultant neurosurgeon at Barbados' Queen Elizabeth's Hospital. Before operating on Wes's back, Mr Gill expressed astonishment that Wes was able to walk with such a badly damaged spine. The operation was complex and dangerous; the anaesthetists warned him that possible complications included blindness, particularly if the surgery lasted for more than three hours. Wes was in the operating theatre for five and a half hours, during which time Mr Gill 'performed a miracle' on his back. Following the surgery, he was able to walk for miles without the aid of a stick and was fitter than he had been for years.

The euphoria of a return to fitness was short-lived. Just as Wes had finished his three-month course of rehabilitation, he was involved in a serious road accident. Driving in heavy traffic at Top Rock, near St Lawrence in Christ Church, he had slowed to a standstill when a vehicle slammed into his car from behind. His back took the brunt of the impact, leaving him in the same predicament as before his surgery. The risks involved in having a repeat operation were too great; instead, he pays weekly visits to his therapist, Tony Jones, to ease the discomfort. With the aid of a walking stick, he puts on a brave face: 'I count my blessings. I thank God that I have reached 85.'

Of all his many blessings, one which he counts every day is his good fortune in being part of a loving family – from the security it brought to his childhood, to the joy of being a father, grandfather and great-grandfather.

Wes's mother watched him play cricket only once, at Kensington Oval in the Third Test against India in the 1961-1962 series. He took three top-order wickets for 64 runs from 22 overs in the first innings to help West Indies to an innings victory. Lance Gibbs may have stolen the show with astonishing figures of 53.3-37-38-8 in the second innings, but Ione was satisfied with her boy's performance. She never felt the need to watch him again: 'Every ball you bowl, I bowl with you, Wes, so I do not have to be there.' Instead, she preferred to stay at home and keep a written record of all of his wickets as she listened to the cricket commentary on her Redifusion radio. Years later, when her grandson Sean was a jockey, she would listen to every race; just as she had 'bowled every ball' with his father, she 'rode every horse' with him.

Ione set great store by politeness and 'proper' behaviour. When Wes worked for Banks and lived in the company house close to the brewery, a steady stream of colleagues and friends visited him after work and at weekends. He positioned a cooler beside the front entrance so that his guests could help themselves to a beer when they arrived. To his amusement Ione was somewhat perplexed by their practice of taking a drink from the fridge without asking. He explained that he stocked the cooler with beer to make them feel welcome. His mother remained unconvinced: 'I don't think my mother was very happy about that. She didn't think it looked nice. She was all for good manners ... but she loved the guys!'

The Hall brothers recognised how much they owed their mother, and they were continually looking for ways to repay her. These did not always meet with her approval, as Wes had discovered when he left school to provide for her. Her independence again came to the fore in 1992, when Llewellyn and Wes had a three-bedroom house built for her in the smart residential area of Clearview Heights to the north of Bridgetown. After living there for just four months, she asked Wes to bring his car to the house, where she was waiting with four large suitcases packed full of her belongings. She instructed him to load them into the car and to move her back to the house in the government housing area in Grazettes. Although the new house was more comfortable than any Ione had lived in before and her neighbours were friendly, they left for work in their cars in the morning and she saw no one all day. Ione felt lonely and missed being part of a lively, caring neighbourhood. She was sorry to leave, but her heart was elsewhere.

In contrast, life in the housing area revolved around the community, and Ione was very much at the centre of it. She cooked every day and always had enough for anyone who would drop by unannounced. If her window was not open at 5.30 am, neighbours would knock on her door to check on her. Wes lived nearby, and he encouraged her to move in with him, but she insisted on returning to her old home. Wes and his children moved into the house she vacated in Clearview Heights, and they stayed there until he built his current home in 2006. While he was disappointed that his mother did not settle in the house, he understands her feelings, having himself had a similar experience. Home for Wes now is a desirable property in an attractive area, but it saddens him that neighbours have little contact with each other. He misses the sense of togetherness that he took for granted in the bustling neighbourhoods where he grew up:

> I was a lot happier living in communities like The Ivy, St Lawrence or Grazettes Housing Area. At Christmas my mother would bake the pork, and another person cook the rice, and somebody else bake the bread, and we would all come together for the meal. You lose that togetherness when you move out of a community.

For Wes a saving grace was that Ione's death in January 1994 spared her the pain of witnessing the events in parliament which brought his political career to an acrimonious end a few months later. More than 2,000 people attended her funeral. Eight West Indian cricketers carried her coffin into the church, and eight more carried it out. Among the 16 were Sir Garry Sobers, Charlie Griffith, Rawle Brancker, Peter Lashley and Everton Weekes. She had known them all, regularly entertaining them in her home:

> She cooked for them; they all loved my mother. Everyone did. There was always a welcome at my mother's house. No books have been written about my mum, but she was just a beautiful person who did so much good in her life.

Wes and Llewellyn may not have realised it at the time, but their grandmother was as loving as she was keen on discipline. She believed that obedience and Godliness went hand-in-hand, and her strictness was her way of making sure they grew up in the right way. Even in old age she would admonish her great-grandchildren. They had plenty of opportunity to heed her wise words, for she died in 1979 aged 99, missing by just six months the Governor-General's traditional 100th birthday visit. The last time Wes saw his grandmother, she told him that she 'was tired and going home' and that he was to keep on looking after his mum. Three hours later, Ione called Wes to confirm that 'she's gone'.

After leaving St Giles' school and completing an apprenticeship in printing at *The Barbados Advocate*, Llewellyn took up a job with a firm of printers in Manchester. He left Barbados for England in 1956 when he was 20, and in 1964 he joined his sweetheart Myrna in Toronto, where he has lived ever since. Coincidentally their three children, Jackie, Neil and Gregory, were born in 1966, 1968, and 1974, the same years as Sean, Kerry and Remi respectively. Despite many years of physical separation, Wes and Llewellyn have remained close, and their relationship is as strong as ever: 'I have always been there for him, and he has for me.'

Wes's younger sister Margaret has three boys, Nigel, Martin and Stephen, and her grandson Rashad Armstrong is an outstanding young wicketkeeper-batsman who plays for Carlton in the BCA first division. Wes has high hopes that he will play for Barbados.

The divorce of their parents was difficult for Wes's children, especially the older two, who were aged eight and six at the time. Wes drew on his own experience for guidance. By being an absentee father, Fred unwittingly instilled in Wes the resolve to be an attentive one: 'That was the gift that he left me, and the only thing I could do for him was to be a good father to my children.' After the divorce Wes prioritised the children's education and family stability and kept the family together as much as possible. Sean lived with him from the age of nine; Kerry and Remi joined him when they were 18 and 16 respectively. Until then he collected them from their mother's house every Friday evening, and they spent the weekend with him. They all went to good schools, and he took them with him on overseas engagements, exposing them to mind-expanding experiences and places. The children are appreciative that the parting was honourable and without acrimony. Undoubtedly the maturity with which their parents handled the situation helped to dispel tension, and all of them share a close, loving relationship with both their mother and father.

> I do not think, from what they say, that I could be faulted as a father. I am lucky that my children all get on so well and have turned out to be so well adjusted. I hope that's a reflection on how they were brought up.

Wes's children have given him untold pleasure, and he is very proud of them all. John (his first child, who was born and grew up in Canada), Sean, Kerry and Remi all followed different career paths and achieved great success.

Although he was a good schoolboy cricketer, Sean's overriding passion for horses made it unlikely that he would follow in his father's footsteps. He has been riding horses since he was eleven and won his first race at the Garrison Savannah at the age of 14. On leaving school two years later, he became a full-time jockey and rode successfully overseas, in Martinique, Jamaica, Trinidad, India and Australia (on the recommendation of the great Australian jockey and trainer, Scobie Breasley[1]). Sean rode numerous winners in Barbados, including horses owned jointly by Sir Garfield Sobers and Wes. After retiring as a jockey Sean travelled to the Woodbine

---

[1] A.E. 'Scobie' Breasley (1914-2006) rode five Melbourne Cup winners. He also won the Derby twice and the Prix de L'Arc de Triomphe once before embarking on a successful training career.

racetrack in Toronto to further his knowledge. He gained experience at various stables before becoming assistant trainer at Laurie Silvera Racing Stables. He did a great deal of work for the British owner Robert Sangster, whose horse *Rambrino*, trained by Sean, won the 1996 Barbados Gold Cup. Aged 29, Sean became – and remains – the youngest trainer to win the race. Back in Canada he achieved success as a trainer, breeder, owner and equine therapist, before in 2009 he returned to Barbados, where he works at the Garrison Savannah stables: 'Sean is the hardest worker I have known; he gets up at four in the morning to get to the track.' He is a talented songwriter, and many of his songs have been recorded by singer John Glock. Sean's daughter Chivon and son Courtney live in Toronto, and in 2016 Wes became a great-grandfather for the first time when Chivon gave birth to a baby girl, Azeelea.

At the Christ Church Foundation School Kerry showed much promise in the classroom and on the athletics track, where her natural talent for sprinting was 'inherited from my dad'. After attending sixth form at Combermere, she obtained a BSc in management studies from The UWI's Cave Hill campus in Barbados. She went on to gain her master's degree at Florida International University in Miami before returning to Cave Hill to complete a PhD in tourism history in 2002. Subsequently Dr Kerry Hall has compiled a cv spanning public and private sectors: her posts include Chief Tourism Development Officer in the Ministry of Tourism and International Transport and Director of People Development and Training at the Five Diamond Sandy Lane Hotel. As an independent consultant she has worked on local and regional tourism projects and delivered presentations on tourism-related topics throughout the Caribbean and as far afield as Mexico and Nigeria. She has co-authored a coffee-table book called *Island in the Sun: The Story of Tourism in Barbados* and crafted a White Paper on the development of tourism in Barbados for the period 2012 to 2022; this was adopted as the national policy paper by the government. She has held numerous other high-profile roles, including most recently Chief Executive Officer of the Barbados Tourism Product Authority and Director of Tourism Development, where she advised the Minister of Tourism and International Transport. Via her social media platform, *Tourism Overhall*, she aims to make a positive difference to the lives of Barbadian people by ensuring that tourism is 'a catalyst for social and economic transformation that benefits all'. In the words of her father: 'She gets things done!'

Remi, 'the baby of the family', achieved academic excellence at school and university, where his tutor at Barbados Community College, Wes's friend John Boyce, pronounced him 'a genius'! He continued his studies in the USA, where he pursued his passion for electronics and gained a degree in electrical engineering at a leading engineering college, ITT Technical Institute-Miami. After moving back to Barbados, he has performed various engineering and IT roles: for 16 years he was the 'problem solver' at Grantley Adams International Airport and currently works for the Ministry of Health. His father is proud to declare 'there is no electronic device or appliance that he cannot fix'! Quiet and unassuming, Remi is an accomplished surfer and swimmer.

The boys' names reflect Wes's non-cricketing heroes: Sean was named after Sean Connery, with the middle name 'Eusebio' in honour of the great Portuguese footballer of the 1960s. In similar vein Remi's middle name was a homage to the legendary Brazilian footballer Pelé, whose real name is Edson Arantes do Nascimento, 'so we called him "Edson" because it was the only part I could spell!' The choice of 'Kerry' was more spur-of-the-moment, inspired by a short visit to Ireland, where Wes and Shurla fell in love with the country and the people.

Wes jokes that when it came to naming his daughter, he is pleased he chose not to adopt the approach of Brian Lara, whose daughter is called Sydney in recognition of his first Test century, a magnificent 277 at the Sydney Cricket Ground in 1993: 'I was the first West Indian to take a hat-trick. That was at Lahore – my daughter is happy that she is known as Dr Kerry Annalisa Hall!'

Wes had an older son, John, who was born in Canada in 1964: 'He was the glue in the family. He got on better with the other three than they sometimes got on with each other.' Wes attended John's marriage to his fiancée Frances in Canada, and in 1995 they had a son, Jazz, the second of Wes's three grandchildren. In March 2007, on the first day of a family trip to Barbados, John took his son to the beach. The two of them were playing in the surf when John collapsed and died. Frances and Jazz returned to Toronto, and shortly afterwards Wes, Kerry and Remi accompanied the body back to Canada, where they joined Sean and the family for the funeral. Wes delivered the eulogy. At the time he was comforted by the outpouring of sympathy from around the world. His faith has helped him to come to terms with his acute pain and continues to provide solace in darker moments.

John's legacy lives on in the person Jazz, who was just twelve years old when his father died. He went on to obtain a business degree and works successfully as a music producer in Toronto.

Wes's grandfather James Ingram and his brothers, Brigham and Lewis, had 43 children between them. Unsurprisingly therefore, on his father's side, Wes is related to many families, including the Adams, Croneys, Ingrams, Kings, Niles, Simpsons, Stoutes and Youngs. Perhaps the best-known of the family is Alison Hinds, a descendent of the Ingrams who is one of the most popular and successful soca[2] artists in the world, known throughout the Caribbean as the 'Queen of Soca'. Of his maternal grandmother Louise's six siblings, her four brothers went to work as labourers building the Panama Canal. Two of them returned to Barbados, and the other two settled in Panama and Cuba respectively. The Bowens, Broomes, Burtons, Collymores, Halls, Marshalls, McCleans and Taitts are all relatives on his mother's side. With such a huge extended family, it is not surprising that the family reunion in 2017 was the first time Wes met several of the 168 relatives who attended. One of the guests was Wes's cousin Maxine McClean, who served in government as a leader of the senate and was the minister for foreign affairs and trade between 2008 and 2018.

With his European and African ancestry, Wes understood the concept of race from a young age: 'My father's family was like my West Indies team – a rainbow coalition.' It is unsurprising, therefore, that Wes grew up to be tolerant of the differences between people and developed an enlightened approach. Race as it pertained to black and white never occupied his mind; he just saw people who happened to be of a different colour. At Combermere, when Wes met the headmaster Major Noott and Mr Hughes and the other masters, he was not unsettled by the sight of white men; in fact, he regarded the kindness and encouragement he received from them as normal behaviour. He integrated easily with British people from when he was a young man and got on well with the white supervisors and managers at Cable & Wireless:

---

[2] Soca – 'Soul of Calypso' – began in Trinidad in the 1970s as an upbeat variant of calypso. It is now a popular mainstream musical genre throughout the Caribbean.

To this day I still have a close relationship with English cricketers, folk in Accrington and also in Australia. The people I met from all over the world confirmed to me that race is a social construct and not a biological reality. It is who you are that matters, not where you come from or what you look like. We are all created in the image of God.

Racism was so deeply embedded in every aspect of life in colonial Barbados that it was part of the 'normal' state of affairs. However, as a boy, Wes had no reason to suspect that anyone might think any differently to him about race, so he remained naively oblivious to the existence – or the concept – of racism. Obviously the reality of the situation dawned on him as he gained an understanding of how the island's institutions operated systems of privilege and exclusion based on the colour of a person's skin:

My grandfather James and his two brothers were sons of a Scotsman. They had white complexions, and they could have played for any of the white cricket clubs in the island; the only clubs I could join were Empire and Spartan.

In the wake of the 2020 killing of George Floyd by police in the United States, Wes applauds the lead taken in the fight against racism by cricketers and other sportsmen, particularly Michael Holding and Lewis Hamilton, a man he greatly admires. He believes in the power of education in combating prejudice, with schools and especially parents bearing responsibility for ensuring that the message is delivered loud and clear to youngsters.

Wes reflects that in order to play in South Africa prior to 1992, he and his teammates would have to have been declared 'honorary whites': 'I loved my grandfather, but you cannot call me an honorary white. Simply put, I am a proud black man.'

Wes endorses Nelson Mandela's assertion that sport – more than politics – is capable of building bridges. As a West Indies player in the only multi-racial team in the world, he had witnessed the power of cricket in overcoming society's racial taboos: 'With blacks, whites, Chinese, Indians and Caribs[3], we were a combination of races and creeds in a world that

---

[3] Caribs were indigenous to the Lesser Antilles islands (which include Barbados). They originated from Mainland Caribs who migrated from South America to the islands around 1200.

was yet to recognise the importance of ethnic diversity. West Indies can stand tall as a pioneer of multi-culturalism.'

Hence, cricket was of unique importance in helping to shape race relations in the Caribbean. Wes proudly refers to the first session of the April 1972 Test at Port of Spain between West Indies and New Zealand. There were four West Indians on the field, representing the four major territories and four different ethnic backgrounds: West Indies' opening batsmen were Roy Fredericks, a black Guyanese, and Geoff Greenidge, a white Barbadian. The umpires were Ralph Gosein, a Trinidadian Indian, and Douglas Sang-Hue, a Jamaican of Chinese descent: 'Where else in the world could that happen? We had all cultures, religions and colours.'

Cricket is also the only sport where West Indies competes as one nation. There have always been inter-territory differences, but together they have been able to produce numerous powerful West Indian teams capable of being world champions in all forms of the game. Hence, West Indies achieved far greater prominence and success in cricket than in any other sport, and cricket has earned a special place in the hearts of the Caribbean people. It is widely accepted that pride in the West Indies team helped to forge the national identity which was a factor in the development of the region.

Wes's simple hope for the future is expressed in the paraphrased words of Martin Luther King Jr, from a speech[4] delivered in 1963, but still relevant in the context of racial struggles in USA and elsewhere: 'My children will one day live in a world where they will not be judged by the colour of their skin but by the content of their character.'

[4] American Civil Rights leader Dr Martin Luther King Jr (1929-1968) gave his 'I Have a Dream' speech in Washington DC on 28 August 1963.

25

Lessons Learned from Cricket

Wes attributes much of what he achieved in later life to lessons learned on the cricket field:

> The first thing that cricket taught me at the age of eight was to separate opinions from the facts. It was only an opinion that I could not go to Combermere or play for the West Indies, but the facts are that not only did I play for the West Indies, I was a chief selector, manager for many years, president of the WICB and West Indies representative on the ICC board.
>
> There has been little that I have done in my life in which cricket did not play a part; a funny thing to say but it's true. It affirmed the values and discipline my grandmother and mother taught me, principles that have guided me throughout every area of my life. Those values and discipline enabled me to handle relationships and the pressures of life – everything! Lessons I learned in my cricketing career guided me when I was in management. They guided me in parliament, just as they did in preaching.

As a player – even as a youngster on the 1957 tour of England – he developed theories on various themes, based on his 'cricket education'.

Success – and failure

Wes drew on his experiences in cricket for his thoughts on what constitutes success and on the qualities needed to be successful. Supreme excellence requires a combination of talent and what he calls an 'instinct for perfection', and as such it is attained by the fortunate few cricketers whose instinctive genius allows them to perform outrageous feats. After the inevitable mention of Sobers, Wes points out that, although such excellence may be out of reach for the vast majority of people, everyone can achieve success. He defines success not as an isolated triumph but a sustained high level of performance, with new goals continually set in the drive for improvement. Ability and discipline enable individuals to perform at a high level; success is achieved by those who are driven to set new goals in their quest for improvement. His theory owed much to his great mentor Frank Worrell, who encouraged his players to adopt a 'winning determination' in the pursuit of perfection.

Conventionally, of course, failure is seen as the opposite of success. Wes begs to differ. He views failure not as a single cataclysmic event but a series of small reversals that will culminate in a serious problem if they are allowed to build up unchecked: 'Failure is a building block to success. It provides knowledge, because if you never failed you would never learn anything ... you can use failure to your advantage.'

Wes noted that players can put in great performances – the occasional marvellous innings or five-wicket spell – but become great players only when they do it consistently. Throughout his cricketing career, he was continually reminded that this requires constant thinking and analysis. Drawing on the lessons of early struggles, he reconstructed his entire approach to bowling, and thereafter he was meticulous in preparing a plan of attack for opposing batsmen, particularly those who had caused him problems in the past. Hence he found that learning from his 'failures' was immeasurably more useful than the success of taking five wickets against a moderate batting side in bowler-friendly conditions.

Vision

In addition to its simplest meaning – the ability to see – vision can also be defined as the ability to imagine the future and to act accordingly. As a Christian Wes believes this derives from the biblical definition: a supernatural revelation occurring between heavenly and earthly beings. The concept of vision has played an important part in Wes's life, beginning with his revelation as a young boy.

Individuals' perceptions of success are influenced by their different visions. In a cricketing context, both an opening batsman who is striving to average 50 and a tail-ender trying to improve his average to 15 will have achieved success if they realise their targets. Wes refers to an often-quoted extract from the *Old Testament, Proverbs, 29.18*: 'Where there is no vision, the people perish.' His interpretation is that vision shows how we can adapt and change to overcome challenges; therefore vision is the driver of progress.

Faced with competition from other sports, cricket has been required to adapt and change dramatically on an organisational level and on the field. In recent years structural changes have delivered a 'product' that would have been unimaginable in Wes's playing days. Particularly the various 20/20 competitions – with flashing bails, fireworks, loud music, dancers and 'X-factor substitutes' – would not have been recognisable as cricket even 20 years ago. Unimaginable, too, would have been the vast revenue generated by the new formats and, by extension, the vast sums of money earned by top players. Cricketers' roles also have changed beyond recognition. Scoring runs quickly has become the principal requirement of batsmen, and a bowler's prime objective is containment. Players have been creative in developing their skills in order to remain competitive: armed with thick, heavy bats, batsmen have invented a range of daring strokes such as reverse sweeps and 'ramp' shots. A bowlers' repertoire is likely to include slower-ball bouncers – which would previously have been considered bad bowling – cross-seam deliveries and yorkers.

In a sport steeped in tradition, the innovations face opposition from both within the game and sceptical supporters who see them as a threat to cricket's traditional skills and values. Unlike many players of his generation, Wes appreciates both sides of the argument. He salutes the vision that led to changes which were necessary for the game to flourish commercially, and he welcomes the introduction of a colourful spectacle with the emphasis on entertainment and excitement. Raising the profile of the sport has delivered a vast new audience, placing cricket in a healthier financial position than ever before, with a long-overdue increase in player rewards. Positives are tempered with a note of caution. The greatest fear is that the purest form of the game will become marginalised. A generation raised on a diet of short-form cricket is less likely to appreciate – and therefore pay to watch – the ebbs and flows of a Test match played over several days.

From a playing perspective, further growth of 20/20 cricket – and fatuous, dumbed-down spin-offs such as 100-ball cricket – is likely to undermine the game's traditional skills. Occupation of the crease by batsmen and wicket-taking for bowlers will become less relevant as priorities shift to scoring and economy rates respectively. Again Wes has concerns regarding the implications for Test cricket, in particular the demise of technically correct batsmen:

I am very distressed having seen some of our young players in the nets; the batsmen try to hit every ball for six. A shot-a-ball is alright for 20/20 but not for a Test match. People seem to feel you've got to be swiping to make runs. No! The Ws, Graveney and Cowdrey would have found ways to play correctly and still make runs in one-day cricket. Great players adapt ... that is why Smith, Kohli, Sharma, Root and Williamson are so consistent in ODIs.

Despite being backed up by 'funky' field placings and an astonishing improvement in the standard of fielding, bowlers have struggled to keep pace in a format where big-hitting and high scoring are at a premium. The desire of spectators – and hence sponsors – to see the ball repeatedly pumped into the stands often reduces a bowler's role to little more than that of a bowling machine, and Wes bemoans the uneven contest between bat and ball in 20/20 cricket. It saddens him that the art of true fast bowling is likely to become a thing of the past:

> Of course, that type of cricket favours batsmen, because I can be bowling at 95mph on the off-stump, get the edge I was looking for, and the ball flies off the big bat for six. When that happens, you adapt as a bowler, and that means reducing your pace or finding another way.

In his professional career, Wes played in just a couple of limited-over List A[1] matches, and he regrets not having the opportunity to prove himself in the format. Applying the simple logic that he picked up more wickets when batsmen attacked than defended against him, he is confident that he would have been a prolific wicket-taker. As for his economy rate, he feels he would have had that covered too: 'I would give batsmen no width and nothing in the slot, so these guys with big bats couldn't just stand up and swing at the ball'. His stock tactic would have been to bowl at pace at the batsman's body, forcing him to hit the ball in the air, with variation in the form of the occasional yorker and a ball delivered from wide of the crease angling into the right-hander or across the left-hander. Sadly, the outcome of a confrontation between Wes and the modern 20/20 superstars will never be known; however, he is confident that with his pace, 'They would be in trouble if they were attacking every ball!'

[1] List A refers to international and domestic one-day matches of between 40 and 65 overs per side and therefore excludes 20/20.

The recent trend of players forsaking Test cricket for a career in 'white-ball cricket' leads Wes to sound a further note of caution over the pace of change:

> A player coming towards the end of his Test career can have a pay-day for two or three years and not wear himself out physically ... that is a good thing. But we have seen so many changes in cricket, that it is possible for a boy to come along and say that he doesn't want to play Test cricket at all, and he will make very good money in his career playing ODI and 20/20 cricket. Instead of playing five long days, bowling 30 overs in an innings, why wouldn't he bowl four overs – or ten in a 50-over game – earn more money, have less chance of injury and have a longer career? So that is where we have to be careful of change; world cricket has to look carefully at these things.

From turning himself into a fast bowler, to bowling the final over in crucial Test matches, time and again throughout his cricket career, Wes displayed vision and the determination necessary to succeed. In his subsequent careers his uncommon vision has revolutionised organisations and changed lives for the better. In Trinidad the Wes Hall League and SERVOL may have been conceived by Hugh Henderson and Father Pantin, but Wes was immediately able to share their visions and enhance them with his own. He implemented initiatives for workers at Banks, and he battled against the odds for a seat in parliament. In government he introduced imaginative innovations such as Gospelfest and his wholesome tourism programme; he embraced the concept of sports tourism; and his policies yielded record increases in visitor numbers. He brought a player-focused approach to team management and a raft of fresh thinking to the role of WICB president. From pursuing his dreams as an eight-year-old to accepting the call from God, Wes has shown himself repeatedly to be a man of vision in every sense.

Preparation
Pursuit of a vision to its successful conclusion can rarely be attained without preparation. Preparation is something that a player is able to control, and as such Wes believes that there is no excuse for under-preparing, either physically or in terms of acquiring knowledge.

Practising skills until they are finely honed is obviously essential for any professional sportsperson. This requires many hours on the training ground, and no one is a bigger advocate – or better advertisement – for this type of hard work. His grandmother regularly reminded him that 'practice makes perfect'. Although Wes appreciates the sentiment, he prefers the variation 'perfect practice makes perfect': 'because if you're practising the wrong thing, you'll end up being perfectly wrong'.

Efficient, target-focussed training cuts out unnecessary effort and makes it easy to monitor progress. Without a defined objective, the hard work will be wasted. The Ws taught him that the point of net sessions was to groove good habits until they became second nature and that whatever he did in practice would be replicated in a match. A bowler who charges to the wicket and bowls no-balls in the nets will bowl no-balls in the middle.

As a 19-year-old the time Wes spent with George Headley helped him to regather his thoughts when he was doubting himself after the 1957 England tour. He encourages young players to follow his example in seeking knowledge and the cricket authorities to take the initiative by facilitating the process.

Formal classroom learning can sometimes fail to equip young people with the ability to adapt to the real world. Wes gives the example of the difference between teaching mathematics and teaching cricket. At Combermere in 1950 Wes learned Pythagoras' theorem. That theorem holds now, just as it did in 1950, and will in 100 years' time. In contrast, a look at how cricket has evolved reveals a game barely recognisable from 70 years ago. Players need to be flexible in order to adjust to changes in cricket, and this is difficult for youngsters whose learning experiences have centred on immutable facts. As a further complication a cricket match presents a dynamic environment with an infinite number of moving parts. Unlike Pythagoras there is not one situation on a cricket field that will ever be exactly replicated, and this poses difficulties for young players whose minds have been trained to solve problems with clear-cut answers. The closest Wes can come to solving this conundrum is to recommend that a young cricketer avoids over-complicating matters and sticks to the basics. He or she will then be able to maximise their control of a situation and gain confidence. The ability to think on your feet cannot be taught; it can be acquired only through experience. Therefore batsmen should not try to play many ambitious shots until confident in their ability to stay in, and only then should they look to be more expansive. New skills should be built on the fundamentals of the game: for example, opening the face of the bat slightly to deflect the ball square instead of playing it straighter requires only minor adjustments in technique.

Relationships

Within a team setting, it is impossible to realise goals without the help of others, and cricket taught Wes the importance of healthy working relationships. When he played for West Indies, he saw his teammates as part of his extended family. In those days, and with Test series often infrequent, 'You were longing to get back to see the boys. That took us a long way.'

Team spirit and togetherness are crucial to success in any sport. Like baseball, cricket is unusual in that it features individual contests within the team framework, making it impossible to 'hide' on the cricket field. To be successful, a player needs to take responsibility and relish the prospect of testing himself. Wes viewed challenges as opportunities, a mindset due in part to the confidence that accompanied his status as a top-class bowler but also a reflection of his desire to serve, in this case for the benefit of his teammates. In return Wes expected others to aspire to the standards that he set for himself. He demanded consistency from his teammates, with everyone having confidence in one another; if a good performance one day is followed by a poor one the next, then the player in question is a liability.

Wes sets great store by the relationships he had with his two fast-bowling roommates, Gilchrist and Griffith. He talked cricket for hours on end with them both, exchanging information and helping to solve problems together. Having teammates whom you like and trust, and who become friends, can only be of benefit to the team:

> That's why they put batsmen together and fast bowlers together: Charlie or Gilly would spot something in my bowling or tell me things about a batsman that I hadn't noticed, and *vice-versa*. If you're a young batsman, and you have just made a couple of ducks, how are you going to feel when you go back to your room, with no one to talk to? When I was struggling in 1957, Gilly was there to encourage me. The Ws; Ramadhin and Valentine; Sobers and Collie Smith; Haynes and Greenidge; and the fast bowlers in the 80s ... they all roomed together and helped each other.

A good rapport with the opposition is also important. On the cricket field Wes gave no quarter, but he realised that it was possible to be a tough competitor and still show respect to his opponent. He tried at all times to remain mindful that the batsman or bowler he was facing from 22 yards was first and foremost a human being. Friendships with many of his fiercest on-field adversaries lasted long after their playing days were over. A quote from Tom Graveney is typical:

> ... an outstanding athlete, a hostile bowler and one of the nicest people ever to have played the game. Play a good stroke off his bowling, and he would applaud you and mean it. He was a fierce competitor on the field, but a generous one.

Another great batsman, Hanif Mohammad, is equally profuse in his praise:

> Wes Hall was one of the most fearsome fast bowlers that I ever faced, though he possessed a temperament unlike other quickies, for he was a very gentle and generous cricketer; the reason why he was extremely popular with crowds.

Charlie Griffith, a man who knew him probably better than any other player, considers Wes 'the kindest, most likeable fast bowler that there has ever been ... he wouldn't harm a fly.'

Tributes like these echo Worrell's sentiments in the foreword to *Pace Like Fire*. Playing hard and respecting the fact that your opponent also is trying to do their best, led to Wes developing a refreshingly balanced view of sporting confrontation. Lessons learned in the cut and thrust of battle on the cricket field later defined his conduct towards 'adversaries' in other walks of life. Barbados Workers' Union official LeVere Richards is a prime example: Wes managed to negotiate effectively for his employer Banks while maintaining an excellent relationship with Richards.

Communication

Effective communication is essential in any relationship, and Wes regards Frank Worrell as the greatest communicator he encountered in his cricketing days. Worrell captained West Indies in 15 Test matches, and his calm authority and sympathetic treatment of his players inspired loyalty and moulded a group of multi-talented individuals into a formidable unit. He led by example, sharing information with the players and asking them for their thoughts; in return they bought into his captaincy. Wes heeded the lesson and found that it applied in all situations:

> Information is the oxygen of democracy. If you share something with your team, and your team understands you, they will follow you, because you have shown that you value them. If you're the supervisor, it makes no sense to keep information to yourself and let everyone else bang their heads against the wall.

Worrell treated them all as individuals, seeking them out so that he could better understand them – and be understood. His handling of Wes in the final over of the tied Test may appear harsh, but it was a perfect illustration of his man-management skills; he knew that Wes was a robust character and treated him accordingly. From the way Worrell captained Wes, and the challenging career path he oversaw, it was obvious that Worrell saw special qualities in him. A quote from 1965 reveals the extent of the captain's regard for his fast bowler, 'a deep thinker ... who has made a tremendous contribution to the planning of the West Indies cricket "battles" over the past six years.'

Often in his life Wes has encountered people who confuse 'making noise' with the two-way process of communicating, in which receiving and transmitting are of equal importance. If they are to develop an understanding, teammates must be aware of each other's thoughts and needs, and that awareness is gained only by listening to them. Since he was a young cricketer his ears have been his most useful asset:

> As a junior on the team I listened to the great players, and I adapted accordingly and took responsibility for my actions. As a government minister I wanted feedback, and I listened attentively to the civil servants in my office, which enabled me to analyse a situation and then take responsibility for making the best decision. That is good communication.

In business, cricket administration, parliament and the Church, Wes was called upon repeatedly to deliver speeches and sermons. He is fortunate that public speaking has always come naturally to him, and his addresses are stimulating, entertaining and sincere. And notoriously long! Unlike one-to-one communication or talking in small groups, there is little scope for direct feedback when speaking to a large audience, and Wes developed a technique for connecting with his listeners. He picked out a random handful of individuals in the crowd and 'talked' to them, concentrated on their reaction and made sure that they understood and were interested in what he was saying. He worked on the theory that if this sample was engaged, others would be too. Again Worrell's example was influential. Worrell preferred to talk to his players individually, but on the occasions when he addressed the whole team he always talked *to* rather than *at* them, so that each player felt that he was part of the conversation.

When Wes was a boy growing up in Barbados, and during his cricket career in the 1950s and 1960s, the world was a far simpler place. Before the days of mobile phones and the internet, and with computers in their infancy, communication largely involved physical interaction and the telephone. Cutting-edge telecommunication equipment of the type Wes operated at Cable & Wireless was hopelessly slow in comparison with today's digital technology. Over recent decades, the extraordinary advances in communication technology have presented new challenges, and Wes is dismayed by the impact computers and mobile phones have had on relationships. He laments that 'the cell phone in Barbados is now part of our national dress. If you make the mistake of giving a teenager a cell phone without restrictions, you are in trouble.' This is one of the few topics where Wes adopts the older generation's default position that things were better in the old days. He feels that such an attitude is more likely to alienate than benefit the person it is intended to help and that young people need to be treated carefully. It is the older person's responsibility to move towards them in order to pass on the benefit of his/her experience:

> As you grow as a cricketer, and you grow as a man, you need to be in a position to help the others coming along, recognising that things may not be the same as they were in your era. That is something I learned in my time as a player from people like the Three Ws.

Pressure

The ability to cope with pressure is essential for success. Although Wes was blessed with natural confidence and the desire to tackle challenges, no one could prepare themselves for the situations he faced in his career. Apart from the two famous make-or-break final overs, for years he shouldered the pressure that went with being the leader of West Indies' pace attack, and perhaps most impressively, after the 1957 tour of England, he overcame crushing pressure by toiling alone for months on end to save his career. Without doubt cricket taught Wes how to handle pressure.

Coaches can instruct a player how to bat or bowl, so that he or she is well prepared, but once out in the middle it becomes a question of how pressure will affect the player's ability to reproduce those skills. For Wes there was no magic answer. He relied on his strength of character to see him through difficult situations:

> You could get pressure on the field or off it. Getting hate mail is pressure off the field. On the field, when a coach has told you to do this and do that, and you go to Calcutta or Melbourne in front of 100,000 yelling people and the batsmen hits you for three fours, all that the coach has told you goes out of the window. You're no longer thinking, emotions take over, so you've got to be strong enough to be master of your emotions. When pressure arises, you simply have to find a way to derail it before it runs over you and destroys you. And the way to achieve that is through belief. It's a matter of mental toughness, finding a way to be a master of yourself ... mind over matter and have faith in your ability.

The suffocating nature of pressure causes players who lack self-belief to make irrational decisions and mistakes, which can then turn the most favourable position into defeat. Hence, ability to cope with pressure is probably the single most important factor in making or breaking cricketers – and other sportsmen. The brutal truth is that talented players who can perform well under pressure become great players, while those who continue to make wrong choices under pressure, remain talented, but unfulfilled. This was recognised by Frank Worrell, who would be interested less in how good a player was, than how he played under pressure.

Handling pressure is one side of the coin; the other is creating it to undermine the opposition. 'Build pressure' may be a modern-day slogan, but it was a strategy used by Wes and his teammates in the 1960s, based on their knowledge of the opposition's strengths and weaknesses. Whether attempting to frustrate a batsman by bowling a conventional line and length, or intimidate him with short-pitched bowling, the objective was to make him feel uneasy, force a mistake and take his wicket.

The intense pressure which accompanied playing cricket at the highest level may have been discomforting, but Wes saw it in perspective. He acknowledged his good fortune in being tested in the sporting arena rather than a theatre of war or having to perform life-saving surgery. Subsequently he has been able to deal with intense pressure in many high-profile positions, shouldering responsibility and refusing to be daunted. The importance of pressure – and how it is handled – cannot be overestimated.

Having selected a handful of 'headings' to illustrate the importance of lessons he learned from cricket, of far greater importance was the lesson learned from cricket by the West Indian people – about themselves and their place in the world.

26

Cricket, Citizenship and Independence

The part played by cricket in the development and democratisation of the West Indies owes much to many individuals, but Wes identifies three men as being inspirational driving forces: Learie Constantine, C.L.R. James and Frank Worrell.

Constantine was indeed an estimable man. Born in Trinidad in 1901 – the same year as James – he was a fast-bowling all-rounder who played 18 Test matches between 1928 and 1939. In 1928, against England at Lord's in West Indies' first-ever Test, he became the first West Indian to take a Test wicket. From 1933 until his retirement he and the Barbadian Manny Martindale formed the first of many fearsome West Indian fast-bowling partnerships.

On and off the cricket field Constantine led the way for West Indians in England. In 1928 he joined Lancashire League club Nelson. He was the first West Indian to play in the leagues, and his success encouraged other West Indian stars to follow. He settled in England permanently and, after his cricket career, he devoted himself to fighting racism and discrimination on behalf of his countrymen in Great Britain. He studied law and was called to the bar in 1954, before returning to Trinidad where he successfully sought election to parliament. He moved back to Britain in 1961 as Trinidad and Tobago's first High Commissioner in London and was knighted the following year. In 1969, two years before his death, Constantine was awarded a life peerage. Throughout his life he was a vociferous proponent of equal rights and a respected and influential voice in political circles in the West Indies and Britain.

Irrespective of racial and political considerations behind C.L.R. James' relentless campaigning in support of Frank Worrell's captaincy, the decision to eventually appoint him was unquestionably the correct one on cricketing grounds. Before the 1960-61 tour of Australia James demonstrated his extraordinary vision when he challenged Worrell and his team to effectively put an end to colonialism. Subsequently much was made by social commentators and historians of the role played by cricket in the awakening of a Caribbean consciousness that led to independence.

Although Wes was only in his mid-20s at the time, he appreciated more than most the wider implications of West Indies' success, as Charlie Griffith recalls in his autobiography:

> In an interview with John Arlott at the end of the 1963 tour, Wes told Arlott that he hoped that our success would do something to ameliorate the position of the West Indian in Britain and create some respect for him. Wes is happiest when he can discuss matters of this kind. In the hurly-burly of international cricket some West Indians, confused by fame and fortune, often forget their humble origins and their responsibilities. Wes Hall is not one of them.

On 6 August 1962 Jamaica became the first Caribbean colony to gain independence. Trinidad and Tobago followed shortly afterwards. In 2012 Wes was invited to speak at the Trinidad and Tobago Cricket Board's 50th Anniversary of Independence awards ceremony. He attended with his daughter Kerry and chose as the theme of his address the relationship between cricket, independence and citizenship in the Caribbean region. The following is an extract from that acclaimed speech:

> Now we were educated by C.L.R. James, who taught us that cricket in the West Indies is a game and must be compared with other games; it is an art and must be compared with other arts – ballet, drama and dance. Lord Constantine and Sir Frank Worrell, drawing on their vast experience of life and playing in the cricket leagues in England opined – and we concur – that cricket in the West Indies is a metaphor that mirrors cultural, political and social change. A regional integrator; a unifying force; a microcosm of life.
>
> Apart from sacred worship, nothing rouses the deep passion of West Indian people like cricket, particularly when we became the embodiment of world cricket supremacy from 1962-1968 and 1980-1995.
>
> Ladies and gentlemen, to speak about the importance of West Indian cricket is to speak about why West Indians have embraced, developed and domesticated and perfected a culture that was in fact an import from Britain. So we should thank the British for giving

us the opportunity to revolutionise their culture and to create in the process an entirely different game.

Do not think for a moment that West Indian cricket is not a new development. Its logic, values, artistry, morality and spirit are very different from other cricket cultures in other countries. We have to recognise this and understand the significance of it, for we create a different game, because we have a different role for cricket to play in our society.

We expect our cricket to be an ultimate democratic space; that is why the WICB does not support discrimination in our cricket facilities and wishes to encourage the involvement of women at all levels.

So cricket, in my view, is all about building a democratic sensibility for all. It is a social space that is community at its most refined. That is why we fought against the prejudice of race and class and do so against gender by insisting that every West Indian who participates in our culture is equal. The only colour we recognised in our dressing room was maroon.

That is why Lord Constantine and Sir Frank Worrell were so very important; because they were dealing with the wider picture, and the wider picture is the development of the West Indian people. That is what cricket is all about – the development of the West Indian people in every sense. Their national development; their cultural development; their spiritual development; and their artistic development. It is a special kind of development; the kind that says we are building a civilisation in which there are rules about justice and equality.

A civilisation in which the community – yes, the man and woman in the street – is at the centre of things. So we are talking about building a democratic civilisation that is deep within our history, so that cricket is a critical training ground for this kind of civilisation.

The British may have used cricket to preserve their elite culture, but we must use it to break down that culture and give power to the people.

For this reason I am aware that when I became president of the WICB I was part of the tradition of Constantine, C.L.R. James and Worrell, who wanted to put the citizen at the centre.

Look at our cricket culture in the 1950s when I started to play at Test level. I was aware that every kind of West Indian had played for us: Indian, African, white, Jew, Chinese, Syrian, all kinds of mixed-race people, and now we have a Carib from Dominica. Cricket for us has a room for everyone, because that kind of house is consistent with our philosophy of development.

Brothers and sisters, do you realise that in my playing years, the West Indies cricket team was the only multi-racial outfit in the international arena?

Do you realise that we were a rainbow coalition in a world that had not yet begun to understand the beauty of ethnic diversity?

Do you realise that the cricket team was a mirror in which we saw what the independent nation should look like?

The philosophy which celebrates the principle 'One for all, all for one' was what we tried to normalise. It was the idealism to which I was committed.

Let me conclude on this note:

When we talk of West Indian cricket as a development tool for our people, we are speaking of the importance of cricket to something much bigger than itself. What is that something?

It is the West Indian people. Their nation. Their collective consciousness, our identity and the culture we have crafted out of our harsh history.

All of this became clear to me shortly after the facts surrounding the 1960 tied Test were made known. I knew the importance that Frank Worrell had attached to that tour. I knew that the Federation was in difficulty. What I did not know at the time was that C.L.R. James had written to Frank to let him know that if he and the boys showed that West Indies was ready to manage its own affairs, it would signal the end of colonialism. What a prophecy!

Worrell, Constantine and C.L.R. James understood those things. They represented the link between cricket, independence and citizenship. They were enormous, yet cricket was bigger.

Can you imagine that we were just playing in a cricket series, and the future of the region was tied up in the outcome, and the five million West Indians understood that independence needed a grand psychological advantage? And cricket was expected to provide it! The indomitable spirit of the West Indian people, as they supported the West Indies team, caused a wave of nationalism which made independence easier for the citizenship to accept.

To this day, with over 50 years of close contact with West Indies cricket, I do not believe that I know half of what there is to know. The literature that our scholars produced – from C.L.R. James, Prime Minister Michael Manley, Professor Sir Hilary Beckles and Tony Cozier – is the richest literature in the world, and all of it speaks to the magnificence of being a West Indian in a world that gave us so little but in which we created so much.

As we look to the future, I maintain that the relationship between cricket and the national consciousness will evolve but will stand firm in spite of talk about the fading of West Indian cricket culture and the competition from other sporting activities.

Cricket is not here to compete with other sports. As James said, it is a game and must be <u>compared</u> to other games; it is an art-form and must be <u>compared</u> with other arts. Cricket is here to offer West Indies youth and the wider community a value system and a wider reference base to bring order to our society.

Yes, we recognise the impact of sports globalisation, but I maintain that the nation will be more important in the age of globalisation than ever before, and that is why our cricket which is so linked to our national identity will continue to grow. The truism is that in this globalised world, these young awardees, as we congratulate them, must be taught that to be successful, they must be competitive, creative, consistent and adapt to the world's changing conditions. They are the key elements of our survival.

I thank you for your graciousness and hospitality, which can only be exceeded by our gratitude and our capacity to absorb it. God bless all of you. God bless the West Indies.

Wes felt it was the duty of his generation to build on the progress made by his predecessors, and he followed the lead of Constantine and Worrell in making the transition from leading international cricketer to politician serving in parliament. Throughout his political career he was noted for his independence of thought and progressive, people-centred policies, and consequently he can join those two great men and James in having established the link between cricket, independence and citizenship.

27

A Crowning Moment

A rare piece of good fortune to emerge from the wreckage of 2020/21 is that the delay in finalising this book allowed the inclusion of a special chapter in Wes's story. On 29 November 2021, the eve of the 54th anniversary of Barbados' independence, a statue in his honour was unveiled at Kensington Oval.

The ceremony was attended by many of the great and the good of Barbadian society and, although Covid restrictions limited numbers and some tributes were relayed by video link, the occasion was a great success. The following extracts from a few of the evening's speeches convey the mood of a major milestone in Wes's life, as his statue took its place alongside that of Sir Garfield Sobers outside the Kensington Oval cricket ground. Inspired by a thrilling photograph which for many years has had pride of place in the Hall family home, the bronze sculpture captures Wes in full flight a split-second before delivery, with his left leg high and left arm pointing skywards. Commemorating Wes in this way was the brainchild of Chris de Caires, Chairman of the 2007 Cricket World Cup Barbados Committee. For four years, from inception to completion of the project, he dedicated himself tirelessly to the task, raising funds from private donors, liaising with sculptor Jason Hope and advisers from the cricket world and working with the American Bronze Foundry in Orlando, Florida, the company responsible for the bronze casting of the statue. After thanking those who had helped turn his dream into reality, de Caires concluded: 'Sir Wes, there's a lot of love out there for you, and I hope we've managed to incorporate some of that love into this statue.'

The love and respect felt for Wes within the game were articulated by West Indian former greats, including Michael Holding, Sir Clive Lloyd, Sir Charles Griffith and Sir Garry Sobers. Holding spoke as a player managed by Wes:

> As a manager of so many tours that I was part of, you were exemplary. You were in charge. We *knew* you were in charge, but

you managed to carry that message without putting on the veil of an intimidating boss. As a confidant to a young man wondering about life, you were parental, and I'm sure all the players you managed, appreciated those qualities. And another thing, Chief: you had our backs. Thanks for that!

In those days tours were littered with functions that could be a bit boring at times, but as a team we always looked forward to your speeches, as we knew you would bring some life to proceedings, and we would always be proud of what you had to say ... and, of course, how you said it! Chief, congratulations, and I'm proud to be able to say: 'You're a friend.'

Tributes from beyond the cricket world were led by Mia Amor Mottley, the Barbadian Prime Minister, who spoke in praise of his 'absolute gentlemanly behaviour':

I happened to be in the Parliament of Barbados as a senator, sitting in the gallery in what will still be probably one of the most tense moments in the parliamentary history of Barbados; one that required extraordinary courage, especially from someone whose very instinct was always to be the consummate team player. On that evening, you taught me – as you quoted from the bible – that above all else, the future and the stability of this country must rank above anything else. I therefore this evening would like publicly to commend you, not as one of your peers but as one who, from being a young child, has admired you and been influenced by you. In spite of our being on different political sides, it never stopped you from reaching out to me as a young politician. The guidance I got from you was the same as I got from those who belonged to my side. That speaks volumes to me. Those of our generation, whether as cricketers, as politicians or just as Bajans, would do well to understand and learn from the example of your life and the example of your character.

Of all the excellent speeches that evening, one stood out. In her professional capacity Kerry is well-known as an excellent public speaker, and her tribute to her hero and father, delivered on behalf of herself and her brothers, captivated the audience:

Of all your long list of achievements, here is one that didn't make the cut, but this is your biggest achievement to date to us, your children: we give you the title of the world's greatest father. You have inspired us to reach for the stars and live life the way it is supposed to be lived – to the fullest. You are a man of humility and integrity. You are the ultimate team player, the ultimate people person. For our whole lives we have had a front-row seat to you devoting your life to being of service to mankind. To always champion the cause of the faceless and the voiceless; always treat people as equals and show them respect, no matter their station in life; never to judge a man by his ZIP code, where he went to school, his lineage, the colour of his skin or the size of his bank account, but by the strength of his character. And most importantly, to have the courage of your conviction, to fearlessly stand up and speak out for what is right and just, even if you stand alone.

The photograph on which the sculpture was modelled is our favourite picture in the world ... it is the epitome of a super-athlete because that is what you were – a super-athlete. As a child, I always looked at this picture in awesome wonder, because to me it was the fusion of the power of a locomotive and the grace of a ballerina. It's humanly impossible for those two forces to exist in the same space, but Daddy, you managed it! And now, present and future generations will also be able to benefit from this sight, this beautiful statue, with you in full flight, a wondrous sight for time immemorial.

After listening to the many tributes, it was left to Wes to round off the evening with his speech before the unveiling of the statue. He began by thanking the sculptor:

My friends, people like me from the proletariat learned to dream big and to achieve some accolades but not a statue! Jason Hope has done a great job, and Jason, in thanking you, I wish to say that you are a fertile amalgam of the young and brilliant, and that my gratitude is beyond measure. When ordinary people do extraordinary things and are received with approbation, then they leave a memorial for young men and women, that they too can write their names on history's page.

276

Chris de Caires is one of the nicest men I have had the opportunity to work with. He not only conceptualised this momentous task, he single-handedly managed the fund-raising. I wish to say from the bottom of my heart that I really appreciate those Barbadians who have come on board and made sure this statue would be here for all Barbadians to see. Chris, I am eternally grateful to you for your time, and for completing this job, and I want the donors to know that I am very humbled by the immediacy of their response.

I am now in my winter season, and I am ok; I just want to say to you that when the time comes, I am going to lay down these trophies that people all over the world gave to me, I am going to lay them down and I am going to wait for that crown which The Lord, the righteous judge, will give me on that day.

Amid a fanfare and a burst of flash photography, the ribbon was cut by the Prime Minister, Mia Mottley, to reveal the magnificent eight-foot statue in all its glory.

28

The Last Word

Both on and off the field, Wes performed with honour, humour, good grace and humility. Driven by his overarching desire to serve, he has never given less than 100 per cent to any endeavour he has undertaken; not surprisingly, the ledger of his life shows a substantial credit. Each of his calls was unexpected and took him in an unforeseen direction, yet he responded dutifully and with energy, initiative and passion. He continued striving to learn long after leaving the classroom, as his burning appetite to extend his horizons drove him to seek fresh challenges. The result has been a lifetime of achievements:

> I am very happy that a boy from Station Hill, The Ivy, St Lawrence, Grazettes Housing Area – the areas I lived in growing up – can have done those things. I have been privileged to meet some *real* people: when you talk about Errol Barrow; when you talk about Nelson Mandela; when you talk about Muhammad Ali, you are talking about great men. And also Gerard Pantin, Ian Clarke and Butch Stewart ... they may not have been as famous, but they were great men. How many people have been fortunate enough to meet all those great people? Not just to say 'Hello' but to sit down and talk to them. I met the Queen three times on tour as a player and once as a manager; I met her here in Barbados when I was a minister. How many people have met the Queen five times?! Nobody asked you where you were born. It doesn't matter where you come from, but where you are going. I have truly been very blessed. No matter how talented you are, you miss your blessing if you want it packaged, if you expect it to come to you. You have to make it happen.

Wes made it happen. Few people, and probably no other cricketer, can claim to have accomplished so much in so many diverse fields as Wes Hall. Although he did not directly control the sequence of events that took him to his goals, he believes that he facilitated them by aiming high and working hard, and putting his faith in God:

I must confess that when I look at my cv and see what I have achieved .... you could not do that without God. I often ask the question of God: 'Why me? Why not somebody else? I couldn't understand, I wasn't born to this. But you are born to anything that you put your mind to. Ability does not guarantee success; it must be backed up with a strong work ethic, and God's grace does for you that which you cannot do for yourself. I have had my problems in cricket, in parliament, in my personal life. You get problems, sometimes not of your making, but religion has been my resuscitation. I know that fear and faith cannot occupy the same room. Why? Because it is like light and darkness. My faith in God is strong, and fear is extinguished. All that has happened in my life is in the past, I rise every morning with excruciating pain in my back, but the most important thing is – thank God – that I rise and live for the Lord.

CAREER STATISTICS
TEST MATCH RECORD
1958/59 – 1968/69

BATTING AND FIELDING

M	I	NO	Runs	HS	Ave	100	50	Ct
48	66	14	818	50*	15.73	-	2	11

BOWLING

Balls	Mdns	Runs	Wkts	Best	Ave	5wi	10wm	SRate	Econ
10421	312	5066	192	7-69	26.38	9	1	54.28	2.91

SERIES BY SERIES BOWLING

		Balls	Mdns	Runs	Wkts	Best	Ave	5wi	10wm
1958/59	India (a)	1330	65	530	30	6-50	17.66	2	1
1958/59	Pakistan (a)	605	18	287	16	5-87	17.93	1	-
1959/60	England (h)	1418	49	679	22	7-69	30.86	2	-
1960/61	Australia (a)	1158	14	616	21	5-63	29.33	1	-
1961/62	India (a)	1006	37	425	27	6-49	15.74	2	-
1963	England (a)	1068	26	534	16	4-39	33.37	-	-
1964/65	Australia (h)	876	19	454	16	5-60	28.37	1	-
1966	England (a)	1053	35	555	18	4-105	30.83	-	-
1966/67	India (a)	438	10	266	8	2-54	33.25	-	-
1967/68	England (h)	732	29	353	9	4-63	39.22	-	-
1968/69	Australia (a)	607	5	325	8	3-113	40.62	-	-
1968/69	New Zealand (a)	130	5	42	1	1-34	42.00	-	-

BOWLING AGAINST EACH COUNTRY

	Balls	Mdns	Runs	Wkts	Best	Ave	5wi	10wm
Australia	2641	38	1395	45	5-60	31.00	2	-
England	4271	139	2121	65	7-69	32.63	2	-
India	2774	112	1221	65	6-49	18.78	4	1
New Zealand	130	5	42	1	1-34	42.00	-	-
Pakistan	605	18	287	16	5-87	17.93	1	-

FIRST-CLASS RECORD
1955/56 – 1970/71

BATTING AND FIELDING

M	I	NO	Runs	HS	Ave	100	50	Ct
170	215	38	2674	102*	15.10	1	6	58

BOWLING

Balls	Mdns	Runs	Wkts	Best	Ave	5wi	10wm	SRate	Econ
28095	800	14273	546	7-51	26.14	19	2	51.45	3.04

FIVE OR MORE WICKETS IN AN INNINGS

7-51	West Indians v Glamorgan	Swansea	1963
7-54	West Indians v East Zone	Jorhat	1958-59
7-69	**West Indies v England**	Kingston	1959-60
7-76	Queensland v Victoria	Brisbane	1961-62
6-22	West Indians v Essex	Southend-on-Sea	1963
6-29	Queensland v South Australia	Brisbane	1961-62
6-49	**West Indies v India**	Kingston	1961-62
6-50	**West Indies v India**	Kanpur	1958-59
6-75	Barbados v British Guiana	Bridgetown	1963-64
6-90	**West Indies v England**	Georgetown	1959-60
5-20	**West Indies v India**	Port of Spain	1961-62
5-41	West Indians v Baroda	Baroda	1958-59
5-48	West Indians v Tasmania	Hobart	1968-69
5-60	**West Indies v Australia**	Kingston	1964-65
5-63	**West Indies v Australia**	Brisbane	1960-61
5-76	**West Indies v India**	Kanpur	1958-59
5-77	Queensland v Victoria	Melbourne	1961-62
5-87 [†]	**West Indies v Pakistan**	Lahore	1958-59
5-121	Queensland v New South Wales	Sydney	1961-62

[†] Including a hat-trick

SCORES OF 50 OR MORE

102*	West Indians v Cambridge University	Fenner's	1963
88	Barbados v Indians	Bridgetown	1961/62
78	West Indians v Victoria	Melbourne	1968/69
55	Barbados v Nottinghamshire	Trent Bridge	1969
50*	**West Indies v India**	**Port of Spain**	**1961/62**
50	**West Indies v Australia**	**Brisbane**	**1960/61**
50	Queensland v Victoria	Brisbane	1962/63

Acknowledgements

This biography of Wes Hall would not have been possible without a great deal of assistance.

I would like to thank the publisher, John McKenzie, for inviting me to write the book and for his continued support and encouragement.

John Wisden and Co Ltd kindly gave their permission to use quotes from *Wisden Cricketers' Almanack*. Thanks are also due to Philip Bailey and Cricket Archive for their help with statistics; and to David Lloyd for very kindly writing the foreword. The assistance provided by Stephen Chalke was invaluable.

I would like to thank Wes's children, Sean, Kerry and Remi, for welcoming me so warmly and for their co-operation and positive input throughout.

A special word of thanks is due to Wes's family friend Cora Cumberbatch, who spent many hours with him, patiently reading through the manuscript and typing out his thoughts and recollections. Much of the input provided by Wes is the result of their collaboration.

Finally, I would like to express my gratitude to Wes himself, who could not have been more supportive. Over the course of my trips to Barbados, I was a regular visitor to his home and was granted unlimited access and time with him. His infectious enthusiasm knows no bounds and, despite occasional ill-health, his commitment has never wavered. It has been a joy to get to know him and a privilege to work with him.

Paul Akeroyd
Surrey, England
September 2022

Bibliography

Ackerly, Doug, *Front Foot! The Law That Changed Cricket* (AFN, 2016)

Ambrose, Curtly with Sydenham, Richard, *Time to Talk* (Aurum, 2015)

Beckles, Hilary, *Cricket Without a Cause: Fall and Rise of the Mighty West Indian Cricketers* (Randle, 2017)

Benaud, Richie, *A Tale of Two Tests* (Hodder & Stoughton, 1962)

Eytle, Ernest, *Frank Worrell* (Hodder & Stoughton, 1963)

Fingleton, Jack, *The Greatest Test of All* (Collins, 1961)

Gilchrist, Roy, *Hit Me For Six* (Stanley Paul, 1963)

Gibran, Khalil, *The Prophet* (Knopf, 1923)

Griffith, Charlie, *Chucked Around* (Pelham, 1970)

Hall, Wesley, *Pace Like Fire* (Pelham, 1965)

Lloyd, David, *Around the World in 80 Pints* (Simon & Schuster, 2018)

Manley, Michael, *A History of West Indies Cricket* (André Deutsch, 1988)

Marqusee, Mike, *Redemption Song: Muhammad Ali and the Spirit of the Sixties* (Verso, 1999)

Richards, Jimmy & Wong, Mervyn, *Statistics of West Indies Cricket 1865-1989* (Heineman Caribbean, 1990)

Ronayne, Michael, *Test Cricket Tours: No.5 West Indies* (the author, 1984)

Ross, Alan, *The West Indies at Lord's* (Eyre & Spottiswoode, 1963)

Sandiford, Keith, *Famous Cricketers Series – No.61: Wes Hall* (ACS, 2001)

Tennant, Ivo, *Frank Worrell: A Biography* (Lutterworth, 1987)

Weekes, Everton & Beckles, Hilary, *Mastering the Craft: Ten Years of Weekes 1948-58* (Universities of the Caribbean Press, 2007)

Wisden Cricketers' Almanack, various years

INDEX   *(Members of Wes Hall's family are omitted)*

A

Ackerly, Doug 134
Adams, Jack 35-6
Adams, Jimmy 231,235
Adams, Tom 199
Adderley, Sam 13
Agard, Adrian 207
Alexander, Gerry 44-6,65,
67-71,78-9,86-7,90-1,
93,95-6,98,164,174
Allan, David 160
Allen, David 120-3
Allen, Gubby 134
Alleyne, Ivor 38
Alleyne, Stephen 237
Ambrose, Curtly
205,227-30
Arlott, John 270
Armstrong, Gregory 204
Arthur, Owen 176
Arthur, Tony 219-20
Asgarali, Nyron 46
Ashe, Arthur 203
Atherton, Mike 230
Atkinson, Denis
37,40,45,60,64
Atkinson, Eric
40,45,60,66,74,88-9

B

Babb, Vernon 18
Bacher, Ali 205,217,234-5
Bailey, Trevor 51,86,133
Baird, Lucille 214
Baker-Welch, Maizie 201
Baksh, Vaneisa 239
Banfield, Bert 194,196
Barnes, NW 35,38
Barrington, Ken
118-9,126,128,168-9
Barrow, Errol
11,186,198-202,217,278
Barrow, Nita 217
Baskin, Billy 210-3

Baskin, Catherine 210-3
Beckles, Darcy 194
Beckles, Hilary
144,176,238,273
Belgrave, Elliott 246
Benaud, Daphne 92
Benaud, Richie
86,91-5,97,134,169
Benjamin, Kenny 228,230
Benjamin, Winston
226-8,230-1
Bishop, Ian 228-30
Blackman, Collis 196
Blackman, Harold 75,220-1
Blades, Colin 238
Blake, Jacob 255
Boltz, Ray 213
Bonitto, Arthur 104
Bonitto, Neville 104
Boyce, Ernest 40,43
Boyce, John 253
Boycott, Geoff 151-2
Bradman, Don
57,87-8,92,134
Bradshaw, Delisle 203
Brancker, Rawle
23,25,31,37,137,189,
196,215,222,250
Branker, Ken 42
Brathwaite, Roger 240
Breasley, Scobie 251
Broodhagen, Karl 33
Broomes, Ivan 215
Brown, David 166
Browne-John, Ann 238-9
Burge, Peter 102
Burke, Jim 86
Burnham, Forbes 108,185-6
Butcher, Basil 67,117-8,
143,151,175

C

Cadogan, Grantley 11
Callender, Victor 25-6

Camacho, Steve 234,236
Campbell, Sherwin 230
Carew, Joey 151
Carrington, Avis 16-7
Cash, Bill 208
Challenor, George 57,132
Chanderpaul, Shivnarine
233,235
Chandrasekhar, Bhagwat 165
Chang, Herbert 112
Chappell, Ian
134,154-5,169
Clarke, Ian
190-1,193-4,196,278
Clarke, Lionel 211-2,214
Close, Brian 119-20,127-9
Cobham, Judith 224
Collier, Jack 7,82
Constant, Pat 92
Constantine, Learie
8-9,132,152,175,269-73
Contractor, Nari 66,116
Cook, Geoffrey 55
Coppin, O.S. 30
Cowdrey, Colin
42,49-51,119,121-2,126,
128,132,151,163,169,260
Cowper, Bob 130
Cozier, Tony 92,215,273
Cuddihy, Russ 7
Cuke, William 211,213-4
Cummins, Cecile 208
Cunningham, Mr 36

D

Daniel, Wayne 195
Davidson, Alan
93-4,132,163,169
Davidson, Betty 132,169
Davis, Charlie 109
Davis, Ian 106
Debeger, Les 196
de Caires, Chris 277
Depeiaza, Clairmonte 37,45

Dewdney, Tom   45,51,89
Dewhurst, Lindon   7
Dexter, Ted   55,118,
     126,128,131,163,169
D'Oliveira, Basil   169
Donovan, Billy   41
Douglas, William   198

E

Edwards, Richard   153,156
Egar, Colin   90-1
Eland, Jim   7,83-4
Ellcock, Ricardo   31-2
Evans, Godfrey   24
Eweling, Reverend   55
Eytle, Ernest   53

F

Farnum, Ken   48
Fazal Mahmood   73-4
Fingleton, Jack   91-2
Flanagan   57
Floyd, George   255
Ford, Doug   101
Francis, George   132
Franklin, Kirk   207
Fredericks, Roy   256

G

Gabriel, Richard   109,112
Ganteaume, Andy   45-6,111
Garner, Joel   190
Garnes, Shirley   224
Gaskin, Berkeley   68,156
Gibbs, Lance   9,57,89-90,
     108,115,117,119,132,
     136,139,142,145,151,
     154,156,163,168,248
Gibran, Khalil   236
Gilchrist, Roy
     43-5,51-2,54,64-74,78,
     82-3,88-9,115,136,162,
     170,215,242-3,247,263
Gilkes, Al   217

Gilkes, Sonny   38-9,188
Gill, John   247-8
Glock, John   252
Goddard, John
     44-5,60,78,172-4
Golding, John   148
Gollop, Avril   219
Gomes, Larry   109-10,112
Gomez, Gerry   173
Gosein, Ralph   256
Gover, Alf   53
Graham, Billy   213
Grant, Neville   18
Graveney, Tom
     42-3,49,152, 155,
     163,168-9,260,264
Greaves, Evelyn
     199,219-20,242
Greaves, Philip   186
Greenidge, Geoff   256
Greenidge, Gordon
     194,239,263
Griffith, Charlie
     9,78,88-9,115-20,124,
     126-9,132-4,136-7,139,
     142-3,145,151,153-4,
     156,161-3,166,196,
     250,263-4,270,274
Griffith, Clyde   75
Griffith, Herman
     37,59,63
Grimmett, Clarrie   56
Grout, Wally
     90-1,94-8,102,131
Gupte, Subhash   69

H

Hadlee, Richard   163
Hall, Michael   242
Hamilton, Lewis   255
Hanif Mohammad
     65,73-4,264
Hardikar, Manohar   68
Harper, Roger   233,235

Harvey, Neil   163,169
Haynes, Desmond   214,263
Haynes, Martin   17
Haynes, Richard   221
Headley, George
     8,56-9,87,132,
     171,173,217,262
Headley, Rena   56
Henderson, Hugh
     108-10,180,261
Hinds, Alison   254
Hinds, Paula   203
Holder, Vanburn   194
Holding, Michael
     239,255,274-5
Holford, David   31,156
Holt, JK   63,145,173
Hooper, Carl   233
Hope, Calvin   207
Hope, Jackie   7
Hope, Jason   274,276-7
Hoy, Colin   90-1
Hughes, Gwyneth   30
Hughes, Ronnie   23-30,34,
     39,46,54,102,254
Hunte, Conrad
     8,67,98,117,136,145,218
Hunte, Miss   22
Husbands, Hudson   219

I

Imtiaz Ahmed   60
Ince, Godfrey   48-9,51,75
Innis, Errie   25
Inverarity, John   154

J

Jackson, Ewart   224
James, CLR
     87,92,133,139-40,269-73
John, George   132
Johnson, Len   102
Johnson, Vic   198-9,201
Jones, Tony   248

Jones, Bobby 206-7
Jones, Prior 144
Jordan, Cortez 116
Joseph, Clarvis 237

K
Kallicharran, Alvin 175
Kanhai, Rohan
  8,44-6,54,73,96-7,99,
  101-2,117-8,132,136,
  142,145,155,158,175
Kelly, Frank 102
Kennedy-Green, Michelle 92
King, Frank 25-9,43-4
King, Lester
  115,145,153,156
King, Lord 207
King, Tony 238
Kline, Lindsay 90,98-9
Knight, 'Huffie' 18
Knowles, Billy 39-40,190
Kohli, Virat 260

L
Lara, Brian 111,169,226,
  228-30,234-5,253
Lashley, Peter
  25,30-1,37,92,250
Lawrence, Roy 124
Lawry, Bill 154
Layne, Ed 245
Layne, Edward 208
Leacock, DJ 190-1,194
Lillee, Dennis 61,135,163
Lindwall, Ray 62,133
Lloyd, Clive 8,108,145,
  193-5,197,226,236,274
Lloyd, David 7,81,83-4
Luther King, Martin 256
Lynch, Sylvia 219-20

M
McClean, Clesbert 26
McClean, Maxine 254
McDonald, Colin 130

Mackay, Ken 90,102,130
Madray, Ivan 175
Malinga, Lasith 136
Mandela, Nelson
  204,217-9,255,278
Manley, Michael
  51,70,185-6,273
Mark, Derek 7
Marqusee, Mike 144
Marshall, Malcolm
  170,194,215
Martindale, Manny
  8-9,132,269
Mascoll, Clyde 32
Mason, Frank 45
Mathias Wallis 60
May, Peter 49-51,77-8,
  80,161,163,169
Mayers, Anthony 38
Mayers, Colin 38,210,213
Mayers, Robert 38
Meckiff, Ian 96-7,99
Milburn, Colin 143,167
Miller, Cecil 219
Miller, Keith 36,91,133
Misson, Frank 90
Morgan, David 244
Morris, JO 17
Mottley, Mia 16,275,277
Muhammad, Ali
  143-4,148,218,278
Mullins, Miss 16
Murray, David 112
Murray, Deryck
  114,121-2,147
Murray, Lance 147
Murray, Sonny 114-5,147
Mushtaq Mohammad 74

N
Nanan, Nirmal 112
Nash, Malcolm 208
Nasim-ul-Ghani 74
Nehaul, Patricia 218
Nelly, Marjorie 210

Nettleford, Rex 238
Noott, Cecil
  22-3,26,30-2,35-6,51,254
Nurse, Seymour
  8-9,92,125,136,143,
  157-8,165-6,215

O
Oliver, Sylvester 43
O'Neill, Norman 93,169
O'Reilly, Bill 56-7

P
Pantin, Clive 180
Pantin, Gerry
  179-84,201,261,278
Parks, Jim 119,169
Peirce, Noel 40,186
Pinder, Rawle 41
Pollock, Peter 235

Q
Queen Elizabeth II
  30,54,158,216,278

R
Rae, Allan 62,138,171
Ramadhin, Sonny
  8,45,50-1,115,132,138,
  141,143,154,171,173,263
Ramkisson, Dudnath 112
Ramnarine, Dinanath 242
Richard, Adriel 243
Richards, LeVere 192-3,264
Richards, Viv 8,169,175,
  197,217,226,236,239
Richardson, Peter 49
Richardson, Richie
  226,228-9,233-6
Rihanna 33-4
Roberts, Andy
  195,226,230,239,241
Robinson, Buster 158
Robinson, Eddie 7
Robinson, Oscar 21

Robinson, Robina 111
Rodriguez, Willie 151
Root, Joe 260
Roper, David 225
Ross, Alan 128
Rousseau, Pat 237,239-40,244
Rushton, Derek 7
Rushton, Frank 7,82

S

Sahadeo, Boya 112
Sandiford, Erskine 202,218-21
Sang-Hue, Douglas 256
Sangster, Robert 252
Scott, Francis 25
Scott, Winston 188-9,198
Seacole, Mary 30
Sealey, Clyde 26
Sealy, Austin 204
Sealy, Elvin 232
Sealy, Harry 23,30
Shackleton, Derek 25,120-2
Sharma, Rohit 260
Sheppard, David 214-5
Short, Peter 186,229
Simmons, David 196
Simmons, Keith 220
Simpson, Bobby 93,131-2,163,169
Simpson, Meg 132
Singh, Charran 77
Singh, Swaranjit 69-70
Smith, Alan 131
Smith, Allan 226
Smith, Cammie 62,92,196
Smith, Collie 45,263
Smith, Geoff 160
Smith, Ian 184
Smith, Ivan 54
Smith, Robin 228
Smith, Steve 260
Smith, Sydney 154
Snow, John 135,143,170

Sobers, Garfield 8,18,25,33,36,45,52-3,60, 62,65,67,77,81,88,90,93-4, 99,101-5,108,117,120, 124,132,136-40,142-5, 149-56,158,165-9,171, 175,184-6,196,203-4,208, 239,250-1,257,263,274
Sobers, Gerald 18,105
Solomon, Joe 94,98-9,175
Statham, Brian 51,77,133
Stayers, 'Charlie' 115
Stewart, 'Butch' 223-5,236,278
Stollmeyer, Jeffrey 107,153,173
Surti, RF 114
Swanton, EW 41-3,60,170
Sweeney, Hope 89
Symonds, Peter 203

T

Taitt, Branford 75,187,199-200
Taitt, Eustace 22
Tarilton, 'Tim' 57
Taylor, Jaswick 67,74
Thomson, Jeff 136
Thorpe, Graham 230
Titmus, Fred 119-20,143,169
Trotman, Leroy 220
Trueman, Fred 51,54,77, 118,120,133,135,163
Tshwete, Steve 205
Tull, Louis 17
Turner, Glenn 155
Tyson, Frank 133,170

V

Valentine, Alf 8,45,50-1,90,93,96,115, 132,138,141,171,263
van Troost, Andre 231
Virgin, Roy 163

W

Walcott, Clyde 8,43-4,46,48-53,79,132, 137-8,141,146,164,170-7, 194,196,215,235,260,262-3
Walcott, Muriel 175-6
Walcott, Keith 37-8
Walrond, Errol 245
Walsh, Courtney 205,226,230
Walters, Christopher 192
Walters, Doug 154,169
Ward, Eugene 146
Warner, RSA 112
Watson, Chester 39,78,88,115
Weekes, Carl 181
Weekes, Everton 8,28-9, 40-1,43-4,46-53,59,76,79, 92,132,138,141,164,171-7, 239,241,250,260,262-3
Weekes, Lionel 208
Weir, Ernest 41
Welch, Pedro 187
White, Crawford 27
Wieland, Bob 241
Wilkinson, OH 18
Wilkinson, Sam 32
Williams, Beatrice 13
Williams, 'Boogles' 42
Williams, Eric 182,184-6
Williams, John 75
Williams, Lionel 25-6,28,43
Williamson, Kane 260
Wintle, George 106-7
Wood, Wilfred 29-30
Worrell, Frank 8-9,45, 49,53-4,62-3,72,75,78-9, 86-110,113-4,116-25,128-9, 131-3,138-41,144-7,161, 164,167,171-7,186,201, 231,258,260,262-7,269-73
Worrell, Velda 146-7,175

Y

Yarde, Basil 213
Yearwood, Lewis 238

Also Available From

J.W. McKENZIE BOOKS

12 Stoneleigh Park Road, Ewell, Epsom, Surrey KT19 0QT

Tel 0208 393 7700

www.mckenzie-cricket.co.uk

SIR EVERTON WEEKES: AN APPRECIATION
by Tony Cozier

An appreciation of the great Barbados and West Indies batsman by the author and broadcaster who became the voice of West Indies cricket.

62-page softback, £12

Also in a limited edition of 125 hardback copies
signed by Everton Weekes and Tony Cozier, £100

SIR GARFIELD SOBERS: THE BAY LAND'S FAVOURITE SON
by Keith A.P. Sandiford

An account of the early life of Garfield Sobers
in the village of Bay Land in St Michael, Barbados,
by a fellow Barbadian and school friend.

104-page softback, £15

Also in a limited edition of 125 hardback copies
signed by Garfield Sobers, Keith Sandiford and Tony Cozier, £100